Bill Murray's previous publications include *Glasgow's Giants: 100 Years of the Old Firm*; *The Old Firm: Sectarianism, Sport and Society in Scotland*; *Football: A History of the World Game*; and *The World's Game: A History of Soccer*.

MAINSTREAM *SPORT*

BHOYS, BEARS AND BIGOTRY

THE OLD FIRM IN THE NEW AGE

BILL MURRAY

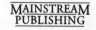

MAINSTREAM
PUBLISHING

EDINBURGH AND LONDON

First published in 1998 by
MAINSTREAM PUBLISHING PROJECTS
Edinburgh

ISBN 1 84018 810 3

Revised and updated, 2003

A catalogue record for this book is available from
the British Library

Typeset in Garamond
Printed and bound in Great Britain by Cox &
Wyman Ltd

*For Else in Holland, who is somewhere there at
the beginning of it all,
Liz (Morag) now in New York, who has lived
through so much of it,
and Duncan in Australia, who is beginning to see
what it is all about.*

Contents

Preface

Since *The Old Firm* came out in 1984, the changes in world football, and not just Scottish football, have been little short of revolutionary. In Scotland the arrival of Graeme Souness at Ibrox and his subsequent signing of the Catholic player, Maurice Johnston, have been two of the most hysterical media events in Scottish sport, and since then Rangers have gone on to equal Celtic's record of winning nine Scottish League Championships in a row. Since the arrival of Souness and the signing of Maurice Johnston several people have suggested that I update *The Old Firm*, as its central theme is the way in which Celtic and Rangers have developed as champions of their respective communities, Celtic of the Catholic-Irish, Rangers of the Protestant-Scots. In the last two chapters of that book I was critical of Rangers for their refusal to play Catholics, and suggested that signing a Catholic would no more upset their Protestant identity than Celtic's many Protestant footballers had affected their Catholic identity.

The Old Firm came out in a revised and updated version in 2000. *Bhoys, Bears and Bigotry* originally appeared as *The Old Firm in the New Age*, the new title taken from one of the chapters of that book. It concentrates on the period from the arrival of Souness at Ibrox, a period that has a certain poetic wholeness, beginning with a Rangers team that refused to play Catholics and ending with a Rangers team that could contain more Catholics than Protestants in its first 11: a revolution indeed – and in the strictest sense of the word.This updated version adds two chapters to cover the period since the failure of Rangers to beat the Stein record of nine league flags in a row, a season that was followed by the departure of Fergus McCann, and in many ways marked the end of an era in the history of the Old Firm. Since then the two clubs, despite their strenuous efforts to 'ban bigotry', have come under scrutiny in an unprecedented way from new organisations and political figures determined to stamp out sectarianism. This is the subject matter of much of the two additional chapters.

The Old Firm was my first foray into sports history, a long way from my original research speciality, the French Revolution, but since then I have merged my interests in French history and sports history by studying the relationship between sport and politics in France in the years before the Second World War, particularly workers' sport and the Nazi Olympics. I was diverted from this when I was asked to write a history of football and that took up several years and resulted in two books on the subject. In the course of this research I became even more aware of the importance of the part played by the Scots in the spread of the world game than I had originally thought, and had no qualms about emphasising this; and throughout it all the unique relationship of Celtic and Rangers came into ever clearer focus.

The present book takes up the story of Rangers and Celtic where I left off in 1984, but it is more an impressionistic work than a long haul involving years of research. I have tried to avoid going over ground covered in *The Old Firm* (and *Glasgow's Giants*), but I cannot assume that all readers of this book will have read the earlier works, and so where necessary I have recapitulated or referred to what was said there.

All those who helped me with these books have helped with this one. As always I must thank La Trobe University: terrible things are happening to universities at the moment, but I have been left free to pursue my interests; Carol and Heather in the History Office; the staff of the university library; and my colleagues who have all been as sympathetic as ever to what for many of them is still an esoteric topic. In Germany, Arnd Krüger and Ulrich Matheja offered their usual support; and in Holland, Else Bongenaar, someone who plays an unspoken part in this book (as in *The Old Firm*) most kindly found the material in the Dutch press relating to Pierre van Hooijdonk. Friends and colleagues in the Australian Society for Sports History have tolerated my eccentricities and sharpened my thoughts. Anthony Bidgood kindly copied several issues of his collection of *Tiocfaidh Ar La* for me. Don Ferrell continued to help me through the mysteries of electronic communication, easing the onset of panic when I thought I might have lost a file. I have also continued to enjoy the encouragement of family and friends in Adelaide, where Rosemary McKay flies the Scottish flag with inexhaustible pride; and my daughter Morag, better known as Liz, now in New York but who spent a year in Scotland caught up with one side of the Old Firm.

Others have helped by sharing their knowledge of the Old Firm and the Scottish football scene. I must first record my thanks to Jack Webster who, although he has not had much to do with this particular book, has been a constant source of encouragement and help to me since he first read the original manuscript of *The Old Firm* back in 1983. Others were generous with their time in a two-week period in November 1997: of those who expressed no objection to being named it is my pleasure to thank Gerry Dunbar, Roddy Forsyth, Michael Kelly, David Low, Kevin

McCarra, Archie McGregor and Gerry McNee. I wrote to the chairmen of both clubs and was accorded a long and productive discussion with Fergus McCann. Peter McLean, Celtic's public relations manager, provided me with a mountain of relevant material, while Joe Sullivan made helpful comments on what I had written. John Greig, public relations manager of Rangers, took time out from a busy schedule to answer many of my queries and very kindly arranged for me to join a tour of Ibrox stadium at short notice. Rangers director Ian Skelly invited me to watch an Old Firm match from the rarefied atmosphere of the Club Deck, after which I had a long conversation with former Rangers manager David White. The editor of *Follow, Follow* did not reply to my letters. At the University of Strathclyde I had further illuminating conversations with Callum G. Brown, Richard J. Finlay and Rangers fan John Young. At Mainstream, my thanks to Bill Campbell for permitting a rescheduling of the deadline, and to the editorial department who handled all the consequent changes with good humour and professional skill.

My most immediate and greatest debts go to three people who have given more of their time to my work than any individual has a right to expect. Graham Walker, an unwavering Rangers fan through the darker days into the recent triumphs, has discussed many aspects of Scottish football with me, before, during and after matches, and made many incisive comments on an early draft. Roy Hay, grandson of a Celtic great from early in the century and who is still suffering from his beloved Ayr United's rejection of David Murray in 1988, has constantly tried to beat sense into me at the same time as he improved what I have been trying to say. He also read an early draft, but it is not his fault if some of my excesses remain uncurbed. Once more, however, my greatest debt is to Pat Woods, in this book more than any other. Quite simply I could not have written it without Pat, as he has kept me constantly supplied with information on the Old Firm in between my trips to Scotland since 1984. Again he has read the drafts with meticulous care and saved me from many errors. My judgements are my own, as is my way of expressing them, and from these, in this book more than in any other, Pat remains totally absolved.

Bill Murray
January 1998

In addition to the usual culprits who have helped me with this revision and update, especially Pat who came out of self-imposed retirement to set me straight on what I have said, Graham who had only just come down to earth after the treble, and Roy who overcame jetlag and set aside other more important tasks to keep me in check, I must thank: Doreen Montgomery of the Glasgow City Council, Alison Logan of Sense over Sectarianism, Helen Miller and Peter McLean of Nil by Mouth for providing me with reams of printed material and discussing various issues with me; the Rangers Football Club for sending me its publicity material for Pride over Prejudice; Michael Grant who offered some interesting thoughts as a voice from the north; John Manning of the Jock Stein Celtic Supporters Club of Melbourne who has kept me up to date on the team he follows from the other side of the world; Norrie Paton with whom I share an interest in Burns and football; and 'wee John', my brother who still sees the foibles of the old country with friendly eyes undimmed by years and distance, and all my other friends and family on both sides of the world.

June 2003

Introduction

On the evening of 7 May 1997, Rangers Football Club beat Dundee United by a single goal from Brian Laudrup to win their ninth consecutive Scottish League Championship title. It was the culmination of a frenetic season in which the champions and their eternal rivals, Celtic Football Club, collectively known as the 'Old Firm', fought out what was virtually a private battle, with the eight other teams in the Scottish Premier League acting as little more than a backdrop. It was a historic victory for Rangers, who thus equalled the nine consecutive League flags won by Celtic under Jock Stein in the years between 1966 and 1974, a period in the shade of their Glasgow rivals that had haunted the Rangers faithful ever since. In the course of laying that ghost to rest Rangers had also laid to rest another ghost from their past: their refusal to play Catholics, which the club once thought was necessary to preserve its Protestant traditions. This sectarian policy was already an anachronism in Scotland of the mid-1980s, but in the world of global television and the financial rewards that went with this, sectarianism was not only an irrelevance, but a potential barrier to playing in the ever more lucrative European competitions. The first steps in modernising Rangers and setting them on the road to domestic success and regular entry into the top European competition came with the appointment of Graeme Souness as player-manager on 7 April 1986.

Souness's arrival at Ibrox Park, the famous ground of the Glasgow club, created an unprecedented buzz of interest from a media for which the arrival and departure of football team managers to the rhythm of success and failure had become a routine event. Certainly Rangers was not a club that made a habit of sacking managers, although there had been five in the two decades before the arrival of Souness, a reflection of the failing fortunes of the club, above all its failure to keep up with Celtic. All but David White of these managers had been from 'traditional' backgrounds, committed to the club's Protestant past and prepared to maintain the old values. The new man had no such previous connections, and this suggested that something new was in the air. Those expecting, or fearing, great changes, were not to be let down.

Souness was brought from Sampdoria in Italy in a coup that was carried out swiftly, cleanly and in remarkable secrecy, despite the fact that on three separate occasions he had said that the only thing that might bring him back to Scotland would be as a manager of Rangers. No one took him seriously – except David Holmes of Rangers. He was a world-class player who had represented Scotland on many occasions, but he was also known to be tough and ambitious, a man who liked to get his own way. In signing him Rangers were clearly intent on revolutionising a club that had been labouring well below its potential, its reputation clouded over by its unspoken tradition of never playing a Catholic footballer. In modernising Rangers Souness's success was shattering, and as the 'sleeping giant' aroused itself and adapted to the rapidly changing economics of British football, their traditional rivals Celtic were left floundering in their wake. Worse, one of the pedestals on which they had based their moral superiority was about to be knocked from under them.

When *The Old Firm* was published in 1984, I thought it would be only a matter of time before Rangers gave in to the pressure to break with their past and sign a Catholic. Those closer to the pulse of Scottish football dismissed this as unlikely. Then came Souness with his cosmopolitan background and well-publicised boast that he was a football mercenary, interested only in winning. For many Rangers die-hards winning was not the only thing; more important was to win without playing Catholics. This was an attitude that took Souness three years to break down, but even before then he had embarked on changes at Ibrox that were nothing short of revolutionary.

For Rangers, 1984 was not a particularly auspicious year, and certainly not a particularly happy one. For their supporters, who were failing to turn up at Ibrox by the tens of thousands, there had been little to lighten the long darkness since the triple Championships of 1976 and 1978. Other clubs would have been happy enough with the successes Rangers had in these intervening years; but Rangers are not another club. In 1984 the man who had won them these successes was back, although the much revered Jock Wallace was not to be the miracle-man the faithful hoped he would be. Celtic during this time were also still in the shadow of the great teams that had set them on the way to nine successive League titles, called the Lisbon Lions after their even more memorable feat of winning the European Cup in 1967 against Inter Milan in the Portuguese capital.

A 'New Firm' was said to have come into being in the early 1980s, as Aberdeen won three League Championships and three successive Scot-tish Cups, as well as a European trophy in 1983, while Dundee United played some sparkling football, won the League in 1983 and came within an ace of European success in 1987. Together they challenged the dominance of the two big Glasgow clubs. It was a short-lived challenge, and their failure to draw crowds as large as those who came to watch even a mediocre Rangers or Celtic game, showed that it was not just the quality of the football that drew Scottish supporters to watch the Glasgow giants.

In 1984 the disasters at Bradford, the Heysel and Hillsborough were in the near future, and the hooliganism that played a role in the second of these disasters was a blight on the game – less so in Scotland, where the strict laws against alcohol at matches introduced after the 'Hampden Riot' of 1980 went a long way to easing this problem. Attendances at football matches throughout most of the football world in the early 1980s were on the decline, and in Scotland Rangers and Celtic were playing to well below their usual crowds. Football was said to be in a crisis, and although a cure was at hand it had many features worse than the disease. Football in 1984 was on the brink of a revolution, as independent television companies fought the state monopolies and used football as a bait to attract subscribers or customers to watch their programmes. In this they were assisted by the new cable and satellite technology that brought football instantaneously to a global audience, a new market, exposure to which the owners of the advanced technology sold to eager sponsors.

In the aftermath of the disasters at Bradford and Brussels, football was snobbishly dismissed by one newspaper as a slum sport played by slum people in slum conditions. Within a decade the image of the game had changed, as a new class of spectators came to watch matches from the comfort of the completely renovated and all-seated stadiums that were one of the outcomes of the report into the Hillsborough disaster of April 1989. Some of the richest football clubs accepted the Taylor report with the ideological spur that in this way they would get rid of the fans some of them regarded as scum, attracting instead to their corporate boxes a clientele who found through football a means of pursuing their commercial interests. Football was becoming fashionable, attracting people who could afford the steep increases in prices that went along with creating the new stadiums. By the 1990s football stars were sought after as never before to sell products on television to people who might never have been inside a football ground. This was not new, but it was on an unprecedented scale; footballers from the earliest days had given their names to help sell products in which they had had little interest, such as the non-smoking Stanley Matthews who used to sell cigarettes in newspaper advertisements in the 1950s, while Denis Compton appeared on billboards throughout the country selling Brylcreem. But these were exceptional sports stars and Denis Compton was better known as a cricketer than an international footballer. And neither Compton nor

Matthews enjoyed the hero-worship of the stars of stage and screen, a gap that has closed slightly in the 1990s.

Football in the 1950s was still seen as the game of the working class; and while it has never been a completely working-class game, it has always had an appeal to the less well-off, as an avenue of escape for those with talent in their toes and as a cheap form of entertainment for those who could only afford to watch from the terraces. The condition of the working class itself changed steadily in the years from the 1950s, and the changes in football grounds reflected this in part. But there were other forces at work, as those who have always seen a commercial advantage in the game's popularity took advantage of its global reach to recreate it in an image closer to their corporate ideal: from the late 1980s football had to be made fit to set before the new class of yuppies (to use a favourite term of the time) who had just discovered the game.

The 1980s, the decade of Thatcher in Britain and Reagan in the United States, has been praised or denounced as the decade when the rich were taught to despise the poor with an easy conscience, the 'greed is good' philosophy that reigned supreme as individuals, companies and corporations set out to market and make a profit from anything they (or someone else) owned. Football teams were to the fore in this as they sold their jerseys, their names and their traditions in the pursuit of more wealth. In the new post-modern world bigotry was a nuisance if not an irrelevance, and there was no way that a modern company could operate out of a 'biscuit tin', as was said disparagingly of Celtic – mainly by their own supporters. Rangers and Celtic, so often partners when it suited their commercial interests, came to separate terms with the new age, the one with considerably more success than the other, to such an extent that the growth of Rangers in financial terms and their success on the domestic front threatened to put an end to any serious rivalry from Celtic.

It had been otherwise in that other tumultuous decade from the mid-1960s when the cultural revolutions convulsing the Western world left Rangers exposed as a sectarian sore in a world where bigotry in all its forms was coming under attack. Blacks in the United States rejected the racism that was their daily lot; indigenous peoples revolted against their colonial masters, women set out to claim an equal place alongside their menfolk, and soon homosexuals would come out of their closets. It was the decade of peace and love-ins, of protest marches against the Vietnam War and in favour of a world in which the rights of the community were upheld against the greed of the individual or the privileges of the few. In Northern Ireland marchers protesting the violation of basic civil rights were met by the forces of Protestant privilege, sparking a virtual civil war in which the British Army had to be brought in to protect the Catholics.

In Scotland, the continued refusal of Rangers to employ Catholic players came under attack, increasingly as they refused to admit they had such a policy, and the situation in Northern Ireland worsened. During this time the public image of Celtic continued to improve as they won the European Cup in 1967 and bestrode the Scottish domestic scene with flair and panache through to 1974. More significantly Pope John XXIII, with the reforms of Vatican II (1962–65), brought the Catholic Church into the twentieth century and a new period of ecumenism was opened up. In this period, too, from the late 1950s to the early 1970s, the number of Catholic students at Glasgow University increased three-fold and comprised one of the largest student bodies in the United Kingdom. For the first time ever, perhaps, Celtic were openly praised by all sections of the Scottish press, although the paranoia that had been nurtured over the century could not be erased so easily.

Celtic's success on the field and a series of setbacks to Rangers on and off the field, brought their sectarian practices in regard to not playing Catholics increasingly under criticism. Celtic, who had always played Protestants, although they refused to let the direction of the club fall into non-Catholic hands, were able to occupy the moral high ground. All this was challenged with the arrival of Souness, irrevocably so when he signed the Catholic player Maurice Johnston in July 1989. A historic breach had been made in the Old Firm rivalry, but two individuals could not dissolve the hatreds of nearly a century overnight, and one of the world's great football derbies proceeded into the glitzy new age of global sport with its own challenges to face.

1. The Greatest Club Game in the World?

Anywhere in the world where Scots have gone – and that is just about everywhere – you will find Celtic and Rangers supporters. The big clubs of Spain, Italy and England have their fans around the world, but it is doubtful if any of them have such a devoted and widespread following: few have had such unbroken loyalty over the decades, and none of them owe their popularity to the polarisation that exists between the two sets of fans over religion.

A South American *hincha* (fan) is said to have been the first to make the claim that you can change your wife or your religion, but two things you can never change are your mother and your football team. He was speaking of football fans in Argentina, but he could have been speaking for fans all around the world: not least those of Celtic and Rangers. In the years before the Second World War, when the British game was still held in awe throughout the football world, Rangers or Celtic could at various times lay claim to being the best club team in the world, although it is a claim that has no solid foundation, as the club games played on the continent at that time were not treated seriously by the British and foreign clubs very seldom visited Britain. In Britain itself, the Celtic team that won six Championships in the first decade of the century could hold its own with any English team; and the Rangers team that dominated the inter-war period usually came out on top in their regular glamour friendlies with Arsenal in the 1930s. In the decade after 1966 Celtic and Rangers set up a remarkable record for a country as small as Scotland, by then reduced in football terms to a size more commensurate with its population, the rest of the world having taken over the game the British had invented and done so much to promote.

During this time Scotland held two European trophies: in 1967 when Celtic won the European Cup and in 1972 when Rangers won the European Cup-Winners' Cup. A week after Celtic won the European Cup in Lisbon, Rangers came within a toe-poke of making it a Scottish double of European trophies when they lost by a single goal in extra time in the European Cup-Winners' Cup to a Bayern Munich side that included three young stars who would take it to world acclaim – Sepp Maier, Franz Beckenbauer and Gerd Müller. Three years later Celtic again reached the final of the European Cup, but fell to Holland's Feyenoord, arrogantly believing they had won the trophy after they had outclassed England's Leeds United with victories in both legs of the semi-final – in the second leg in Glasgow before a record 133,961 spectators. In the evening of 19 April 1972 Glasgow hosted two European semi-finals: in the European Cup-Winners' Cup a crowd of 80,000 at Ibrox saw Rangers eliminate Bayern Munich on their way to a confrontation in the final with Moscow Dynamo in Barcelona, while 75,000 at Celtic Park saw the home team eliminated on penalties by Inter Milan. Celtic reached another European semi-final, in 1974, but would have to wait nearly 30 years before again attaining such heights; despite the changes at Ibrox after 1986 there has been only one lonely season (1992–93) when Rangers revived memories of the glory days of Scottish participation in Europe.

It was Rangers and Celtic who were to the fore in pioneering the armies of travelling supporters for away games in Europe. Celtic fans travelling to Lisbon for the 1967 European Cup final supplied enough stories to fill a book (which the journalist Gerry McNee duly wrote), many of which involved the ingenious stunts thought up about how to get there – and then get back. With Europe a regular part of the football calendar some fans of the two clubs had to work out complicated itineraries on how to get to the midweek game on the continent and then back to Scotland for the League game on the Saturday – and in some cases convince their boss that they had good reasons for absences from work. By the 1980s cheaper air travel eased some of these difficulties, but others could still arise. When Rangers were scheduled to play Dynamo Kiev in the first round of the European Cup in September 1987, some of their fans overcame the visa restrictions by joining the Scottish Communist Party and signing up for an official tour that conveniently coincided with the Rangers visit.[1]

Despite the glamour of Europe, however, it is their games with each other that most fire the passions of the Bears of Rangers and the Bhoys of Celtic – also known as the Huns and the Tims, the former an unfriendly reference to the Rangers supporters and now judged politically incorrect, the latter accepted by the Celtic supporters. The relationship between the two teams mystifies the minds of more rational mortals, but is real enough to keep up a constant stream of anecdotes and reminiscences. Two stories from Stephen Walsh's *Voices of the Old Firm* highlight the peculiar relationship between the two teams: Rangers were playing a League match at Ibrox on 23 October 1971 when it was announced that Partick

Thistle were beating Celtic 4–0 in the League Cup final at Hampden Park. Joyous Rangers fans immediately left Ibrox, commandeered all the taxis they could and made their way across Glasgow to join the Jags supporters in exulting at the humiliation of a Celtic team more used to sweeping away all before it.[2]

The other comes from the end of the 1982 season when Celtic were playing St Mirren at home, and needing a point to win the League. Aberdeen were playing at home to Rangers that same day, and if they won by a four-goal margin and Celtic did not pick up the point they needed, the Dons would win the League. When the half-time score came through from Pittodrie that the Dons were winning 4–0, instead of angst at Parkhead, where the score was 0–0, Celtic fans started to cheer, hoping the Dons would pile on the agony, even, it would appear, at the cost of their own League flag.[3] As it was, they won 3–0 to take the title in comfort.

LOCAL DERBIES AROUND THE WORLD

Local 'derbies', the particularly tense confrontation of two teams in close geographical proximity, are part of the life-blood of football. They are almost as old as the game itself, spreading out from villages to towns and then within towns, and ultimately to nation against nation or nations within nations. From the earliest times, local heroes have emerged for their sporting skills, carrying the hopes of those without their abilities but only too willing to identify with them. From the late nineteenth century followers of football teams were devising ingenious ways of supporting their local heroes and wearing their colours, and loyalty soon took precedence over the quality of play. Today teams of exquisite skill, be it in Africa, South America or elsewhere, have played before half-empty stadiums while sell-out crowds have watched more boring or blood-and-thunder encounters involving their national or local teams. In Scotland from the 1890s, Rangers and Celtic thrived in opposition to each other, attracting support from all over Scotland and even beyond its borders, leaving other teams in the competition far behind. The basis for the success of the two clubs certainly included skill, but the passions that inspired the fans were tribal at worst, pride in their communities at best. The Rangers/Celtic club game, the Old Firm, has been called (by Scots) the greatest club game in the world; but leaving aside what is meant by 'great', it is unique in its religious basis.

At the turn of the century football in Britain was far in advance of the rest of the world, although Europe and most of Latin America would eventually catch up. From the beginning of the century Argentina and

Uruguay in South America, and Hungary and Austria in Europe, played the most ferociously contested national rivalries outside the United Kingdom. Uruguay, with a population of two to three million, shares with Scotland a small population and a totally disproportionate impact on the world game – Uruguay through to the 1960s was arguably the world's most successful football nation. Uruguay also shares with Scotland a domestic league dominated by two big city rivals: Nacional and Peñarol. However, unlike the Old Firm, who have occasionally been dislodged from the top spots in Scotland, the stranglehold of the two big Montevideo teams is almost complete. Neither has a clear-cut ethnic identity, Peñarol having long since lost any Italian origins that might have set them against a 'purer' Uruguayan Nacional. In Argentina the Boca Juniors–River Plate derby has no ethnic base: both began in the poor Boca district of Buenos Aires, but when River moved further west into a more affluent suburb they attracted a slightly wealthier support. Long before Rangers started the fashion in Scotland in the 1980s, the Argentines were prepared to spend a fortune to attract star players, and River Plate became known as The Millionaires for their free-spending on players in the 1930s; in the 1940s they produced arguably the best forward-line in the history of the game, known as 'La Máquina'.

Football flourished later in Brazil than it did in Argentina, Uruguay or Chile, and it came with the acceptance of blacks into the all-white socially exclusive teams who had run the game before the 1920s. Vasco da Gama, of Portuguese origins, first broke the ban, and their success through playing blacks was soon followed by other clubs, most notably Flamengo, founded as an independent football team in 1911 when they broke away from the Boating Club of which they had been a part. Fluminense, founded in 1902, also from a Boating Club, signed a few blacks in the 1930s, but they were treated in a most patronising way and the club never sought nor won the support of the poor in the way Flamengo did. The Fla–Flu derby, however, became the biggest in the world, with regular crowds of over 150,000 to see the games, and a record 177,656 spectators in 1963. This was made possible by the construction of the Maracaná in 1950, to house the World Cup of that year. Some Scottish crowds came close to 150,000 in the late 1930s; but the most an Old Firm game attracted was 118,730 to a Ne'erday game (the name given to the traditional New Year's Day game between Rangers and Celtic, now more often played on 2 or 3 January) at Ibrox in 1939 – thousands, however, were locked outside that day. The previous Ne'erday game had seen a record 83,500 squeezed into Celtic Park, while at Ibrox in the late 1930s and late 1940s, Old Firm games attracted crowds of up to 95,000, with 105,000 for a League Cup game on 16

October 1948. These were the peak days of attendance at football matches in Britain, when safety was taken less seriously than it is today, although crowds for the big games were usually limited by ticket to 134,000 for Hampden, the national stadium.

In Britain and Europe there are equally tense local derbies, but as in South America and outside Northern Ireland, few of these are based on opposing ethnic, cultural or religious foundations as was the case in Scotland between Rangers and Celtic. Players of Nürnberg and neighbouring Fürth in Germany in the 1920s refused to travel in the same train to play for the national team, and the Czech teams Slavia and Sparta have been rivals throughout their one-hundred-year history. In Belgium, where the linguistic divisions are the source of savage enmities, no team emerged as champion of the Flemish-speaking regions in opposition to a team representing the French-speaking Walloons. In the beginning, all teams had French names and the national and most local administrations conducted their affairs in French. But from early in the century a process of 'Fleminising' the game and converting clubs back to Flemish titles has restored the linguistic and cultural predominance of the Flemish teams. Moreover, the Belgian national team, which has performed some minor miracles in recent years, is one of the few Belgian institutions which has won the support of the entire nation.[4]

Italy is another country where regional differences have been overlooked when the 11 men of the Azzuri take the field; but at the local level the confrontations can be bitter: teams from the wealthier north against those from the south, but more importantly two teams from one town or a town close by. In Rome, Lazio are sometimes seen as having a slightly more middle-class following than their eternal rivals, Roma. When Lionello Manfredonia arrived at Roma in 1987 after ten years with Lazio and two with Juventus, a club almost as hated as Lazio by Roma fans, the Ultras of the Southern Curve split in two between those who wanted to accept Manfredonia and those who hated him for having worn the colours of the enemy. It was a split much worse than any that developed at Ibrox after the arrival of Maurice Johnston to play for Rangers, a man of alien faith who had also worn the colours of the enemy.

HAKOAH AND THE MUSCULAR JEWS

Most local derbies are cross-town rivalries with little class, ethnic or above all religious antagonisms. Before the Second World War, however, there were several prominent Jewish clubs which had to live with the anti-Semitism of their rivals, but no single rival emerged to champion the anti-Semitic cause – others on the political stage performed this task only too successfully. In Spain, clubs representing provinces with different ethnic bases, especially Castilians, Catalans and Basques, have set up bitter rivalries, but they all share the same religion.

The association of religion and football goes back to its early days, when the 'muscular Christians' sought to win over the souls of would-be converts by encouraging their enthusiasm for football. Churches, along with pubs, were often at the origins of clubs that are still well known today; Aston Villa and Everton in England, Queen's Park, Hibernian and Celtic in Scotland, are just a few of those prominent today that had religious origins. Jewish clubs were founded in the 1890s in Europe, but it was not until 1909 and the founding of Hakoah in Vienna that a Jewish club came to challenge the elite continental clubs.

Hakoah was founded as a refuge from the anti-Semitism that scarred the city of dreams, a multi-disciplined sports club devoted to demonstrating that Jews were neither weak nor water-shy, as popular prejudice had it. The club produced some brilliant swimmers who were often accompanied by their wrestlers and weight-lifters who stood ready to battle with or dump in the pool those who were too vocal in their anti-Semitism. But it was the football team that was the pride of the Jewish community, winning games with a bruising style that deliberately set out to deny the weakling stereotype. Hakoah have since lost the glamour they had in the mid-1920s, when they won the first professional Austrian League Championship in 1925, much to the anguish of the many anti-Semites in the Austrian capital. They lost many of their best players to 'the rich uncle in America' after tours of the USA in 1926 and 1927, and struggled in the 1930s, finally to be crushed when the Nazis absorbed Austria in 1938. Along with FK Austria, which was seen as the team of the liberal Jews, they were faced with the general anti-Semitism so prevalent in Austria at this time, although no specific team emerged to challenge them on an anti-Semitic basis.

In view of the fate that awaited them, it is impossible to overestimate the reality of race hatred against the Jews of Europe, and ridiculous to claim that the insults at football matches involving Jewish teams was no more than '90-minute racism', but there were occasions when winning rose above prejudice, giving pause to question the depth of feeling behind the chants and slogans voiced at sports meetings. One fan whose team was saved from relegation by a Hakoah victory, and who was more used to expressions like 'filthy pigs' when referring to Jews, congratulated Hakoah with a mumbled, 'Well done, Herr Jew.' And it was not unknown in games between two Jewish teams for the followers of one or other to let loose insults that in any other situation would have been denounced as anti-Semitic.[5]

The closest Europe came to a local derby based on anti-Semitism was with Ferencvaros and MTK in Hungary. Ferencvaros, or 'Fradi' as they are popularly known, were a Catholic and more working-class team, and their rivalry with MTK, one of Hungary's first clubs, had a strong anti-Semitic streak. MTK went the way of other Jewish teams in Europe when the Nazis and their allies came to power, and when the Communists took over in the years following the defeat of the Nazis, neither MTK nor Fradi was in favour, the one for its bourgeois origins, the other for its association with fascism. In the Netherlands, several Jews were involved in the founding of Ajax Amsterdam, but they have never been a particularly Jewish team, no more so than Tottenham Hotspur in England, whose Jewish connections are incidental. In the contemporary fashion for football hooligans to take on Nazi postures, Ajax have been denounced as 'Yids', a title that many Ajax supporters (like those of Spurs) have been happy to accept, even though they are not Jewish. And no team in the Netherlands ever looked like gaining fame because it hated Jews. In Hungary Ferencvaros fans have renewed full-throated anti-Semitism in their terracing repertoire, an indication as much as anything of the sad state into which a once great football nation has sunk. And so far as Jews having to disprove that they are physical or moral cowards is concerned, the establishment and subsequent history of the state of Israel in 1948 has put paid to that stereotype.

CATALANS AND BASQUES

It is in Spain that the most intense football rivalries based on ethnic identity have been formed, particularly with those clubs that represented the separatist ambitions of the Catalans and the Basques. These reached a new intensity when General Franco, whose one redeeming grace was that he genuinely loved football, promoted Real Madrid as the regime's ambassador abroad and the champion of Castilian centralism at home. He was much more successful in convincing the innocent abroad that his regime was a reflection of the all-white purity of one of the greatest teams in the history of the game; but at home the Catalans and the Basques were not won over to the regime that came to power, after three years of civil war, in 1939.

Franco, especially through his friend Santiago Bernabeu, who had devoted all of his adult life to the club, favoured Real Madrid. He fed his impoverished subjects a constant feast of football: non-stop games from South America on television on May Day, the traditional day for workers' celebrations; newspapers using up to six times their space on sport in preference to politics; and overall a general policy of 'footballising' the masses in the hope that their minds might be taken up with matters other than their misery. Against the rebellious provinces Franco was pitiless in his attempts to impose his dictatorship. He banned the Catalan and Basque clubs from displaying symbols of their ethnic identities, forced them to change their names, usually from the English origins to Spanish, and forbade the use of the Catalan and Basque languages. This was impossible to carry out in the culture of football, and under the protection of the crowds at the stadiums FC Barcelona (CF Barcelona under Franco: that is Club de Fútbol instead of Fútbol Club – originally Foot-Ball Club) in Catalunya and Athletic (Atlético under Franco) Bilbao flaunted the colours and chanted their provincial slogans and hatred of Madrid. Since Franco's death in November 1975, however, much of the Barcelona/Real Madrid rivalry is based on sporting success. Under the dictatorship – and even before – it was not so, and provincial pride underscored all games between El Barça and El Madrid.

FC Barcelona's community identity with Catalunya is one of the most deep-seated and mutually supportive in the game, although not all of its supporters would agree with the goals of the more extreme separatists, especially since the restoration of local privileges to the 'autonomous provinces' in the new Constitution of 1978. The Catalan national identity can be compared more readily to Scottish national ambitions than to those of a local club, and unlike Celtic, who refused to have their jerseys numbered because it sullied the hoops but surrendered when it came to commercial graffiti, Barcelona have refused, despite the millions this would bring in, to have the colours of Catalan pride besmirched by a sponsor's name. The makers of the shirt have an identifiable logo, however, and in the world of commercial exclusives this played a role in the astronomical sums offered to the young Brazilian superstar, Ronaldo, where a rival shirt maker was involved in subsidising the fortune that could have taken him to Rangers, except that he chose the less lucrative but more competitive Italian League and Inter Milan.

If Barcelona's identity can in some way be compared to that of Scottish nationalist ambitions, those of the Basque clubs perhaps bear some resemblance to that for a united and republican Ireland: certainly that is how the Irish Republican Army like to see it, and in February 1996 an IRA spokesman appeared at a meeting in support of Basque independence at the stadium of Athletic Bilbao, a meeting in which Basque terrorists (ETA) were to the forefront with their familiar black hoods and guns. It is also how the pro-IRA Celtic fanzine *Tiocfaidh Ar La* sees it, praising their militancy and the killings that have accompanied their struggle for independence – presumably down to the murder in July 1997 of the young politician held as a hostage and whose death brought millions of angry Spaniards together as no other event had done. *TAL* encouraged Celtic supporters to take an interest in the Basque struggle, and when watching Basque clubs on television to give them a shout of 'Gora ETA Militar', the equivalent to 'Up the 'Ra' (Militar (M) being the equivalent of P for Provisional in the IRA).[6]

Basque claims to independence are stronger than those of either the Scots, the Irish or the Catalans, in that their culture is based on a language totally different from that of the Castilian centralists. Not surprisingly then, the Basque clubs are even more fiercely independent, and for a long time most of them refused to employ anyone who was not a Basque. Unlike Rangers, who surrendered their all-Protestant identity in 1989, Athletic Bilbao refused, even under threat of relegation, to bring in non-Basque players to help the club.

Bilbao's strict Basques-only policy began in 1919, 21 years after the foundation of the club, and not only was it restricted to Basques, but Basques born in the province of Vizcaya, that is to say players born within 80km of the club, a population of about three million. Not only that, but the players had to have parents and grandparents born in the region. Despite this policy, they have never been out of the Spanish First Division and have been the most successful of the Basque clubs; in recent years, however, when they have been threatened with relegation, they have relaxed their policies and play Basques without restriction, even French Basques.

The other powerful Basque club, Real Sociedad de Saint Sebastian, had a Basques-only policy, but this included anyone born in the Basque country, so that the son of an immigrant could be accepted. This has relaxed even further in recent years, and like Bilbao they have always been prepared to employ foreign coaches or managers, which they see as an honour to the club. (Even in the more enlightened commercial days in Scotland one might wonder whether Rangers supporters would regard the appointment of a Catholic manager as an honour.)

FC Barcelona, on the other hand, have welcomed foreign players and coaches since their inception in 1899, and despite teams that have included few Catalans over the years, this has in no way affected the club's Catalan identity. The club has nurtured a healthy relationship with the community, and once a week the stadium and its magnificent museum are open for free to the public. In Scotland, Celtic found early in their history that Protestants playing for the club did not dilute their Catholic identity; it is only in the past decade or so, however, that Rangers have found out what others had been telling them for years: that Catholics or even Englishmen in the team's colours would not destroy what they stood for.

The Spanish game has other notable reflections of the situation in Scotland. Although one of the wealthiest regions in Spain, and although FC Barcelona has for a long time been one of the richest football teams in the world, it has suffered from a persecution complex developing into a paranoia that goes back to 1911 and has lasted even into the time of Johann Cruyff. There are no cries of 'masonic conspiracy' here, as regularly accompany setbacks to Celtic in Scotland, especially as the most prejudiced treatment against Barcelona came in Franco's time, when Freemasonry was crushed with a fanatical fury. 'Political refereeing' even gave rise to a new word in the Spanish language: a '*Gureceta*' for an outrageous refereeing decision. It came from a quarter-final second leg Cup game in June 1970, when Emilio Gureceta, the referee in charge of the game, awarded a penalty to Real Madrid against Barcelona for a foul committed well outside the penalty area.[7]

In recent years, presidents of Barcelona and Real Madrid have refused to be seen inside each other's stadiums, but while Rangers and Celtic directors have often felt uncomfortable as guests at away games, and at the beginning of 1998 antagonisms between the owners of the two clubs surfaced in the press, the closest either club has come to a ban on the other was on one occasion when David Murray, the Rangers chairman, refused entry to Celtic supporters.

One thing the Basques, Catalans and Castilians have in common, however, is their faith. They have private chapels in their grounds; the players can cross themselves to their heart's content anywhere they like, and they are even proud to have the Pope as one of their members. Only in Scotland (and to a lesser degree Northern Ireland) did a team of specific ethnic, in this case religious, origins, draw a single rival based on opposition to these origins. The strength of Glasgow Rangers grew and fed on its anti-Catholicism, which in turn stoked the fires of Irish nationalist and religious passions, to create the aptly named business based on bigotry. For a long time, indeed until the 1980s, this was a profitable concern. Now it is the business that comes first and the crowds who are filling the remodelled stadiums at Ibrox and Parkhead come for the spectacle and not to satisfy some basic tribal urge. Or so the new management hopes.

THE HATE THAT SURPASSES ALL UNDERSTANDING

Even if the religious divisions of Celtic and Rangers were to become irrelevant, the rivalry between the two big clubs would continue to be accompanied by a mutual hatred: it seems to be the way of the world and an inescapable element in the human spirit. Count Otto von Bismarck,

the Prussian architect of a unified Germany in 1871, once remarked that
he was sustained in his life by two things: the love of his wife and his
hatred for Ludwig Windthorst, the leader of the (Catholic) Centre Party.
For all the devotion that fans claim to have for a particular team, this is
a love that often has to be nurtured by hatred of a close rival. At times
this can reveal a sickness that has more to do with the psyche than
football: Torino fans praising those of Liverpool for killing Juventus fans
at the Heysel in 1985; Liverpool fans abusing those of Manchester
United with reminders of the dead bodies on the runway in Munich in
1958; Nigerian players taunting Ethiopians with gestures to their mouths
and stomachs mocking their hunger; London fans in the 1980s flaunting
pound notes and designer underwear at the fans of clubs from the north
of England; Italians from the north dismissing those from the south as
'niggers'; the list could go on, through to the Dutchman who claimed
that the happiest moment in his life was after the World Cup final in
1974 when he heard that a German celebrating his country's victory over
Holland had fallen from a balcony and killed himself.

Not so very far removed from Bismarck, then, was the Hearts fan with
whom I shared 90 minutes of a Hearts–Hibs game shortly after the
appearance of *The Old Firm* in October 1984. I was introduced to him
soon after the game began as he urged Hearts to 'Get stuck into them
fuckin' Taigs!' ('Taig' is an insulting word for a Catholic; 'Fenian' is more
common in the West of Scotland) – and eyeballed me provocatively
when I turned to see who was bellowing in my ear. This invitation to
discuss the nature of sectarian rivalry took up much of the remainder of
the match, and at some time in our debate the Taigs became Catholics.
But as my new associate concluded, somewhat at a loss to explain in any
positive way his attachment to Hearts (whom he saw as the capital's anti-
Catholic equivalent to Rangers): 'You've got to hate somebody.'

Hitch your hatred to religion and you have a holy cause, and it doesn't
matter whether you attend a particular church or are terribly concerned
about the nature of the Trinity or the real presence at the mass. But it
would also be wrong to ignore the religious elements in the support for
the two teams: religion has always been about more than matters
spiritual, and the hand of history that has hung over most countries is
not so much dead as a source of sustenance in large parts of Scotland.
The vast bulk of the Rangers support is Protestant, as that of Celtic is
Catholic. That these terms should be used in a secular sense is not a
contradiction in terms: logic or even sociological discourse over the
nature of religion or class holds very little interest for most football fans,
above all those of Celtic and Rangers. Few fans would want it otherwise.

2. A Catholic Comes to Ibrox

For some people the 'Glorious Twelfth' is in August and marks the opening of the grouse season; for those who know better, the 'Glorious Twelfth' is in July and commemorates the anniversary of the Battle of the Boyne, when King William of Orange defeated the deposed Catholic King James VII and preserved the kingdom from popery. It is an event remembered by some with more fervour than Independence Day in the United States, the famous Fourth of July, or the Fall of the Bastille in France, and all three were drawn together in 1989 for different reasons. In that year the Americans were still paying homage to the bicentenary of the introduction of their Constitution, while in France the nation was celebrating the bicentenary of the French Revolution which was about to reach its climax on 14 July; in Scotland, however, minds were fixed on other things as the sporting world still reeled from the events of 10 July, when the Rangers Football Club presented to an astonished media gathering their latest signing: former Celtic player Maurice 'Mo' Johnston, who claimed to be a Catholic and as such was of the faith that some Rangers fans, encouraged by the board, vowed should never darken the Protestant soul of the Ibrox club. He was not, as most reports said, Rangers' first Catholic signing, or even their first major signing who was a Catholic, but apart from two Catholics signed by accident and a couple of junior signings, one of whom, John Spencer, was on the brink of first team selection, he was Rangers' first Catholic player since the First World War.

The Scottish media duly concentrated on the actions of the extremists who demonstrated their disgust at the club's surrender of its principles and vowed never to have anything to do with the club while the Fenian played in its colours. But the media were also only too happy to praise Rangers for finally coming through on the promises they had been making for nearly two decades. Few stories in living memory had evoked such interest, and all that was lacking was the timing of the event: two days later, the 12th instead of the 10th, and the Rangers manager, no stranger to mischief-making, could have had more reason to smile at the furore all around him. Indeed the only story that had aroused comparative media attention had been the arrival at Ibrox just over three years previously of the manager himself: Graeme Souness, the man responsible for Johnston being signed.

SOUNESS VERSUS THE PAST

Graeme Souness's arrival as player-manager on 7 April 1986 heralded great changes at Scotland's biggest football club, as the new man wasted no time in preparing Rangers to join the ranks of the great teams not only in Britain but the rest of the world. He was given money to do so that surpassed the spending power of all previous Rangers managers combined. He signed Englishmen, including a black, then moved out to foreign fields to capture talent wherever it could be found. But, until Johnston, no Catholics. Souness was regarded with some suspicion on his arrival. His life abroad and his expensive tastes in clothing and toiletries were not what Glaswegians were used to; but suspicion about his taste in toiletries was as nought compared with the fears held by some that he was not a Rangers man and might take seriously his promise to sign players regardless of their religion.

Previous Rangers managers, like Willie Waddell, Jock Wallace and John Greig, might have said they were willing to sign Catholics, but the faithful knew this was a smokescreen to confuse the media and keep the world body FIFA quiet, and that even if a Catholic were to be signed, as one of them said, there would be no way he would play for the team. Apart from his continental airs, Souness was married to a Catholic, and although she was divorced and as such in breach of the faith, she was bringing her children up as Catholics: there was no doubt that when Souness said he would sign players regardless of their religion, he was serious. He soon learned that this was not going to be as easy as he thought, and the word was passed gently to him to look in other directions. Faced by the dead hand of Scotland's religious past, Souness looked elsewhere, at least until the Rangers following could be prepared for the hammer blow of 10 July 1989. Those unfamiliar with the situation in Scotland (and Northern Ireland) could only be amazed that such an apparently trivial matter could take on such titanic proportions, but it was merely the tip of an iceberg concealing a long history that had to be navigated with care.

It had begun nearly a century before, in the early 1890s, when the long-established Rangers became the first team to put a stop to the triumphal progress of the Celtic Football and Athletic Club, which had been founded just a few years earlier, following a meeting in St Mary's Hall, Calton, on 6 November 1887. From this moment the Catholic community of Glasgow invested their inexhaustible energy in the project, from the Archbishop who, as patron, headed the first appeal for subscriptions in January 1888, to the hundreds of unsung volunteers who constructed a playing field before there was even a team to play on it. Success on the field ensured the support of Catholics throughout Scotland and beyond. It was all the brainchild of Brother Walfrid, a Marist determined to keep the poor free from the temptations of Protestant soup kitchens and to provide a leisure occupation that would save them from apostasy in the dangerous years when they left school and had too much idle time on their hands. The club's pioneers were mainly first- or second-generation Irish, Scots who were happy to be called Irishmen, and the spectacular success of the Catholic club in its early years was a source of great joy to those Catholics of Irish origin who still had not been accepted into the bosom of Scottish society, and indeed often felt rejected by it. By the early 1890s many such Scots were already succeeding in the professions, but in football-mad Scotland, which had known many Catholic teams before the advent of Celtic, it was the triumphant successes of the new team from the east end of Glasgow that most boosted the pride of those who felt like outcastes in their own homeland.

Protestant Scots whose vision of the world was disturbed by the interlopers looked on with some concern, and when a saviour came in the shape of the Rangers Football Club, many of them, taking advantage of improved public transport – trams to take people across the city, ferries to cross the Clyde at Govan and Whiteinch, eventually a subway system that dropped them off right on the Ibrox doorstep – deserted their own teams to follow the one team capable of putting the Irishmen back in their places. That came in the 1893–94 season, when Rangers beat Celtic on four occasions out of the six games they played, losing only once. Rangers, founded in 1872, had progressed rapidly to challenge the giants of the time, Vale of Leven, Renton, Dumbarton and even Queen's Park, but at the time of the founding of Celtic they had struck a low ebb. However, under the growing influence of William Wilton, who was appointed match secretary in 1889, and with their success against the Irishmen, Rangers never looked back.

Both clubs soon saw the financial advantages in playing each other in games where the ethnic edge was clear cut, and it was this commercialism, which the amateur sports writers of the day found repellent, that led to the two clubs being branded 'The Old Firm' in a *Scottish Referee* cartoon of 1904. In the early days it was Celtic who were the more ethnically distinct, for while they were prepared to play Protestants, indeed could not have succeeded without them, the entire ambience of the club was Irish and Catholic: the first patron, whose appeal launched the club, was the archbishop of Glasgow, all the directors, as they would be until the 1990s, were Catholic, and the vast bulk of its supporters were Catholic. The club saw little need to conceal this, any more than it did the support of several of its leading players and directors for Irish nationalism, some of whom were to be found on public platforms supporting the cause. More publicly, the players' jerseys proclaimed the origins and ethos of the club: originally a white shirt with a green collar and the Celtic cross as a logo, this changed to vertical green and white stripes before the famous green and white hoops took over at the beginning of the 1903–4 season. Then there was the Irish flag flying over the ground, green with a gold harp until it was replaced by the tricolour of the Irish Free State after its bloody birth in 1921. Like the players' strips, it was an open proclamation of what the club stood for.

There was nothing religious in the origins of Rangers, and they were Protestant only in the sense that the vast majority of clubs in Scotland at this time were made up of Protestants. They began, as was the case with so many other clubs in the 1870s, out of a boys' kickabout. Like Queen's Park, Scotland's premier club, their founders came from the Highlands, but unlike Queen's Park, who were associated with the Young Men's Christian Association, they had no particular religious connections. Rangers' founders came from the Gareloch, with just that bit more talent and organisational ability than the hundreds of other clubs springing up all over Scotland in the 1870s and 1880s. Games on the Glasgow Green, where they had to compete for space with dozens of other enthusiasts, gradually changed to more prestigious locations in the more prosperous south side of the Clyde before they built their own ground, called Ibrox Park, in 1887. They relocated to the present site in 1899, having built one of the finest sports stadiums in the land.

Being Protestant at this time did not necessarily mean being anti-Catholic, but it was frequently the case, and when this was linked to opposition to Irish Home Rule, the two could come together in a potent mix. Rangers were no more anti-Catholic than most clubs in Scotland in their early days, although some of their more prominent directors were Freemasons and Unionists. The most notable of these was John Ure Primrose, an active Freemason, Unionist and militant opponent of Irish Home Rule, who had a near lifelong relationship with the club and was chairman from 1912 until 1923, the year before he died. He is said to have committed the club to the masonic cause.[1] The year before Primrose became chairman, the anti-Catholic aspects of the club were given a boost when the Belfast shipbuilders Harland and Wolff, with their predominantly Protestant workforce, set up a yard in Govan. Like other giants of the heavy industries in Scotland, the owners were happy to appoint foremen who favoured fellow Protestants when employment was scarce. It was about this time that Rangers' practice of not signing Catholics gradually became a policy.

In the early years of the twentieth century Celtic had the best team in Scotland, possibly Britain, winning the League Championship six times in a row between 1905 and 1910. It was in an attempt to break this deadlock that Rangers signed several Catholics between 1906 and 1908, while Archie 'Punch' Kyle, who played for the club between 1904 and 1908, remained until the 1990s the longest-serving Catholic in Rangers' history, a fact omitted from all the histories of the club until recently. Eventually, from the time of the First World War, Rangers found that they could beat Celtic without Catholics – and in any case the dream of any young Catholic footballer was to play for Celtic. Similarly most young Protestant hopefuls set their sights on playing for 'the mighty Glasgow Rangers'.

In the inter-war period the 'no Catholics at Ibrox' policy strengthened: it never appeared in written form nor was it officially acknowledged by the club, but it was an open secret indulged by the media and welcomed by the supporters, a ban on Catholics that applied not just to players but to any employee of the club. Games between Celtic and Rangers became overlain with quasi-religious overtones and supercharged by the politics of Ulster, so that much of what happened on the field spilled over into the streets, and while the rest of Britain could enjoy its football in conditions of comparative calm, games between Rangers and Celtic became battles – not just rhetorical, and not just of days of yore (1690) – reflecting the tensions in Northern Ireland.

Little of this was to be reported in the secular (that is Protestant) press, which cherished Rangers as one of its own, and Catholics were left to express their grievances in their own papers, but before the reforms of Vatican II, most Catholics failed to see the ways in which their own Church discouraged too close relations with the Protestant community. Catholics certainly had to face prejudice in many areas and often suffered in terms of progress in certain professions, but it was the Vatican that set up the barriers to normal social interaction between Catholics and Protestants, because of its strictures on interdenominational marriages and through its insistence that young Catholics be educated in isolation from Protestants. Much of this was to change with the reforms of Pope John XXIII at Vatican II, when the Counter-Reformation, a relic from the past going back to the Council of Trent (1545–63) was finally brought to an end. The first duty of Catholics was still to follow the faith of their fathers and convert the heretic, but they were now free to travel the road to God along with other Christians, to be judged on what they were in themselves and not as children of the martyrs.[2] More practically, many married Catholics gave up the wearisome game of Vatican roulette and convinced themselves that they could engage in conjugal relations without having to pretend that their aim was to produce a child. It was confusing for the more conservative Catholics, but when later popes tried to crush the liberalism that had been unleashed, they found that it was too late to close the door to the modern world.

It was against this background that Rangers' refusal to sign Catholics began to come under criticism, especially as the Scottish game broadened out into Europe and British football fans showed the world a new brand of hooliganism. In cases involving Rangers fans the sectarian element added a new ingredient. In 1969 the troubles in Ulster, beginning with simple demands for basic human rights for Catholics, exploded into virtual civil war, and Rangers' anti-Catholic image as well as its well-publicised links with Ulster, became a target for a Scottish press that until then had effectively accepted Rangers' ban on Catholics. The matter was compounded when Jock Stein, himself a man of deep Protestant convictions, with family and friends of Orange sympathies (some of whom never spoke to him again after he joined Celtic, a fate shared by other Protestants who wore the colours of the Catholic club), took Celtic from 1965 into their glory days in domestic and European competitions.

In the meantime, the escalating violence in Ireland, and the highly publicised incidents of hooliganism involving Rangers fans, brought the club under a barrage of criticism from all quarters. Apart from a few principled shareholders at annual general meetings, however, the club did nothing about its anti-Catholic image, and the fans who objected to being branded as bigots because of this had to keep their collective anger to themselves. In the early 1960s some Celtic fans, in the spirit of the fanzines to come, published *The Shamrock*, a magazine with a pro-IRA stance that criticised the bumbling way in which the club was being run. Rangers, too, had had magazines put out by the supporters, most notably the *Rangers Review* that came out from April 1947 and then the *Rangers FC Supporters Club Annual* that virtually replaced it from 1950. But these fan magazines were generally deferential to the club, in complete contrast to *The Shamrock* and the fanzines that started to proliferate from 1987. Rangers fans were generally muzzled by the club tradition that silence was the best response to controversy, that the club, being bigger than the man, was always right. Indeed when the break with the past came it was from the club itself: the bigotry expressed in the Ibrox terracing was merely a cruder and more

vociferous expression of the views in the boardroom, and the Rangers
revolution had to begin there, with the clearing out of the old guard as
a first step in modernising the club.

AWAKES THE GIANT FROM ITS SLUMBER

The fortunes of the Rangers Football Club on the eve of the Souness
signing were about as low as they had ever been. Under Jock Wallace,
who had become manager in 1972, Rangers broke the Celtic deadlock in
1975 and won two trebles in 1976 and 1978. But Wallace left in May
1978 after a bust-up with another of the club's stalwarts in upholding the
'traditions' of the club, the former star player and manager, Willie
Waddell. Wallace was replaced by another dyed-in-the-blue Rangers
man, John Greig, who in his first season came within eight minutes of
achieving Rangers' third treble in four years, before a ten-man Celtic
team scored twice to pip them for the 1979 Championship. But the
burden was to prove too much for a young man thrust from being
captain of the club to managing-director overnight, and all Rangers
gained in the rest of the Greig years was a Scottish Cup victory against
Dundee United in a replay in 1981 and a League Cup victory the
following season. Greig resigned on 28 October 1983, saying he was
finished with the game, but he could never leave Rangers and returned
in 1990 as their public relations manager.

The first two choices for Greig's replacement were the men behind the
remarkable resurgence of the New Firm of Aberdeen and Dundee
United: Alex Ferguson and Jim McLean. Neither could be tempted,
Ferguson it was said because he was married to a Catholic and had many
Catholic friends, and as a former player was only too well aware of the
club's feelings on this matter. The man most disappointed by McLean's
rejection of the job was Walter Smith, his assistant, who was to have been
part of the deal. Smith's time would come, however. In the end Rangers
had to settle for Jock Wallace, who had always been the people's choice,
a no-nonsense guts and determination manager whose attitude to
Catholics playing for Rangers was well known. The second coming of
Wallace was to offer no salvation, however: that would have to come
from out of the deserts on the other side of the Atlantic, from Nevada,
where Lawrence Marlborough, grandson of John Lawrence (the self-
made millionaire known as 'Mr Rangers' who was chairman of the club
from 1963 until he resigned for health reasons in 1973) had gone to live
in 1983.

Lawrence Marlborough had little interest in football as a game, but he
was a businessman and this was reflected in his decision to live in the

United States. There he became attracted to the American sporting ethos, where clubs operated as money-making franchises owned by a single individual. It was a different world from that operating in Scotland, but from whatever angle he viewed the club in which he was a major shareholder, it was not maximising its commercial potential. And so he completed a share deal with the Rangers director, Jack Gillespie, in November 1985 that gave him a narrow majority on the board; in return, Gillespie was promised a place on the board for life. Marlborough went on to buy further shares that lifted his control to nearly 66 per cent. It was not done without a few cross words, but his power now allowed him to bring about a bloodless coup whereby three directors were removed in February 1986 and the chairman since January 1984, lifetime Rangers man John Paton, was replaced later in the year by David Holmes, a non-Mason and an employee from Marlborough's own company, John Lawrence (Glasgow) Ltd. Holmes, who combined the posts of chairman and chief executive, was in his private life a Falkirk supporter, and in the revitalised Ibrox business credentials rather than the traditional faith were the first prerequisites. As Holmes set about modernising the club, however, he insisted that 'Rangers belong to the people'. His greatest success was his first: the signing of Graeme Souness, then playing for Sampdoria in Italy.

SOUNESS TAKES UP THE CHALLENGE

Souness came out of the east, like several of his most distinguished forerunners: the legendary Bill Struth himself came from Edinburgh and later moved to Fife; Willie Woodburn also came from the capital, as did John Greig, who as a youngster of 16 when he signed for the club was in tears that it was Rangers and not his own club Hearts that had signed him. Souness, too, came from the capital, but his was a different world, even from that of Greig, who had been born a mere eleven years before him. Born on 6 May 1953, he was endowed with a fair football talent but even more a deep faith in his own abilities. His career became that of the fabled prefab to penthouse, as he left behind his humble beginnings to bestride the international stage with arrogance and class, making an independent fortune that was further boosted when the glazier's son married the daughter of a Liverpool retail millionaire in 1980. His playing career before 1986 was entirely outside Scotland: he openly professed that he was a football mercenary who would play for whoever offered him most money, and in this regard he was quoted as saying he wished he had been born in England.

As a youngster Souness was a lukewarm Hearts supporter with little interest in Rangers. At barely 17 he constantly criticised the manager of Spurs for not playing him in the first team and as a result was sent to Middlesbrough where he had an unhappy spell before signing on in 1978 for a Liverpool team about to reach the peak of its outstanding progress. There he gained a reputation as a world-class player, and following Liverpool's victory on penalties over Roma in the European Cup final in 1984 he went to Sampdoria, not, as most players unctuously claim, to take on new challenges, but as a tax exile. In Italy, unlike many British footballers before him, he felt very much at home in wine bars and classy restaurants rather than drinking in pubs and eating take-away kebabs. In a Scottish jersey he was as committed to the colours as any home-based Scot, a skilled player whose physical approach was in the tradition of Sammy Cox, 'Tiger' Shaw and Bobby Shearer, added to which was an elegance and a cynical violence that made even his own team-mates wince.

Souness made no secret of his Conservative and royalist opinions, and this would cause no trouble inside the walls at Ibrox or among a large number on the terracings. But he was a winner, so committed to coming out on top that it did not matter to him even if he did so with the help of Catholics – he had even played alongside them, at Liverpool and in Italy, while they were not unknown in the Scottish team. Like anyone with an experience of the game beyond Scotland, he knew that the religion or politics of the men wearing the jersey was irrelevant, and as the entire history of the game has shown, with the exceptions of the isolated cases of Rangers and the Basques, the fans of any team are above all concerned about victory: English clubs had welcomed the foreigners from north of the border in the 1880s, and those that queried the social or national origins of their players were soon left behind; Italy and Spain had always signed foreigners with abandon, and the socially sensitive clubs of South America in the 1920s and 1930s had had to swallow their racism and accept blacks. Today, to the benefit of the player if not the country he has left, Europe is home to the best footballing talent in the world, an expression of the desire of individuals to compete at the highest level and the technological changes that make it possible for them to reveal their talents on a global basis.

In 1986 this was not as obvious as it would become even a few years later, so that when Souness went across the border to plunder players from England he took the Scottish sporting public by surprise. Not only did he sign Englishmen, but he signed top-class Englishmen, two of them current internationalists, willing to play for a recognised inter-national manager, on higher salaries than they could earn in England, and above all with the prospect of playing in Europe from which they had been banned after the Heysel tragedy of 1985. Until Souness, the traffic had been virtually all one way across the border, and many Scots took some delight in the process being reversed: never since Falkirk signed Syd Puddefoot from West Ham in 1922 for £5,000 had any Scottish club paid such a fantastic sum of money for an English player. Several Catholic players were on the market at this time, and the grapevine quivered with rumours as to who had been approached and who would be the first one to sign.

One of the first was Alistair Dick, a Scottish youth internationalist then with Spurs, but his family leaked the story to the press, complete with a picture of the young Dick wearing a crucifix around his neck, and so the club dropped the idea. Glasgow-born Catholic, Ray Houghton, then playing for Oxford United, was the first Catholic to be made an offer by Souness, but he was only too well aware of the situation in Glasgow, and went on to sign for Liverpool, while on the international stage he chose to play for Ireland rather than Scotland – his father came from Donegal. Souness also admitted trying to sign Derek Statham of West Bromwich Albion and another Catholic whom he would not name. This was probably Ian Rush, the deadly Welsh striker and former team-mate of Souness at Liverpool, but who was also known at Ibrox to have admitted that one of his lifelong ambitions was to have an audience with the Pope. Rush was then having an unhappy time with Juventus, and when he returned to England in 1988 it was to his old club, despite an offer of £3 million from Souness, by far the most he had offered for a player until that time. Among other Catholics rumoured to have been linked to Rangers were Liam Brady, one of Ireland's finest ever players and later to become a Celtic manager, and Mirandinho, a Brazilian playing for Newcastle, who claimed that Rangers had approached him. And a month before the signing of Mo Johnston Souness tried to secure the signature of John Sheridan of Leeds United and Ireland.[3] Souness was perplexed at this refusal by the more vociferous fans to countenance Catholic players at Ibrox and asked in exasperation while on World Cup duty in Mexico in 1986: 'Do they want a sectarian team or a successful one?'[4]

By signing Englishmen, Souness eased the fears of the faithful, although some of the new arrivals, such as Mark Falco and Trevor Francis, were scrutinised for any giveaway signs that might reveal deep-felt beliefs, such as the parts of their body they touched or the school to which they sent their children. In Rangers' first major signing, Terry Butcher from Ipswich for £750,000, they had no such fears, although even he had to quash any lingering doubts with a public pronouncement that he was not a Catholic: Butcher was a Conservative, implacably opposed to the IRA and anything to do with 'Southern Ireland'. He refused to listen to the Irish pop group U2 for this reason, and when he found out that Jim Kerr of Simple Minds was a Celtic supporter he threw his collection of the band's tapes out of the window.[5] More to the point he was a great central defender, the captain of England who had knocked back an offer from Manchester United to play for Rangers. Along with the goalkeeper Chris Woods, who arrived at the same time from Norwich for £600,000, he formed the backbone of the new Rangers team. Others came and some went, for transfer fees that seemed outrageous at the time but which would appear like peanuts ten years later, while local Rangers stars, Ally McCoist and David Cooper, cursed that they had committed themselves to long-term contracts: Cooper had re-signed the year before Souness arrived and McCoist committed himself to a four-year contract in 1986. By the summer of 1989 Souness had spent nearly £12 million on 28 players, four of whom, Gary Stevens and Trevor Steven from Everton, Richard Gough from Spurs and Maurice Johnston from Nantes, each cost over £1 million.

THE NEW RANGERS

The English imports were welcomed, and Mark Hateley when he arrived in 1990 from Inter Milan – after a failed attempt to get him from Monaco in France in 1987 – soon found that his rumoured comparison of Glasgow with Beirut was as ridiculous as others knew it was – Brian Laudrup would later comment on how much friendlier the Rangers fans were compared to those of Fiorentina, who were as quick to abuse as they were to idolise. Hateley, after a troubled start, mainly caused by injury but not helped by suspicions that he was a Catholic, soon set up a match-winning partnership with Ibrox favourite Ally McCoist, and won over his critics in the East Enclosure with many match-winning performances. None of these players, however, touched the hearts of the Rangers fans the way certain other English players did: above all Graham Roberts, who came from Spurs for £450,000 in December 1986, and won over the fans with wholehearted displays that owed as much to physical commitment as skill. Like some other English imports he cheerily adopted what he saw to be the culture at Ibrox, and lost no friends for the rumoured stories of how he mimicked the Pope in post-match frolics. Above all he won undying fame when, deputising in goal for Woods, who had been sent off in an infamous Old Firm match in October 1987, he conducted the crowd behind the goal in a few choruses of 'The Sash', a piece of pantomime that would not be lost on Paul Gascoigne when he joined the club a few years later. Butcher was also instructed in how to win over the fans, and received an ovation when he visited the Larkhall Rangers Supporters Club and opened with the immortal phrase: 'No Surrender!'

Souness might have been a Unionist and a royalist, but he could make no sense of the anti-Catholicism that hung around the club. Shortly after he arrived, he could not believe the despondency of the players in the dressing-room when in the last game of the 1985–86 season Rangers won a UEFA place in Europe, but then the news came through that Celtic had won the League. About the same time he made a statement he had to go back on in the official *Rangers News* a couple of years later, when he said: 'I don't care if we lose four times a year to Celtic as long as we still win the League.'

Despite all this, the Rangers fans were returning to Ibrox in droves. On 9 May 1986, the night before the Scottish Cup final between Hearts and Aberdeen, Rangers played in the Glasgow Cup final, a fixture that would normally attract a few thousand out to see the club's young hopefuls, but on this occasion it was a sell-out. That it was against Celtic was one of the reasons for this, but more important was the possibility that the new man might make an appearance on the field that night. The pre-season friendlies in the summer of 1986 had to be made all-ticket games, but not only were the fans coming back, they were coming back with a commitment to the club that denied frequently repeated accusations – and by Rangers people themselves – about them being fickle. Nowhere was this better demonstrated than when thousands stayed behind to cheer the club after defeats in Europe, but above all at the end of the 1989 Scottish Cup final when Rangers lost 0–1 to Celtic and the Rangers support refused to leave the ground. So enthusiastic was their support for their losing team that the post-match interviews with the Celtic captain had as a musical background the sound of the massed choir from the terracing belting out 'The Sash' and other songs of joy.

Souness's first two signings were among his best. One was to end transfer speculation surrounding the fate of Ally McCoist by securing the young star to a four-year contract. The other, not strictly speaking a Souness 'signing', but which needed his approval when he was suggested by Holmes, was the appointment of Walter Smith as assistant manager. Smith, whose dream as a youth was to play for Rangers, had to make do with a career with Dundee United, first as an iron-clad defender then as an assistant to Jim McLean, a manager whose success with the limited financial resources at his disposal must entitle him to be ranked among the greatest managers in Scottish football. Smith was 18 when he signed for the Tannadice club in 1966, and completed an apprenticeship as an electrician while playing part-time football. After 18 months with Dumbarton from September 1975 he returned to Dundee United where

McLean took the thoughtful young footballer under his wing. Smith was desperately disappointed when McLean knocked back the Ibrox offer in 1983, and when the second opportunity came he had no hesitation in accepting it. In February 1986 Smith was approached about partnering Souness in the new Rangers, and although he had ambitions to become a manager, and had indeed been approached regarding the top job at Motherwell, St Johnstone and St Mirren, he had no hesitation in joining Rangers. Souness could not have succeeded without the right-hand man who knew the Scottish game intimately, while the calm and outwardly affable Smith offered a counterweight to the volatile and confrontational Souness. Smith's salary as assistant was much greater than he could ever have expected at Dundee United, and more than he would have received even as manager of most Scottish clubs, while his partnership with Souness paid off when he succeeded him in April 1991 and went on to lead the club to its historic nine League titles in a row.

There was one other signing that in a different sense was more significant than that of the two Rangers stalwarts: Mark Walters. In most countries in the Anglo-Saxon world a 'mixed marriage' is one between people of different races: it is perhaps only in Scotland and Ireland that the notion of a mixed marriage is immediately taken to be one between people of different religions, religious bigotry often being regarded in Scotland as stronger than racial prejudice. However that may be, Scotland is no more immune to racial prejudice than other countries, and while racial chants fouled the air at many English grounds in the early 1980s as more and more teams took advantage of the skills of native-born players of Afro-Caribbean background, there is little ground to believe that the situation would have been any different in Scotland. The reception of blacks playing for English teams in pre-season friendlies was at times poisonous, and it is for such reasons that Souness's signing of black player Mark Walters from Aston Villa for £500,000 in late 1987 must go down as one of his bravest signings. Securing the signature of two Jews, the Israelis Avi Cohen and Bonni Ginsberg from Macabbi Tel Aviv, was of no great moment.

Walters was a gifted player, but this would not have protected him from his colour if he had not been wearing a Rangers jersey, or if the club had not given Souness its complete backing. As it is, Rangers fans who did abuse the newcomer were immediately banned from the ground, while the official *Rangers News* came out strongly against anyone who criticised the signing. Unofficially, the new Rangers fanzine, *Follow, Follow*, placed Walters on the cover of its first number with an editorial saying that 'Blue is the only colour that counts', a policy that it would follow in all subsequent editions. In his first game, against Celtic at

Parkhead on 2 January 1988, Walters was met by monkey chants and a shower of bananas, but at Ibrox he was protected by the club and its supporters, and those whose neanderthal tendencies urged them to join in the chants of the opposition just had to contain themselves.

Some transposed their racism to the 'one of ours' variety, as in the Skol Cup final against Celtic in October 1990, when Celtic's coloured player Paul Elliott fouled a Rangers player and was met by the tirade from a Rangers fan to the effect that: 'You're no' even a real black! You're no' even a real darkie! At least we've got a proper nigger! Mark Walters is black! You're just coffee-coloured!'[6] Among Celtic fans, a similar racism could be found in the woman at a Celtic–Hibernian game some years later who pointed at Hibs player Kevin Harper and asked her companion in a matter of fact way: 'Who's the wee coon?' only to be told that there was nothing to worry about as 'Wee Harper's all right. He's a Mick.'[7] Signing Catholics was another matter. And given Scotland's history, under-standably so. But the time had to come. Most people expected a highly rated foreign Catholic – it had long been a joke about what would have happened to a Maradona or a Pelé or any of the big Italian or Spanish stars who were Catholics, if Rangers had wanted to sign them. In the 1970s this was not on, by the late 1980s it was, and it was from the ranks of such foreigners, English or Latin, that most observers thought that Rangers would bow to the inevitable. Instead Souness dropped a bombshell. It was one thing for him to pick a Scottish-born Catholic, and one with a well-publicised hatred of the club, but to sign one who had played for Celtic and claimed to be a true Tim, a Bhoy to his bootstraps, was going beyond the pale. But there he was before the TV cameras on 10 July 1989, looking somewhat sheepish beside a smirking Graeme Souness. As well might Souness have been grinning, for not only had he taken the Scottish public by surprise, he had put one over Celtic. Indeed there was more gnashing of teeth outside Celtic Park than there was burning of scarves outside Ibrox.

MO SURRENDER

On 12 May 1989, as Celtic prepared for their coming Scottish Cup final against Rangers, Johnston appeared before the cameras at Celtic Park in a Celtic jersey professing his love for the club his heart had never left throughout his spell with French club Nantes. The board and the Celtic fans were delighted, but over the next few weeks there developed 'snags' which deteriorated into bickering and threats of legal action over whether or not Johnston was a Celtic player. There were rumours of him going to Rangers and some bets were even taken on this, but on 25 June

Johnston categorically denied that he would join them. On 1 July his contract with Celtic was withdrawn, and it was then that Souness moved in for the kill. The Celtic board was shown up in a bad light, acting like amateurs and giving the appearance that they had lost the player because they would not meet his financial demands, conditions that Rangers had no trouble in agreeing to.

Johnston was not what many Catholics would be happy to accept as one of their own, as his observance of the faith was minimal and his behaviour not that of which the devout would be proud: in this regard he was no Paul McStay or Tommy Burns. Indeed his father was a Protestant, a lifelong Rangers supporter, but he had married a Catholic and had allowed his son to go to a Catholic school. Tainted by his education, Johnston had taunted Rangers fans when he crossed himself in front of them after being sent off in the final of an Old Firm League Cup final on 26 October 1986, and in a biography published in 1988 he declared his hatred of Rangers for their policy on Catholics. In Rangers terms, then, he was a Catholic, and as such a standing insult to the hard core of the Rangers support; worse, he had worn the colours of the Irish/Catholic club, and in the eyes of some Rangers supporters this was as bad as being a Catholic. But against this the more rational Rangers supporters could rejoice in the way Souness had once more embarrassed their rivals, having snatched their prize catch from under their noses. And even among some diehards this not only made the signing more palatable, it was a consolation devoutly to be savoured: the Tims had been stuffed again!

The more immediate reaction was less philosophical, and the TV cameras lined up to see the more outraged Rangers fans arrive at Ibrox to perform the anticipated rituals of scarf-burning and tearing up their season-ticket books; among the other moments of high drama was when a car pulled up outside the ground and laid a wreath mourning the loss of '116 years of tradition'. There were some angry scenes, especially when Souness appeared, but most of the fans milling around were simply stunned. Union Jacks appeared with 'No Mo Here' on them, and a sign saying 'Traitor's Gate' was hung over the main entrance to Ibrox. On the wall near the M8 motorway, FUCK YOUR MO SURRENDER was painted in big, block letters by Celtic fans for the benefit of passing motorists – in the press the expletive was removed out of respect for their more gentle readers.

In fact there were only about 30 calls by fans asking for refunds on their season tickets, while others called in anxiously inquiring about a new season book to replace the one that had either been lost or accidentally damaged. David Miller, secretary of the Rangers Supporters

Association, who was shocked by the signing, expressed his disapproval in a less than convincing statement that this was more for it being Johnston than for him being a Catholic. At the club's AGM held in the Broomloan Stand at Ibrox in August, however, the angry interjections were outdone by the applause from the 2,000 shareholders when the chief executive, Alan Montgomery, blamed separate schools for religious bigotry, and the biggest cheer of all went to Graeme Souness when he explained why he had signed Johnston: he wanted Rangers to be the best. Some Rangers supporters clubs promised never to appear at any game in which Johnston played, while other Rangers fans ludicrously refused to recognise the results in games in which he played – and therefore that Rangers did not win the League in the 1989–90 season. More rationally, a few Rangers fans refused to go back to Ibrox while Johnston was there, but this proved too much for some, who later went along in disguise: the pain of staying away was too much. Rangers continued to play before a full house and there was no serious trouble between pro- and anti-Johnston Rangers supporters such as greeted the signing of Manfredonia for Roma in Italy. At Ibrox it hardly got worse than one section of the East Enclosure singing: 'Mo, Mo, Super Mo, Super Maurice Johnston', while another part sang: 'Mo, Mo, Fuck your Mo, Fuck your Maurice Johnston'. The whole saga was perhaps best summed up seven years later by the Rangers fan in the Rosevale pub in Partick who told the reporter of the London-based magazine *Shoot*: 'My great-grandfather wouldn't have been able to imagine such a thing. My grandad would have been furious. My dad was uneasy about it. Myself? I don't mind who we sign as long as they can play football. And for my son it won't even be an issue.'[8]

The most outspoken opposition to the Johnston signing came from the 'traditional' areas, although they were depleted as the hardliners had already left for Ireland and the big celebrations on the Twelfth. In Northern Ireland itself a meeting of the Glasgow Rangers Supporters Clubs was held in the Whitehead Rangers Club on 23 July 1989, with invitations for two representatives from each of the 97 clubs in Ulster to attend. The packed meeting placed an immediate ban on travel to Ibrox while Johnston was with the club, which affected the 400 regulars who went to the games; they also called on their 6,000 members to boycott Rangers' commercial products and participation in the Rangers Pools. The meeting was anxious to clear itself of any charge of bigotry, claiming reasonably enough that Johnston had treated Rangers with contempt and they were just returning the compliment, but went on to make the rather contradictory statement that their opposition was not to Johnston being a Catholic, but to the breaking of one of Rangers' main traditions.[9]

Among Rangers' Scottish players there was some resentment. A few years later Terry Butcher told how the Rangers kit-man refused to set out Johnston's gear with the other players', or to give him the chocolate bars that were distributed to them. These duties then fell to Butcher as captain, who also noted that the Scottish players found it harder to accept Johnston than the English, above all for the reaction among their friends.[10] Johnston had had troubles enough living in Glasgow before he left Celtic for France, and so he was provided with a safe house in Edinburgh, in fact Graeme Souness's which was empty at the time, with minders to ensure his safety when he made any public appearances. Unlike Salman Rushdie, who at this time was in hiding from the Ayatollah's *fatwa*, Johnston was in hiding from both sides of the religious divide.

Johnston was immediately branded a Judas by the (more polite) Celtic supporters, and a host of jokes appeared along this theme, although one of the best appeared in *Follow, Follow*, where the Rangers fanzine had a cartoon of Johnston confessing before a priest: 'Forgive me, father, for I have signed.'[11] The Celtic fanzines, in honour of his time in France, dubbed Johnston '*le petit merde*' (the little shit), and 35 members of the New Stevenson Celtic Supporters Club, near Motherwell, petitioned to have its name changed to the 'We Hate Mo Johnston CSC'. A *Herald* photographer caught the Union flag at half-mast at Celtic Park on the day of the deed, and asked, tongue-in-cheek, whether this was inadvertence, recognition of the death of Laurence Olivier who had just died, or just a sign of the general distress at the club.[12] And the *Rangers News* was surely not being serious when it reminded its loyal readers in a front-page editorial that Johnston 'was a player who had entertained the Ibrox faithful in the past with his on-the-field skills'.[13] The readers of *Follow, Follow* were evenly split on the matter, but the Major, one of the fanzine's regular contributors, was not amused. In signing 'the wee beggar rat-bag' he claimed some years after the event, the club had 'broken the mould' and for that he could never forgive Souness.[14] On the other hand, the history of the club, co-authored by one of its most devoted fans, makes the enigmatic statement that Souness 'failed to change the nature of things. He was bucking the Scottish establishment, and the Scottish establishment is blue.'[15]

The fans at Ibrox tried to get behind Johnston, and it helped when he scored the only goal against Celtic two minutes from the end of an otherwise undistinguished Old Firm game on 4 November 1989. It also helped that Johnston had a phlegmatic personality with no serious interest in religion or issues beyond the most basic. In this he was like the black American baseball player Jackie Robinson, who was used to break down the racial barrier in the game in the US when he was signed by the Brooklyn Dodgers in 1947. Robinson had the necessary temperament to withstand the abuse he would expect to receive, in his case from his team-mates as much as from his opponents, as well as the fans from both sides, *all* of whom would be against him. Johnston's problems were minor in comparison and in 1989 the vast majority of the Scottish football public welcomed the Ibrox breakthrough.

But Johnston never really fitted in: singing 'The Sash' or mimicking a flute-player would have done little to help his particular reputation, and in November 1991, having lost his first team place, he left for Everton and subsequently a host of other teams. His departure from Ibrox was without any regrets, but nor were there any recriminations: he had, after all, been one of Souness's most successful signings after his first year. Above all, and to the surprise of none but those who had held bitterly to the exclusion of Catholics before Souness, Rangers had signed and played a Catholic and the world continued to turn on its normal axis.

A NEW BEAR AT IBROX

On a regular basis after the arrival of Souness, Rangers supplied the press with a continuous stream of stories, on the field, off the field and behind the scenes. The most startling of these was when it was announced in November 1988 that Lawrence Marlborough's shares in Rangers had been bought up by a hitherto little-known financial genius called David Murray. Like Souness, the 'whiz kid who snapped up the Gers' had had no previous association with the club, but he soon established his personality in such a way that he won over the most cynical of the Rangers followers as he acted in accordance with his claim to hold Rangers in a custodial relationship, rather than as a property from which he would make a profit.

Murray was born in Ayr, and was rejected twice by his home-town club, first when he played in a trial match as a youngster (after which he went on to play rugby), then with an offer to buy it early in 1988, rejected because he was deemed 'too volatile'. Failing to buy Ayr and take them to who knows what heights, he had to make do with a second choice and buy Rangers. His interest in Rangers came through his friend and neighbour, Graeme Souness, who alerted him to the possibility of the Marlborough shares becoming available, and who later claimed Murray as his best-ever signing. On 18 November the first steps were taken and the deal was completed within the week, a certain urgency entering the negotiations when it was heard that the grasping hands of Robert Maxwell were closing in. This was the second time that the fate of Rangers and the criminal then posing as a public benefactor crossed; before Holmes, Maxwell had offered the position of player-manager at Oxford United to Souness.[16] For £6 million Murray had a bargain, although the club was in the red to the same amount, and Souness showed his faith in the future by pledging £600,000 of his own money: in his own words this was his pledge of a lifelong commitment to the club. It was an ideal partnership to keep Rangers to the fore in the world of international finance and, hopefully, on the international football scene.

Murray's father had been a coal merchant and a gambler, which had led to a divorce and his son having to move from Fettes College in Edinburgh back to the state system, so that while he became one of Scotland's richest capitalists he did not fit easily into a conservative right-wing mould. He was named as a likely chairman of the Scottish Conservative Party, but has stated that none of his companies, including Rangers, has ever contributed funds to the Tory Party; he has also retained a social conscience that saw him defend public utilities in the face of privatisation. Moreover, although a convinced Unionist, he has remained committed to the development of specifically Scottish businesses.

Murray's business career began in 1969 when he started work for £7 a week in his uncle's metal dealing firm in Edinburgh, but four years later he had branched out on his own. By 1976, when he was seriously injured in a horrific car accident that put paid to any of his sporting ambitions, his firm, Murray International Metals, was turning over £2 million annually with a £100,000 profit. In 1982 Murray sold 10 per cent of his steel-broking firm for £1.5 million and two years later won the Scottish Business Achiever's Award. When Murray International Holdings (MIH) bought Rangers, the company controlled a network of 36 companies with an annual turnover of £90 million. Murray by then had branched out into several fields, including the leisure industry, but made money mostly on buying and selling property – in view of his father's experience, however, not as a gambler, but by taking calculated risks.

Murray's upbringing in Ayr had given him a liking for football. But at Fettes College in Edinburgh he found rugby more suitable to his social tastes and his financial ambition: there were more useful contacts to be made in rugby than in football circles. Many of his old rugby mates work for MIH, and the deal with Rangers was nothing great in commercial terms, but like Berlusconi with his multi-million dollar empire and a football team that accounted for only a fraction of his profits, there was more esteem to be gained from the ownership of a club that was the pride of the neighbourhood than the ownership of any number of television stations, retail outlets or metal businesses.

The new Souness-Murray partnership was the public face of Rangers, and while it gave most of the club's supporters a sense of pride in a stadium and players who could match the best from anywhere in the world, there were doubts held by some about how far the club had been taken from its roots, not just in the dilution of its Protestantism, but the way in which it was getting away from the ordinary fan with whom the club had always associated itself. Some at the club were happy to get rid of what they called the scum, and the finances of the club dictated that it pander to the new-found middle-class clientele who like to be associated with success, but misgivings were felt by the true Bears whose territory in the East Enclosure was about to be converted to seating. In the battle between the Camel Coats with season-tickets and the Bears who could only afford to pay on the day, there was no contest. Murray insisted that the fans had to be part of his ambitions for Rangers and Ibrox, but in practice this meant the richer fans, and increasingly so as the years went on. But whatever the rumblings of discontent from those who saw themselves as the true fans, there was always consolation to be found in the embarrassment that Rangers' success caused the Tims at the other end of the city, not only in the players who bestrode the Ibrox turf, but the ever-improving Ibrox stadium. Scarcely was Murray in control of the club than he was announcing new plans for the stadium which would take the club well into the twenty-first century. At Celtic Park concern about the failure to match their rivals was stilled by success on the field in 1988 and 1989, but the respite was little more than a lull in what for a long time was a one-sided battle.

3. The End of the Biscuit Tin

Celtic completed their centenary season in triumphant fashion, with a League and Cup double on the field, and off it a brilliant stage production of the club's history, *The Celtic Story*, which played before enthusiastic audiences at Glasgow's Pavilion theatre throughout most of May and June 1988. The following year they won the Cup again, but thereafter a resurgent Rangers swept all before them. Celtic were about to enter the lean years that they had not known since the early 1960s, and, as in the years on the eve of the Stein era, the board came under attack for failing to meet the supremacy of Rangers. This time there was no Stein to inspire the players; nor was there on the board a figure of the stature of Robert Kelly or even Desmond White to lead directors who seemed more intent on preserving their own privileges than building a winning team. Or buying one, which was the essence of the new ethos. The immediate reaction of the Celtic board to the big spending of their rivals was to protest that they would not be stampeded into trying to buy success, and Tom Grant grumbled at the end of 1986 that Celtic would not 'splash out outrageous sums of cash, just because people see Rangers do it'.[1] Celtic were then at the top of the League, playing before large crowds, but by the end of the season they were no longer at the top and four of their best players were seeking their fortunes elsewhere: Maurice Johnston, Brian McClair, Alan McInally and Murdo MacLeod. In income from gate money and transfer fees Celtic had gained much more than they had spent, but, to use the sarcastic phrases that were fast becoming clichés, the 'family club' was ill-prepared to meet the demands of the new age as they continued to work out of the 'biscuit tin' and to expect the players to 'play for the jersey'.

By the 1980s the entire sports world had undergone a commercial revolution that saw its stars earn money on a scale never before thought possible. The dollar rush began with the individual sports in the 1960s, above all in golf where Arnold Palmer and Mark McCormack of IMG (International Management Group), the world's largest sports management business, showed how sports stars could become millionaires through sponsorship and lending their name to a host of commercial products. At this time Wimbledon, still a haven of amateurism, paid for the balls it used, but from 1968 along came the acceptance of professionals, soon to be earning as much as the golfers, and the manufacturers of balls had to outbid their rivals to pay for the privilege of supplying balls for the world's premier tennis tournament. Cricket in Australia was hijacked by the TV mogul Kerry Packer in the late 1970s, the players having been easily seduced from the bosom of the conservative Australian Cricket Board by offers of vastly increased payments compared to the pittance they had been paid previously. Packer's main aim was to replace the government television monopoly with a hyped-up game tailored for his own Channel Nine television audience. By this time the Olympic Games, always a showpiece for the hypocrisy of amateurism, were put on sale to the highest bidder. The world body for football, FIFA, also underwent a transformation when the Brazilian multi-millionaire, Joao Havelange, replaced the former English schoolteacher and referee, Stanley Rous, as president in 1974. It was a shift away from the more honest, but stuffy and conservative British approach to that of a man who had made millions in the midst of scandalous poverty – a metaphor, perhaps, for the changes about to befall the game.

RISING WAGES, FALLING VALUES

The increases in the salaries of British footballers came slowly, even after the abolition of the maximum wage in England in 1961 and the end of the retain and transfer system in 1963. The odd player was immediately promised £100 a week, but few were paid as much as that and even more were sacked to keep the wage bill down. Three of the greatest coaches of this time, all Scots, Matt Busby at Manchester United, Bill Shankly at Liverpool and Jock Stein at Celtic, men revered by their players and each of whom had known hard times in his earlier life, did what they could to keep players' wages depressed: the Lisbon Lions were on £40 a week, much the same as the stars of Manchester United and Liverpool. In Scotland, Rangers and Celtic also believed that players should be on modest wages: Rangers are said to have lost Jim Baxter because they would not depart from the principle of paying all players the same and give him an extra £40 a week, although this was only one of the factors that sent the Rangers hero south; in the 1970s Rangers' spending on players was curtailed by the expense of rebuilding Ibrox; by the 1980s they were falling well behind what players could get in England, losing John McClelland to Watford and Gordon Smith to Brighton, lowly English clubs that were prepared to pay twice that of Scotland's richest club. Before Souness, Rangers' record signing fee was £235,000, to bring

Craig Paterson from Hibs to Ibrox in 1982, while no player was paid more than £240 a week. Jock Wallace left Rangers because he was not given the money to spend on players that he wanted, and Waddell, Wallace and Greig together received less money to spend on players than was given to Souness in his first years in the club. Despite this it is Celtic that have earned the reputation of being a Scrooge, of operating a 'multi-million-pound business out of a biscuit tin'. The label stuck as they fell behind the free-spending Rangers after 1986.

Rangers' and Celtic's ability to call on loyalties denied other clubs has been the source of their playing strength through the years, although the tug of the jersey and the appeal of the dollar have never been clearly disentangled. It was an issue that went back at least to 1893, when the *Irish Weekly Independent* ridiculed the notion that Celtic players played for the jersey ('faith and fatherland' were the words actually used) when everyone knew that they played 'for 30/- a week'. There is much to admire in a player whose commitment to a club is a loyalty beyond that which is owed to a paymaster, but it is a loyalty that has often been abused, and before the 1980s even the most loyal servant could well ask why he should play for the price of a fish supper when champagne and fancy cars were on offer elsewhere. The days of Jimmy McGrory playing for a club that took advantage of his devotion were long over, although Danny McGrain may well have wondered about his rewards after a lifetime devoted to the same club. He was freed shortly after his last appearance at Celtic Park, in a League game against Falkirk on 2 May 1987, without as much as a handshake from the board or the chance to say a proper farewell to the fans.

Celtic lost Kenny Dalglish in 1977, but Scotland was never going to provide a stage big enough for one of the greatest players ever to grace its grounds. They lost Charlie Nicholas in 1983, a one-time denizen of the Jungle, the Celtic equivalent to the Kop at Liverpool or the East Enclosure at Ibrox, who was unhappy with the terms he had been offered. They tried to sell another brilliant graduate from the Jungle against his wishes in 1982: this was when Tommy Burns' contract ran out and Celtic tried – shades of McGrory and Maley in the 1920s – to tempt Arsenal to buy him for £1 million as a replacement for Graham Rix. In the end Rix stayed with Arsenal and Burns, a future Celtic manager then at the peak of his career, signed a four-year contract on £300 per week (£100 more than before) and a signing-on fee of £18,000, to be paid in instalments over the period of the contract.[2] Even with the inflation of the 1970s this was a considerable advance on the wages paid to the Lisbon Lions, and more than what was paid at Ibrox – but a paltry sum in comparison with the explosion in wages that was to come.

It was not only the players who had reasons for complaint at what the centenary history of Celtic called 'fiscal restraint': Celtic's managers found it a constant source of frustration. Billy McNeill, who spent his entire playing career at Celtic and who was captain of the team throughout the Stein years, was dismissed as manager in June 1983 because he had asked for a contract and indicated that he was not satisfied with his salary. A man of the older generation, he nevertheless felt frustrated by the restraints placed on him so far as buying players was concerned, and he had several battles with Desmond White who had weightier matters to consider, such as the amount of money the club was spending on youth trips, scouting, travel expenses and petrol consumption – while less kindly fans would add the amount of money coming through a particular turnstile. Even in the 1990s, as Michael Kelly tells us of his days as a Celtic director, the club's financial largesse did not extend to car phones and decent catering.[3]

McNeill and White devoted their lives to the one club, but their running battles finally led to a parting of the ways. McNeill's successor, David Hay, ran into similar problems, and when he travelled south in the 1986–87 season in search of players to bolster the defence he was told by chairman Jack McGinn through the columns of *Celtic View* that if he wanted them he would have to finance them out of his own pocket. When the club asked him to resign so that they could maintain the fiction that they had never fired a manager, Hay refused and was discarded, as one of his family said, 'like a piece of garbage'.[4]

McNeill was reappointed to the club at the end of May 1987, in a cloak-and-dagger affair in a Clydebank carpark that excited the imagination of the tabloids, but which was too late to prevent the departure of four class players who were Celtic to the core, but who now headed for more profitable pastures down south or across the Channel. This time around McNeill was given some money to spend on players, but in trying to counteract the spending spree at Ibrox, Celtic were trumped at every turn: on the same day as they bought Frank McAvennie from West Ham in October 1987 for a record £800,000, Rangers paid nearly double that amount to bring Richard Gough from Tottenham Hotspur. It was a story that would be repeated many times over the next few years.

FAITH OF THE FAMILIES

There is much to admire in a club whose board sees itself as the custodian of a set of ideals rather than of being the trustees of a profit-making conglomerate, but none of this means anything if they fail to satisfy the appetite of the fans for titles and trophies. Before Souness, the Rangers board comprised a small group of men who had often been successful businessmen but who were above all devoted to the club – for a long time they were all former players. These men saw themselves as the keepers of a trust, a sacred trust even, of a Protestant heritage which was interpreted by their fans as much as by their enemies as being anti-Catholic. The Celtic board on the other hand, was dominated by a few families devoted to upholding the cause of the Catholic/Irish community and their descendants and friends. By playing Protestants and employing Protestants in various capacities they were able to claim that they were not a Catholic club: what this means is 'exclusively' Catholic, for the entire ethos of the club is steeped in its origins. No one exemplified this more than Robert Kelly, a man of deep principle, justly proud of his club's role in Scottish society, who at the time of the great flag flutter in 1952 urged Catholics to become better organised and to wield an influence in proportion to their numbers as the early pioneers had done. In a speech to the Glasgow Province of the Knights of St Columba in February 1952 he praised that body as an example of how Catholics could fulfil their duties 'to make sure that Catholic laymen, in whatever profession they have been called, exert their influence to the fullest possible extent'.[5] According to his nephew, Michael Kelly, there were suspicions in the early 1960s that he was trying to create an all-Catholic team;[6] and through to the modern era being a Catholic was a plus for any player who came to Celtic Park.

Of the two families that have dominated Celtic since its earliest days, the Kelly name goes back to the signing of star player James Kelly from Renton in 1888. This is often given as the basis for the club's early playing success. Kelly went on to become a director and chairman of the club from 1909 to 1914, staying on as a director until his death in 1932. His son, Robert, took his place on the board and became chairman from 1947 until shortly before his death in 1971. The Kelly name was carried on by his nephew, Kevin, who joined the board on his uncle's death and became chairman in 1991. 'Bob' Kelly was succeeded by Desmond White as chairman, and when the latter died in 1985 the White name was carried on on the board by his son, Christopher.

The Whites were not original members of the club, but in some way they can claim this through John Glass, who more than any other individual was responsible for establishing the club's success off the park in the early years. Glass, who never missed a committee meeting and who was chairman of the club before it became a limited liability company in 1897, died in 1906. He was replaced by his protégé, Tom White, who at 22 years of age was one of the youngest ever directors of a football club. White also inherited Glass's shares. He took over as chairman from James

Kelly in 1914 and remained in that position until 1947, when his son Desmond joined the board. The other name that made up the Celtic family was Grant, represented on the board at the time of the Souness takeover by young Tom, who was brought onto the board in March 1985 in a move to ensure that the power he wielded through his large shareholding was used in the proper way.

Tom's great-grandfather, James, had been one of the original directors, a businessman from Northern Ireland who had made his fortune in the drink trade, but who had been better known in his day for his forays into stadium construction than for anything to do with the team. James Grant died in his native Ireland in 1914, leaving his large shareholding to his son, John, who later emigrated to Canada. When he died the shares were inherited, among others, by his sister, Felicia Grant who lived in Toomebridge, Northern Ireland, and who, through a complicated succession of inheritances, including those of Tom Colgan who had been a Celtic director, ended up in the 1960s with the biggest block ownership of shares in Celtic: 1,705 fully paid and 1,752 half-paid. Although this did not pose a direct threat to the Kelly/White block ownership, Robert Kelly in particular was careful to court her friendship. Although she never threatened to use her share power, she never relinquished it. When she died in Belfast in 1973 her shares passed to Tom Grant's father, from whom he inherited half on his father's death in 1979, with voting control over the other half. There were other Grant shares in Canada, and they would play a key role when moves were undertaken in the 1990s to seize control of the Celtic board from within.

Celtic shares were closely controlled by the majority shareholders, who did not allow them to be traded on the open market, a precautionary measure taken by Tom White in 1933 to keep out 'undesirable outsiders' – more specifically to stall what he feared might have been a threat to the board from the growing shareholding of Willie Maley. The directors ran the club as a family trust, and while that 'trust' was seen to be in the interests of the larger Celtic 'family', and the team did well, there were few complaints. During this time Bob Kelly and Desmond White studiously and honestly portrayed the image of a club that cared about its supporters, many of whom had come from impoverished social circumstances. Against this background, Celtic baulked at expensive moves on the transfer market or grandiose schemes of stadium develop-ment, and the club did what it could to ensure that its poorer followers could afford games at Parkhead. Neither Kelly nor White seem to have made any money out of the club, and Kelly in particular was more interested in its traditions than its bank balance. In 1956 he expressed concern, in view of the way the game was expanding into floodlighting

and international club football, that 'the big clubs will grow bigger and
the middle and smaller clubs smaller, with the possible weakening of the
whole structure'.[7] He was appalled by the abolition of the maximum
wage in England in 1961, and how this would lead to excessive demands
by the players. Faced during this time by one of the best Rangers teams
of any era, he refused to match them by entering the transfer market. In
doing so, however, but even more so by trying to manage the team by
using Jimmy McGrory as a front, he committed the inexcusable sin of
letting the club fall behind Rangers. This he expiated, faced by growing
fan discontent, with the appointment of Jock Stein as manager in 1965.

With the unprecedented success of Stein, the Celtic board was under
no pressure to modernise the club, and Desmond White continued to
treat the supporters as the same battlers who had followed Celtic from
windswept terraces and rudimentary facilities for decades. By the 1980s
the Catholic community in Scotland was no longer that of the
immigrants seeking roots and a place in society as was the case with their
predecessors a century before, nor even that of those in the inter-war
period suffering the worst of a depressed economy in which Protestant
bosses looked after their own and were respected for it. By the 1960s
'The Grip' was more an excuse than a barrier to promotion and Catholics
were firmly entrenched throughout the professional and managerial
layers of Scottish society.

The situation of the average fan was changing throughout Britain and
other advanced capitalist countries, where class lines were no longer as
clear as they had been before the consumer revolution began in the late
1950s. The ranks of the middle classes were swelling as more people
depended for their living on white collar jobs and technology took over
some of the more onerous tasks performed by manual labour. On the
domestic front dishwashers, electric blankets and other appliances were
within the reach of most and cars were no longer a luxury. Living
standards were improving, for most people, but not all, and the gaps were
widening between those in work and those out of work. In less than two
decades from 1970 employment in many of Glasgow's engineering
enterprises was devastated, including 40 per cent of the jobs in
shipbuilding and marine engineering, and while the new shopping
centres with their coffee shops and wine bars added a welcome touch of
class to the city, the peripheral housing estates with their rootless youths
and the country's cheapest heroin remained an urban desert to remind
the better-off that all of Glasgow was not smiling better in the 1980s: the
rich were becoming increasingly richer and the poor more desperately
poor – and forgotten.[8] But there were enough people who saw themselves
as better off to support governments committed to helping the rich.

Celtic and Rangers of the 1980s then, still had supporters who found in football a passion and a leisure pursuit that suited their pocket. But there were others who were not so willing to put up with the conditions that had been borne so stoically by their fathers. This was a reality that Rangers, with their all-seated stadium and the higher prices that went with it, grasped more readily than Celtic. Even Celtic supporters on meagre incomes themselves called out for the club to match the spending at Ibrox, above all on players, as a life of eternal torment at the hands of the Huns was too horrible to contemplate.

THE 'GERS GO MARCHING ON

In Souness's first full season at Ibrox, 1986–87, Rangers won the League for the first time since 1978; they also won the League Cup, but went out of the Scottish Cup in a sensational 0–1 home loss to Hamilton Accies in the first round. Celtic won nothing that year, although they came second in the League and lost the Skol Cup final to Rangers in controversial circumstances. David Hay was replaced by Billy McNeill, in Celtic terms the equivalent of John Greig and Jock Wallace put together. 'Caesar' made a triumphant return to his old club with a team that was as close to being all-Catholic as any in Celtic's history. Unlike his Ibrox rivals with all their high-profile Englishmen, McNeill's team in its first year was the embodiment of the Celtic ethos – although they too had their Englishmen, the Yorkshireman Mick McCarthy and Chris Morris from Cornwall (both of whom were Catholics).

The Rangers 'mercenaries' adapted quickly to their new environment, and welcomed with exaggerated fervour the passions of the Old Firm games. Nowhere was this more enthusiastically demonstrated than at the second Old Firm game of the second Souness season, at Ibrox on 17 October 1987. It was in this game that two Englishmen, captain Terry Butcher and goalkeeper Chris Woods, were ordered off and Graham Roberts, who had deputised in goal, was reported after the game for incidents missed by the referee. Celtic's import from England, the Scot Frank McAvennie, but playing in his first Old Firm derby, was also sent off. It was a dramatic confrontation where Rangers pulled back from 0–2 down to draw 2–2 in the last minute with their depleted team. The major sensation was still to come, however, when the matter was brought before the Procurator Fiscal of Glasgow, Sandy Jessop, and Rangers and Celtic jointly employed Len Murray (a Celtic supporter in his private life) to defend the players against charges that they had engaged in conduct 'likely to provoke a breach of peace amongst spectators'. In addition to the offences for which the players were sent off and for which

Roberts was reported, incidents involving Roberts and Peter Grant of
Celtic were noted, but not acted on: this was when Roberts, deputising
in goal for Woods, 'conducted' the Rangers fans in singing sectarian
songs when Rangers equalised, and when Grant crossed himself
'provocatively' after he had scored his goal. In the cases that went to
court, Woods and Butcher were convicted and fined: McAvennie was
discharged and the case against Roberts was adjudged 'not proven'. For
Archie Macpherson, a veteran reporter of Old Firm games, this one was
no worse than many of those he had seen in his day: there was never any
serious danger of the crowd becoming involved and the Crown had
overreacted. Football, he claimed, was being taught a lesson and the four
players brought before the court, far from being 'a threat to law and
order, were being made scapegoats in a politically hostile environment'.[9]
The blundering of Prime Minister Thatcher into football in the wake of
the Heysel disaster was a temporary glitch in the game, but the use of
television cameras to pick up incidents on the field missed by the referee,
and the intervention of the police, were to become a regular part of the
landscape.

In the meantime, Rangers were saved from a barren 1987–88 season
on the strength of a penalty shoot-out against Aberdeen in the final of
the Skol Cup on 25 October 1987. A late equaliser when the score was
3–2 for Aberdeen climaxed a pulsating encounter and sent the game into
a scoreless extra time. Iain Durrant scored the all important goal from the
spot. Celtic made an early exit from the Skol Cup, but went on to win
the League and then added icing to their 100th birthday cake with a 2–1
victory over Dundee United in the Scottish Cup. They won the Cup
again in 1989, 1–0 against Rangers in a scrappy game in which a late goal
by Terry Butcher was mysteriously disallowed. Celtic reached the Cup
final the following year but were deprived of a third successive Cup
victory when, after a scoreless draw with Aberdeen, the Dons won on
penalties, 9–8.

On such a slender thread hung the fate of manager Billy McNeill,
whose problems on the field were complicated by the growing turmoil
off it. He was not helped by events on the other side of the city where
Rangers were beginning to strike a winning combination and Souness at
last started to curb the appalling behaviour on the field that had marked
his first two seasons with the club. In 1988–89 he set Rangers on the way
to their successive League flags, and repeated the Skol Cup triumph
against Aberdeen, this time with a more convincing 3–2 victory. The
Dons had their revenge the following year, in 1989, but then Rangers
won the League Cup in 1990 with a win over Celtic. The elusive Scottish
Cup would have to wait until 1992. In games between the two clubs,

Rangers outclassed Celtic in the first Old Firm game of the 1988–89 league season with a 5–1 victory at Ibrox in August 1988 that sent the fans into delirium. A few of the more historically aware, however, regretted that Souness eased up on Celtic quarter of an hour after the interval, being content to stroke the ball around with arrogant disdain of the opposition rather than increasing the pressure and wiping out the memory of Celtic's 7–1 League Cup victory of 1957. Some fans, including Walter Smith, tried to remind the players of the need to score more goals, but Souness and the English imports knew nothing of bitter memories past and as a result Celtic's victory at 'Hampden in the Sun' remained unexpunged. Celtic won the second league game, but did not win another Old Firm league game until 24 March 1991. A long winter of bitter discontent had set in for Celtic.

Off the field Celtic lagged even further behind. Shortly after the Mo Johnston signing, the accounts to be presented to the Rangers' Annual General Meeting (3 August) for the year ended 31 May 1989 revealed that Souness was earning at least £4,000 a week, Butcher was on well over £3,000 and eight other players were on about £2,000. It was a massive leap in salaries from even a few years previously, and a millennium away from the day back in 1935 when Bob McPhail and Jerry Dawson made their way up the marble staircase to complain about their bonus for an upcoming prestige friendly against Arsenal at Ibrox. The players had been promised a canteen of cutlery if they won, evoking from McPhail the imperishable protest: 'There's no much use having a knife and fork, Boss, if ye canny afford a steak.' Players travelled to games on public transport in those days, but this was changing in the 1950s and by the early 1960s Rangers players could be seen posing proudly outside Ibrox flaunting their wealth with their Hillman Imps and Ford Zephyrs. Nevertheless, like their Celtic counterparts, they were paid little more than double the salary of a skilled worker: they were still part of the world of the people who watched them each week. By the 1990s the football stars were in a different firmament.

For Rangers fans who had invested in the club there was good news off the field as well as on it. Shares in Rangers had shot up from £16 in September 1988 to £40 in July 1989. That no dividend was recommended was of no consequence: Rangers shares were not a vulgar commodity but a source of pride to be shared with others of the faith. Nor were too many people at Ibrox worried about the £7 million overdraft; apart from the club's assets being valued at £23 million, money was tumbling into the club from all directions.

Alan Montgomery, from a working-class background and unlike Souness and Murray a fanatical Rangers fan from his childhood, was appointed as chief executive of Rangers at the beginning of March 1989. His job was to convert the loyalty associated with the Rangers brand name into commercial reality in a variety of fields that would wander far beyond the Ibrox turf. Montgomery came to Rangers from Scottish Television, and the money to be made from the most lucrative of the media was high on the new executive's list. Ian Archer pictured a future that even he no doubt thought he was exaggerating at the time, but which now seems like an understatement. Archer envisaged Rangers in two years time owning golf courses, cinemas, hotels, strings of restaurants and perhaps even old folk's homes. The club already had interests in the sports goods industry, but there was no reason why it should be restricted to the leisure field. Archer went on to suggest that:

> . . . the day may come when you book your holiday through a
> Rangers travel agency, fly on a Rangers aeroplane to the Costa del
> Rangers somewhere in the Med, where the skies are always blue.
>   If you are a Rangers fan, when you settle the bill the bad news
> will be lessened because the profits will be handed over to Graeme
> Souness to buy even bigger and better players for the club.[10]

In the meantime the club was about to embark on an ambitious programme to make one of the grandest football stadiums in Britain even grander. On 30 March 1990 the club unveiled plans for a two-year £11 million facelift, more than half of which would come from the sale to the public of bonds costing between £1,000 and £1,650. These would give the purchaser a lifetime right to purchase a season ticket in the Top Deck that was to be added to the Main Stand. In addition, executive boxes could be bought for £50,000 each. The standing areas would be converted to seating. It was all a long way from the days when David Hope's plans to introduce executive boxes had been stymied by the protests of those who thought such luxury repugnant to the Rangers tradition. In 1989 the fans had a voice they did not have in the 1960s, but the spirited campaign of *Follow, Follow* to try to save the enclosure from seating was doomed by the new ethos of the club and the number of fans able to pay the new fees, or who were prepared to put themselves in hock to do so.

The bond scheme came into operation at the beginning of June 1990, for the well-heeled by a straight payment, for the less well-heeled it was made affordable with easy payments spread over three years on a low-interest credit scheme. By the end of 1992 Ibrox had three tiers in the Main Stand and all-seated accommodation for 45,000 spectators. Inside were catering facilities supplying anything from Bluenose Burgers and

True Blue Crisps in the fast-food sections to top-quality restaurant meals in the thickly carpeted Top Deck, where a myriad of business deals could be completed without any undue distractions from what was happening on the field.

Fans in the still-standing East Enclosure could be heard chanting: 'You can stick your season tickets up your arse', but their cries were lost in the air. In the pages of *Follow, Follow* the hike in prices was criticised, whether it was of the club for suggesting that a mere £4 enclosure ticket would not allow Rangers to buy players like Mo Johnston, or of the journalist Dixon Blackstock, denounced as a 'cheeky bastard' for sneering at people who wanted to buy a Savile Row suit at fifty-bob-tailor prices, especially when, as in his case, he got into all the games for nothing. Such fans showed more logic than realism, and when *Rangers News* on 6 September 1989 tried to justify a hike in prices for a European game against Bayern Munich, in part by pointing out how much it cost to attend a Diana Ross concert, the retort from the fans was that Diana Ross played Glasgow once every four years, while Rangers, apart from playing domestic games at Ibrox at least 22 times a year, had played many European games.[11]

The fans fighting the rising cost of entering Ibrox had as much chance as King Canute against the waves. They eased their frustration by taking it out on Alistair Hood, Rangers' newly appointed police liaison officer. 'Herr' Hood, with many variations on the SS image, became a much hated figure for taking his duty as overseer of fan behaviour somewhat zealously: according to the fanzines he conducted a reign of terror on wee boys who sang loyalist songs and waved patriotic flags.

THE STADIUM: THE SORROW AND THE PRIDE

The changes at Ibrox were spurred on by the Taylor Report on all-seated stadiums following the Hillsborough disaster of April 1989, and by the example of the stadiums that had hosted the World Cup in Italy in 1990. Sadly, it had been a stadium disaster that led to Rangers reconstructing Ibrox to make it the imposing stadium it is today.

Before the majestic new stadium was erected at Celtic Park in the summer of 1996 and completed two years later, Celtic's ground could never compare with Ibrox Park, except perhaps in its earliest days. But from 1899, and above all from 1929, when the redbrick main stand designed by Archibald Leitch was completed, the Ibrox stadium could be seen on the Glasgow horizon, preserved by an order declaring it a building of historical importance in 1980. Celtic Park is affectionately known as 'Paradise'. A popular story attributes the name to an ironical allusion comparing the move from an enclosure adjoining Janefield

cemetery in August 1892 to being like 'leaving the graveyard to enter
Paradise'; but the more authentic reason is the comment by John
McLaughlin that the club was constructing a Garden of Eden out of a
desert.[12] For the times this was an impressive, even palatial ground, with
its two tracks, one for athletics and one for cycling, whose high banking
gave spectators an excellent view. But it would soon be surpassed by
Ibrox.

Despite the imposing main entrance to Ibrox before the 1970s, the
bulk of the spectator accommodation, like that of most grounds in
Britain, was deplorable, but less deplorable than most and infinitely less
so than Celtic Park. Celtic chairman, Desmond White, justified his
refusal to spend money on ground improvements by claiming that he did
not want to put the game beyond the reach of the ordinary supporter. An
admirable sentiment, and based on a social reality when a few shillings
or a lift over for wee (and not so wee) boys allowed tens of thousands of
people to watch their favourite pastime at reasonable cost – and perhaps
to be infected by the football obsession. It was also a reflection of the
social attitudes of the owners of the grounds that simple facilities like
adequate lavatories and protection from the wind and rain were seen as
luxuries wasted on the poor. Nor was safety a prime concern. The rebuilt
Ibrox of the 1930s was at one stage designed to hold 200,000 spectators,
crammed together like sardines; in fact for the record crowd of over
118,500 who came to see the Rangers/Celtic Ne'erday game of 1939,
thousands clamoured to get out, but the police refused because of the
trouble likely to ensue from the thousands still trying to get in if they
opened the gates. Some never saw the ball that day, others only when it
was hoofed into the air. And on that day, as on innumerable occasions
before and after, and in grounds throughout Britain, tragedy was averted
by the crowds, unencumbered by spectator fencing, being allowed to spill
out onto the track.

It took the tragedies of Bradford in 1985 and Hillsborough in 1989 to
force a radical restructuring of the football grounds of Britain. Long
before the Taylor Report, however, Rangers had embarked on plans to
renovate Ibrox, also, alas, as a result of a tragedy on the scale of Bradford
and Hillsborough. This was on 2 January 1971 when 66 Rangers fans
were crushed to death and 145 injured on the infamous Stairway 13 at
the end of the first Old Firm game of that year. It was not the first
tragedy at Ibrox, or on Stairway 13: the first great tragedy in modern
sporting history took place at Ibrox in April 1902 when a wooden
terracing specially built to take additional standing spectators to hold the
Scotland v England international collapsed, plunging 25 to their deaths
and leaving more than 500 injured, many seriously. The game continued,

a mere charade when the players saw the dead and dying bodies stretched out before them at half-time, while until the final whistle fans continued to watch the game clinging perilously to the structure from which others had so recently fallen to their deaths.

From that time on standing accommodation was built only over solid earth. Unlike cinemas and dance halls, which became with football the most popular sources of public entertainment through to the late 1950s, football grounds were not subject to state regulation until the Safety of Sports Grounds Act of 1975.[13] Because of this Rangers were able to ignore the three incidents involving deaths and injuries that foreshadowed the tragedy of 1971: in 1961 (2 dead, 44 injured), 1967 (11 injured) and 1969 (30 injured) on a staircase that was too narrow and did not allow for funnelling, and whose steps were too steep. Ironically the deaths of 1961 resulted in a measure that added to the deaths in 1971, when the wooden palings that had allowed hundreds to burst through to safety was replaced by solid concrete and wooden sleepers which did not give way in 1971. Whatever the faults of the Rangers Football Club before the tragedy – and these were pointed out in pitiless detail by the sheriff at the inquest – the club's response thereafter was swift and to the point, with money from Rangers Pools being poured into the stadium rather than into players. The result was the new Ibrox that ranks as one of the best in Britain today. The Centenary Stand was built in 1973 and complete redevelopment began in 1978 with the razing of Stairway 13 and the erection of what was to become known as the Copland Stand. The Broomloan and Govan Stands then arose as all-seated edifices to surround the pitch along with the imposing old Main Stand.

A plaque was erected to the memory of the victims on the 20th anniversary in 1991. Willie Waddell, former player and manager at the time of the disaster, who performed heroically when he was the first to realise the scale of the disaster, claimed that the new Ibrox was itself an eternal memorial to the victims. The disaster can never be erased from the minds of those who were affected, and aspects of its reporting have troubled other Rangers fans who were never satisfied with the accepted story of what had triggered off the disaster: a late equalising goal by Colin Stein that had fans rushing back up the stairs to see what had happened. No serious observer could have attributed the blame for the tragedy to Stein: the tragedy of 1971 was one that was waiting to happen and all Stein did was to do what he had been paid – and idolised – for. Other Rangers fans simply wanted the truth of the disaster to be known, and spoke up on the 20th and 25th anniversaries, claiming that the accident took place at least five minutes and anything up to ten minutes *after* Stein's goal.

The popular account certainly rings true. With only a minute to go in a goalless game Celtic's Jimmy Johnstone scored what everyone thought had to be the winner. There was jubilation at the Celtic end, and disgust at the Rangers end, where to a chorus of mumbled and not so mumbled expletives Rangers supporters made for the exit at Stairway 13. While they were still making their way down the steep stairs, some with their feet not touching the steps, as had happened on countless occasions before, a roar from the ground signalled that Rangers had equalised. There was an immediate attempt to make sense of the roar: a hesitation, perhaps some tried to get back up the stairs, although this would have been impossible, but in the confused joy, because the triumphant roar was coming from Rangers supporters, someone tripped and the momentum from above set up an avalanche of human flesh.

What now seems more likely is that thousands of Rangers supporters stayed on at the top of the terracing dancing and singing, and it was from their numbers some minutes later that someone stumbled on the steps – there are several references to a man with his wee boy on his shoulders suddenly disappearing. Even among those celebrating so close to the ill-fated stairway, many went home that gloomy night unaware until they heard about it on the radio or television that they had been so close to what was until then the worst disaster in British sport.

Long before the building of the new Ibrox got under way a religious truce blanketed a shocked city as Catholics and Protestants came together in mourning for the victims. It was not to last, and a new level of depravity was struck 20 and 25 years later when silences in memories of the victims, one at Ibrox, one at Celtic Park, were broken by morons unable to be silenced by the bulk of the fans whose attempts to shut them up would only have made the situation worse – as happened when Aberdeen supporters tried to do something about the cretins among their supporters who were ridiculing the silence in memory of the recent death of the Ibrox legend, big Geordie Young, on 10 January 1997.

THE DYNASTIES DO IT THEIR WAY

As the new Ibrox continued to grow in glory, even those who were finding it difficult to get inside were happy to mock the problems at Parkhead, the Rangers fanzines referring to Celtic Park as 'The Piggery' and its fans and players as the Scum, the Beggars, the Bead-rattlers or the Soap-dodgers. This was the modernised version of the odd cartoon from early in the century that had depicted Celtic as the bog Irish and Rangers as being handsome and elegantly attired. It was an image of Rangers that was to be carefully fostered by William Struth, whose attention to detail

and smartness in dress amounted almost to a fetish, but along with the
arrogance, it did give the Rangers players a certain pride in themselves
and the club.

Celtic, on the other hand, cultivated the image of a club that was
founded on charity, caring for the poor and disadvantaged. But in actual
fact, its directors from the earliest days showed a dedication to making
the club a commercial rather than a charitable organisation, much to the
despair of the stalwarts who had built the club from nothing in its first
years. Most notable of these was John H. McLaughlin, Celtic's first
chairman when the club became a limited liability company in 1897, a
man who had an outspoken contempt for the 'street corner loafers' and
'soup kitchen cranks' who thought that they should run the club. These
were the people whose voluntary efforts had built the ground and formed
the brake clubs, the supporters associations of the time, and who as a
consequence thought they deserved some privileges at the club, such as
concessions on season-tickets and a say in how the club was run. These
same fans also revealed another aspect of their idealism when they asked
for a limit to the number of Protestants the club played. This and other
social considerations were overthrown by the hard-headed businessmen
who converted Celtic into one of the first limited liability companies in
football, ensured that shares on offer to the public did not threaten the
control of the board, and paid themselves some of the largest dividends
of any football club in Great Britain.

It was McLaughlin, too, who, supported by Rangers, was behind the
formation of the League in Scotland in 1890 and its logical and intended
consequence in the introduction of professionalism three years later. One
of his main reasons for doing this was to curtail the financial demands of
players who as amateurs were bound by no contract – it was Celtic, after
all, whose amateur players went on strike for better wages in 1891. He
also thought that professionalism would stop money from the big clubs
being redistributed to the poorer. It was also McLaughlin who stood
against those who wanted to create a clearer-cut Catholic image at the
club and who condemned the Irish community in Scotland for its
opposition to the Boer War. No seeker after popularity, he weathered the
contempt of those who feared the club was falling into the hands of 'a
few moneyed speculators'. In short, Celtic's first chairman would have
been very much at home in the football of the 1980s, where money and
not social responsibility was the prime concern. By the time of his death
in 1909, the club's origins in charity had become, in the words of one of
the club's first historians, paraphrasing Shakespeare, 'sicklied over with
the pale caste of gold'.[14]

A football team on an all-conquering run can get away with almost

anything off the field, and Celtic had had enough successes over the years
to cover the fact that the family club was in fact a narrow patriarchy in
which the fans had little say. There had been widespread discontent
against the board in the 1940s when the club underwent one of the worst
periods in its history, and there were protests against Robert Kelly on the
eve of Jock Stein's appointment. By the late 1980s the fans were again on
the edge of revolt as Celtic fell behind Rangers and the board seemed
unwilling or unable to do anything about it. It was apparent that the club
would have to throw away the biscuit tin and attract new millions to the
club, either through a private individual or by opening the club up to the
fans with a share issue. Faced by such unpalatable alternatives, the board
at Celtic Park retired into a defence of their own private interests. Tom
Grant had been brought onto the board because his potential power
through his shares threatened the incumbents – 70 years after the last
Grant had been on the board. Jack McGinn's appointment to the board
as first commercial manager in 1982 seemed to be a departure from the
control by the 'families', and the official centenary history marked his
appointment as 'indicative of a new era in football'.[15] In fact, as Michael
Kelly tells us, McGinn was appointed to look after Desmond White's
son, Christopher, who had joined the board at the same time.[16] Desmond
died in 1985 and the following year Tom Devlin, another long-standing
member of the board, having joined it in 1949, died. The fate of the club
was in the hands of three young scions of the 'families', to whom would
be added Michael Kelly in 1990; but far from displaying the
adventurousness of youth they proceeded to put a shell around themselves as protection from the outside world.

Celtic marked their centenary year with an official history which, superb
though it is in many ways, still has several blind spots. Its author, Brian
Wilson, a former left-wing journalist and now a politician in the Blair
Labour government, took to task those who depicted the Celtic directors
as bumbling but well-intentioned incompetents: on the contrary, he
claimed, writing from the vantage point of the directors' box, they had led
the club through a 'century of honour'. This was not the interpretation of
an unofficial history that came out a year before Wilson's book. Tom
Campbell and Pat Woods, writing with the faith of the faithful for the
faithful, but from outside the official sanctum, told the tale of a club with
a certain gritty grandeur, but painted in the warts, most of which were on
the faces of the club's directors.[17] This the board of the 1980s found
unacceptable; they refused to recognise the 'rogue' history and any other
books by the rogue historians, which were banned from being sold through
any Celtic outlet. Like the works of Trotsky in the Soviet Union under
Stalin, at least two of the best books on Celtic became non-books.[18]

Other devoted fans of the club were rebuffed by the board for their criticisms. In 1989 Gerry Dunbar of the Celtic fanzine *Not the View* offered the club a bust of Jock Stein, commissioned from funds raised by donations to the fanzine. Refused by the 'Politburo' because of the fanzine's uncompromising attacks on the board, Dunbar took the bust to the People's Palace where it was welcomed into what the fanzine considered a place more fitting as a tribute to the 'People's manager' – among the ordinary fans of the club.[19] With the renovations undertaken by the new owner after 1994 a grander monument was promised with the naming of the Jock Stein Stand behind the western goal, completing the improvements to the spectator accommodation at Celtic Park.

One other reason that the 'rogue' history was banished from Celtic outlets was that it represented a threat to the profits of the official history, a minor manifestation of the biscuit tin mentality with which the club was increasingly being associated. By 1990 a coterie of family friends was in no position to meet the demands of a game that was now a global phenomenon, with riches through sponsorship that were beyond the dreams of the most insatiable even a couple of decades previously. Celtic and Rangers were among the last clubs to adopt commercial graffiti on their jerseys, but even they soon succumbed to the financial blandishments of having their once sacred shirts besmirched by a sponsor's logo. By 1984 they were bowing to the inevitable, and ironically the only thing that held this up was the fear by advertisers that their name on one jersey would alienate half their potential customers. The solution, unique in the unlovely history of turning sportspeople into mobile advertising boards, was for the double-glazing firm of C.R. Smith to advertise on both sets of jerseys. This was before Souness, and shortly after he arrived the commercial balance of the two clubs was so disturbed that Rangers sought another advertiser and found one much more lucrative in the brewer McEwans when the agreement with the double-glazier ran out in 1986. From 1988 David Murray swept the club along on his own commercial wave, leaving Celtic washed up on the shore. Help was at hand, but it was disdainfully spurned.

In 1988 an expatriate Scot, who had gone to Canada in 1964 and made himself into a millionaire, offered Celtic a massive financial injection that would have helped the club out of its problems. Fergus McCann was the son of a high school teacher, an avid Celtic supporter who had been one of the most active members of the Croy Celtic Supporters Club. The bulk of his fortune came from organising golf tours from North America, thus cashing in on a leisure pursuit that was another of his passions. His offer to Celtic in 1988 was for a low-interest loan of £5 million to increase the seating capacity of the stadium with a two-tiered stand and provide standing accommodation for 48,000, in return for which he would receive a percentage of the increased revenue this would generate. Although at this stage McCann was not seeking control of the club, his offer was rejected.[20]

After several meetings with the directors, McCann felt he was getting nowhere, and the following summer he wrote to them offering to buy a 51 per cent shareholding at £110/£120 per share. In addition he would invest capital of £3 million in the club and put up the collateral for a further £2.2 million loan. He now wanted the position of executive director, and although he promised the directors that their positions would be safe, the thought of someone outside the families having a controlling interest in the club terrified them. And so the offer of effectively £7.2 million pounds was rejected, while the directors promised to block any attempt McCann made to purchase shares. McCann, having been rebuffed by the board in what he considered a 'rude and unbusinesslike way', approached Michael Kelly in his capacity as a public-relations officer. Kelly was not then a director, but he refused to take on the job: he was too much in sympathy with what he saw as the 'aspirations' of the board. Kelly believes this soured McCann against him.[21] Given the diametrically opposed position of the two men in regard to the question of power the possibility of friendly cooperation between them was highly unlikely, and so it is pointless wondering how a union of Michael Kelly and Fergus McCann might have saved Kelly himself and the bulk of the Celtic faithful from the traumas that were about to befall them.

Other offers came in to help the club, but they were all rejected. Paul Green, a property millionaire living in Jersey, offered to buy the club for £6 million in August 1989 by buying up enough shares to gain a 51 per cent majority. He intended to build a new stadium in the vacant land near the Parkhead Forge complex in which he had an interest, but his offers were never taken seriously. Gerard Eadie, owner of the double glaziers, C.R. Smith, who were Celtic's major sponsor, also thought of buying the club, but decided to back Fergus McCann instead.

While Celtic remained marooned, Rangers went their own way, as the revolution begun by Marlborough and carried forward by David Murray continued to bring success on the field. Rangers fans who had lived through the shadow of the Stein years and beyond rejoiced in the glory of the new-look Bears and the regular trouncing of the Tims, besides which any faults in the Rangers hierarchy were mere peccadilloes. Celtic were allowed no such luxuries as they drifted further behind Rangers, who threatened to make a mockery of the term 'Old Firm'. The strength of the new Rangers was nowhere better demonstrated than by the comparative lack of disruption that accompanied Souness's sudden departure from the club in April 1991. A few weeks later McNeill was sacked for the second time in his career with Celtic, and again the fury of the Celtic fans was directed against the board. Two unsuccessful replacements as manager failed to relieve the situation, while Rangers without Souness went on to even greater domestic success. It seemed as though they could do no wrong.

4. *The Souness Legacy*

Souness's departure from Ibrox was in the manner of his coming: sensational, but clinically pure in its execution. On 15 April 1991, just four games short of the end of the season and with a tense struggle with Aberdeen standing in the way of a third successive League Championship, he told David Murray officially that he had accepted the position of manager of Liverpool. Souness, who had been torn by the temptation of the Liverpool job since shortly after it became vacant with the resignation of his old club-mate, Kenny Dalglish, two months earlier, wanted to stay on to the end of the season. But Murray would have none of it and insisted that he pack his bags and depart forthwith. The man who had said Rangers was the biggest club in Britain and the only one he wanted to manage, a pledge he had renewed just a few weeks before in the official *Rangers News*, was returning to his old club Liverpool, which he now claimed to be even bigger than Rangers. In an interview with *Sportsweek* a few months after his arrival at Ibrox he had specifically stated that: 'Even going back to Liverpool would be a downward step.'[1]

At the press conference held on 16 April, after a curt introduction by Murray, a tense Souness read out a statement saying that he had left for two reasons: first and most important in order that he could be closer to his children who were living in the south of England; and second, because he felt he had gone as far as he would be *allowed* to go in Scotland, a veiled reference to what he saw as his bad treatment by the SFA and the media, and possibly, as it was later revealed, that his spending powers were being curtailed at Ibrox. Certainly, he was on a collision course with chairman Murray because of his abrasive attitude to anyone he disagreed with. There was speculation at the time that Souness could pocket a handy profit on the £600,000 worth of Rangers shares he had bought in November 1988, and now worth about £2.25 million on the open market, but in fact they had been bought under a special agreement with Murray's company that he could buy them back at a prearranged price.

Murray's insistence that his old friend depart immediately was echoed by press headlines that screamed 'Get Lost Souness!'[2] and 'Get Out Now!'[3] It was treatment Souness himself had dished out to players who had crossed him, but when the dust had settled, and while Murray was probably correct in saying that leaving Rangers was the biggest mistake Souness would ever make, the overall verdict of the Rangers fans was that he had been a good thing for the club: he had given them a team to be proud of and had taken them irrevocably beyond the parochial sectarianism that had blighted the club before he arrived.

McNeill's departure from Parkhead a few weeks later was another untidy affair, as the manager was kept wondering about his fate after another trophyless season. The board dithered before the one-time Celtic hero found out in a document leaked to *The Sun* outlining how the club could get rid of him with minimum embarrassment. Six years on and another Celtic hero would depart from Parkhead in acrimonious circumstances, and again for the same crime: failing to win trophies and beat Rangers.

At Ibrox, Walter Smith replaced Souness and led the team to unprecedented domestic success, while at Parkhead Celtic had no one in mind to replace McNeill. Souness went on to prove David Murray's warning correct in every way: after pulling Liverpool down to hitherto unheard of depths he went on to pass an undistinguished two years in Turkey, with Galatasaray, before returning to England in 1996, to all but oversee Southampton's relegation from the Premier League in 1997. In the summer of 1997 the rumour-mongers linked him with a return to Scotland – as manager of Celtic! A Rangers cast-off would hardly have enhanced the image of Celtic, and this particularly bizarre piece of gossip ended when Souness left to manage Italy's Torino, a team with a glorious and tragic past, but then in a lower division of the Italian League. There, he lasted only six games before he was relieved of his duties and, after other European peregrinations, finally settled with Blackburn Rovers. In the meantime, a more mellow Souness has discovered that there is more to life than managing winning football teams.

At Ibrox, however, despite the joy among some of the fans and their celebration that Ibrox was now a Souness-free zone, the final summary was positive. Souness was the man who had signed Walters and Johnston, brave decisions that would have been beyond anyone before him; he had brought top-class players from England and abroad, and although they were never given enough time to mould into a team with a style that their price tags warranted, Rangers won three League flags and four League Cups during his five seasons at Ibrox. Walter Smith wanted to give Souness the credit for the League flag won in a last game decider against Aberdeen in 1991: the Dons only had to draw to win the flag, but collapsed before an ever-improving Mark Hateley and an Ibrox crowd that surpassed itself in acting as a twelfth man that day. Murray was less

generous than Smith about whether Rangers would have won the title
without Souness, but he did recognise that Souness was the man who
had 'turned the big ship round'.[4] On the eve of Souness's arrival, Ibrox
had been noted for its mediocre players playing before sparse crowds who
had come to tell them how awful they were. Included among the chants
then was: 'Ally, Ally, get tae fuck.' Souness's unwillingness to play the
same Super Ally had irritated the same Ibrox crowd who had come to
love the irrepressible Coisty and no one had a wider grin than the star
striker at the news of Souness's departure. He went on to form a
magnificent partnership with Mark Hateley, probably the best at Ibrox
since Millar and Brand or, for those with memories of the cloth cap days,
of Waddell and Thornton.

SOUNESS AND RANGERS

Souness brought the crowds back to Ibrox and he gave the club a new
image. As had been said many times before 1986, Rangers would gain
more supporters than they would lose by playing Catholics, and any who
stayed away for that reason the club was well rid of. Under Souness this
had been shown to be the case. Above all he brought success on the field.
And yet his departure was never actually mourned by anyone – even
David Murray claimed that Souness's abrasive manner was heading for a
confrontation between him and the club: for Rangers it was a good move.

People who have met Souness and those who claim to know him will
tell you that he is a most sophisticated man, an excellent dinner companion with a remarkable breadth of knowledge. There are also tales of
his visits to sick children and of his bedside vigil talking back to a full
recovery the son of a Sampdoria director who was seriously ill following
a car accident.[5] But for the vast majority of us who have nothing to go
by but his public pronouncements and his behaviour on the field, or his
treatment of those in his employ, at least as transmitted through the
media, it is another character altogether that emerges. Souness had never
courted popularity, and said from the start that he would rather be
respected than liked. But even respect is hard to find for a man whose
winner mentality insisted that no one had the right to win but him. This
was the Souness who earned three red cards in his first two seasons at
Ibrox: one during his first game for a brutal attack on George McCluskey
which put the Hibs player in hospital, the second in the game against
Aberdeen that decided the Championship that year, and the third in the
first Old Firm game of the 1987–88 season. A (now famous) tea lady at
St Johnstone's MacDiarmid Park, television sets and dressing-room
furniture felt his wrath after away setbacks, and a runners-up medal was

thrown away in the dressing-room after Rangers lost to Celtic in the 1989 Cup final, accompanied by an angry outburst that he did not collect these.

On the park the players followed his example, and even some Rangers supporters were alienated by the physical attacks on opposing players. The result was an inordinate number of red and yellow cards, while the atmosphere at the Barnum and Bailey Old Firm game at Ibrox in October 1987, when two Rangers players were sent off and one more booked after the game, was determined when Souness refused to let his team walk out onto the field at the same time as Celtic. He gave the press even more to think about when he astonished them by apologising for the behaviour of his players at another torrid Old Firm encounter, on St Patrick's Day 1991, that saw Celtic through to the semi-final of the Scottish Cup. Once more the guilty Rangers were Anglos: Terry Hurlock, Mark Walters and Mark Hateley, for a second bookable offence. Peter Grant of Celtic was expelled for accruing two yellow cards – in the space of seconds – and in total there were three red and six yellow cards flourished. Three more Rangers players were ordered off in the next four League games.

Inside Ibrox Souness brooked no dissent, and after a verbal exchange with Graham Roberts after a 0–1 home defeat against Aberdeen in April 1988 that almost ended in blows (according to popular myth it did), the Ibrox favourite was humiliated by being sent to third-team games around Scotland before leaving permanently for England. Terry Butcher, another Anglo whose whole-hearted commitment to the club in every sense won the hearts of the Ibrox crowd, was forced to leave in November 1990 following a dispute over being asked to play in a Skol Cup final against Celtic, the culmination to a period of friction over the captain's fitness. Like Roberts he left without being given the chance to say farewell to the fans, either on the pitch or in the *Rangers News*. Those with longer memories could recall Souness's treatment of Ted McMinn and Robert Fleck in the early Souness years, while Derek Ferguson suffered similar humiliation: but for many all this was surpassed by Souness's refusal to use McCoist in the starting line-up for most of the 1990–91 season.

Off the park, Souness allowed no one but Murray to challenge his authority. Alan Montgomery arrived at Ibrox to do for Rangers in the commercial field what Souness was doing on the playing field. Unfortunately he was one of those increasingly rare birds at Ibrox, a high executive who had been a fanatical fan in his youth. It appears that his anxiety to be part of the action with the players, turning up at their training camps, appearing in the dressing-room, annoying them by his presence on the team bus, and even offering his advice on who should or should not be playing, led to strained relations between the two powerful egos and a situation where either Souness or Montgomery would have to leave. The players made their opinion felt in what the Souness-friendly *Sun* called 'a multi-million-pound rebellion if Graeme Souness is forced out', headlining the article: 'If Souness Goes, We Go.'[6] It was no contest, and was resolved when David Murray returned from a brief holiday and transferred Montgomery to a less sensitive part of the Murray International empire.

Referees were not the least to feel the lash of Souness's tongue, on the field and even off it. At the end of a Celtic v Rangers game at Parkhead on 29 August 1987, when Celtic won 1–0 and Souness was sent off, he was in conversation near the exit when he was approached by the match referee, David Syme, whom he promptly told to: 'F*** off, you poof,' a remark that he allegedly repeated in front of the match linesman.[7] Three red cards and eight yellow cards saw Souness making several trips to the offices of the SFA, a body for which he had the utmost contempt. This was not helped when they imposed what he thought were tough penalties, and as a result Souness had to watch several games from the touchline even when he was not injured. Standing idle on the touchline often proved too much for him, and in February 1989 he was fined £1,000 and banned from the touchline until the end of the season for swearing at a linesman in a game against Dundee United at Tannadice. In April 1989 further abuse in a Scottish Cup semi-final at Celtic Park against St Johnstone earned him a £2,000 fine and banishment to the stand until the end of the following season. It was while under this second ban that Souness was picked up by the cameras of Scottish Television watching the game from the tunnel at Ibrox during a Hearts game in February 1990; this time he was fined £5,000 and banned from the touchline until the end of the 1991–92 season. Scottish football could indeed do with some redistribution of wealth, but this was hardly the way to go about it, and while Souness felt he was hard done by, at least linesmen at games where Rangers were playing could relax a little knowing that he was not breathing down their necks.

Souness vented his rage against the cameras that had picked him out breaking the touchline ban by refusing STV entry to Ibrox, and even when he was with Liverpool he decreed that comments made to the media were not to be used by STV. Referees, the SFA and the media were an unholy trinity that Souness thought were out to get him at every turn. Several print and television journalists were refused entry to Ibrox or to speak to Rangers players, and some newspapers were totally banned. At Kiev Airport two reporters, from the *Daily Mail* and *The Scotsman*, were thrown off the transit passenger bus on the grounds that it was for

Rangers players and officials only. James Traynor, then of the *Glasgow Herald*, was dismissed as a 'little socialist' for his criticism of Souness for what he saw as bad sportsmanship in a European game against Red Star Belgrade in 1990.

In the early days of the war with the press, the *Sunday Mail* had issued a two-page spread headlined 'Fortress Ibrox' with a mock-up picture of the main entrance to Ibrox with barbed wire and heaped sand bags around it. It was the *Sunday Mail* that had highlighted the story of Souness's admonition to David Syme to depart in the Celtic Park incident of a few weeks before and as a consequence it had been banned. But it was not alone; and only the Scottish-based *Sun*, to which certain Rangers players, including Souness, contributed for lucrative sums, seemed free from the wrath of the Ibrox officials.

The media had much to be grateful for in the Souness revolution, as his free-spending on players and the improvements to Ibrox supplied them with a constant stream of headlines and stories for their columns and sports reports. On a couple of occasions he had reason to be grateful to them, most notably, as Sandy Jamieson has shown, for the way they played down his attacks on St Johnstone tea lady Aggie Moffat, and ignored the near-physical confrontation he had at the same time with Geoff Brown, chairman of St Johnstone.[8] This was in the midst of Souness's turmoil over whether or not to accept the Liverpool position, but, as he had shown long before this, he did not need private problems to provoke attacks by those who criticised him: Souness felt betrayed when the press commented on the negative aspects of his behaviour and criticised the team when it failed on the field. Never before had football so frequently occupied the front pages of not only the tabloid press, but even of papers like *The Herald* and *The Scotsman*. It was part of the increasing appeal of football to a wider social spectrum, part of a circulation war among the tabloids, and always an illustration of the way in which journalism was being reduced to blaring headlines and sensation rather than analysis.

New newspapers have always found it difficult to find a niche in the established market, and serious papers even more so. It is perhaps ironic, nevertheless, that David Murray's unsuccessful venture into newspaper ownership with the *Sunday Scot* in the early 1990s, one of his few business failures, was due in part to the lack of sports exclusives, many of which related to Rangers, with Murray himself apparently not even supplying titbits for his own paper. Not only did Murray reveal nothing of the impending departure of Souness, a matter which was decidedly delicate, but neither did he let it know that Walter Smith would be his successor. Other papers got these stories first.[9]

The most important aspect of Souness's contribution to Rangers came in a measured article from one of the more balanced contributors to *Follow, Follow* while Souness was still at Ibrox. In this article,[10] the writer calling himself 'MacDougall' challenged the almost pontifical position at Ibrox held by Bill Struth, the club's revered manager from 1920 until 1954, two years before he died, aged 81, on 21 September 1956. MacDougall claimed that Souness's legacy was much more important. Struth had certainly done more than anyone else in his 34 years in charge of Rangers to make the club what it was. In the post-war years, however, the methods that had served Struth in Rangers' period of sustained dominance were no longer suitable, as an ageing Struth seemed more intent on having his own way than bringing Rangers into line with more modern methods. As MacDougall reminded the Rangers fans, Struth had been involved in an unsavoury boardroom squabble in 1947 which had ended with the removal of the popular James Bowie because he had wanted a younger man to replace Struth. A few years later, at the end of 1953 when the club faced a slump, an unusual flurry of letters to the press advocated among other things the reinstatement of James Bowie, more spending on new and younger players (instead of floodlighting), while one even called for a boycott of the club if the directors did not brighten up their act. Struth, approaching 80, retired at the end of the season, but made sure he was replaced by someone of his own choosing, Scot Symon, who was guaranteed to carry on his policies. The great Rangers teams of the early 1960s took the pressure off the board for another few years, but failure in the face of Stein's Celtic resulted in an unusual fit of panic in the Rangers board in the late 1960s. Until Souness arrived, however, the club remained firmly anchored in the past created by Struth.

This is not the interpretation of the more traditional Rangers followers, who see Struth as a god-like figure, a spiritual presence still hovering over Ibrox into the 1990s, as he is depicted in the dramatised Rangers history, *Follow, Follow*. The traditionalist Rangers historian, Robert McElroy, continued the deification of Struth, claiming that:

> [Struth] will surely be seen by history as one of the greatest of British football managers, surpassing perhaps even the achievements of Jock Stein with Dunfermline and Celtic, Herbert Chapman with Huddersfield Town and Arsenal, and Matt Busby at Manchester United, all of them in differing [*sic*] eras.[11]

Struth can indeed be compared with Chapman. In the 1930s they were managers of the richest clubs in Britain and the glamour that attached to them. Arsenal, like Rangers linked to Freemasonry, were known as the Bank of England club and from 1933 the two teams played regular friendlies, most of which Rangers won. For both men, too, soccer was a secondary interest. It was said of Chapman that he had little commitment to the game itself, and was more concerned about packed grounds than the spectacle provided on the park. Unlike Struth, however, Chapman was a crafty tactician, albeit with an ultra-defensive outlook. He also had progressive ideas on the development of the game, from the use of floodlighting to the need for systematic coaching and regular contact with continental teams: for such reasons he has to be ranked with his two close friends, the Austrian Hugo Meisl and the Italian Vittorio Pozzo, as one of the three great figures of world football in the early 1930s.[12] Struth was hardly heard of outside Scotland and the best that can be said about his knowledge of the game is that he had the sense to admit his ignorance in this regard and to defer to the senior players.

As for later figures in British football, Matt Busby, Bill Shankly and Jock Stein will always be on a different plane from Struth. These were men who lived and breathed the game for the game's sake, interested in it beyond their own club, men who knew what it was like to carve out a living working down the mines and who shared a sympathy with those who came from a tough background. They were disciplinarians who cared more about how the players conducted themselves on the park than whether they wore beards or ties or polished their boots before the game. But even in comparison with other Rangers managers, as MacDougall pointed out, Souness did more good for Rangers in five years, even considering the different eras from which they came, than Struth did in 34.

By the time Souness left Ibrox he was on much better terms all round than he had ever been, the worst complaints coming from his failure to play Ally McCoist in the starting line-up. Indeed, Rangers were on the verge of fulfilling most of the promise that had always been there. But they were still a long way from winning the prize that had been Rangers' main aim when Souness was brought to Ibrox, and the one thing that had justified all the expenditure: success in Europe as a preliminary to Rangers taking part in a new European Super League.

SUPER LEAGUES AND EUROPE

The logic of football since the earliest days has been for the best to play with the best: apart from ensuring attractive fixtures, this also ensured that the big clubs kept to themselves the money they generated. Once professionalism was established in England in 1885 the players had to be guaranteed regular fixtures to pay their wages. Friendlies and the hazards of cup games were not enough and so the Football League was founded by some clubs from the north of England in 1888. It was not called the English League precisely because it was hoped that Scottish clubs would join it. Its founder, the Scot William McGregor of Aston Villa, openly declared it to be a 'League of the Selfish'. Operating alongside but separate from the amateur Football Association, the aim of the Football League was to protect the interests of the professional clubs under its jurisdiction. A separate Scottish League followed in 1890, and professionalism was recognised three years later. The interests of the big clubs, however, despite the efforts of McLaughlin of Celtic and his Rangers counterpart, were restrained by a prevailing amateur ethos that frowned on trafficking in human flesh and which imposed restrictions that ensured that the weak clubs had as much say as the powerful. One hundred years on and the power structure of the Scottish game still prevailed, albeit with several readjustments of the league set-up, until the breakaway 'Premiership' of the top ten was ratified by the League in February 1998.

On the continent and South America there has seldom been much emphasis on the rich clubs helping the weak, and players were not bound by the conditions in Britain that tied players to their clubs in a virtual feudal relationship: or if they were they were well paid for it. It was one of the ironies of the English-speaking world, and that of the Scandinavian countries, where the Protestant work ethic prevailed, that the virtues of profit-making in commercial enterprises were seen as an evil in sport. In the Catholic countries, by and large, players were paid high wages and treated like stars without any twinges of conscience.

In the 1960s British clubs began to enter the brash new world of continental football, and in doing so adopted many continental practices that were often equated with Catholicism, in particular the desecration of the Sabbath. In England the abolition of the maximum wage in 1961 and the Eastham case of 1963 that ended the retain and transfer system paved the way for the open slather freedom of contract of later years. Scotland had not been bound by the wage ceiling, and the higher wages now on offer in England made playing there an added attraction, although it was the great teams of the 1950s, Hibs and Hearts and Aberdeen, who suffered most, as Rangers and Celtic had always been able to match the salaries paid in England. As well as which they had had the power of the jersey. From this point of view the Old Firm has been a good thing for Scottish football.

By the 1970s Celtic and Rangers had both been drawn into the European football world, and for Rangers this meant compromising their stand as a Christian club that refused not only to play football on a

Sunday, but which would not allow Ibrox to be used for commercial purposes on the Sabbath. Celtic, as a Catholic club, had less reservations about desecrating the Sabbath, but like Rangers before Souness they could still not accept paying continental wages, and like them relied on the services of home-grown players. All this would change: the last knell of the Christian ethos tolling when both clubs told the men of the cloth, who had previously been admitted free to games at either stadium, that in future they would have to pay to get in. As one spokesman for the Catholic Church, Father Tom Connelly (reflecting the always ambivalent nature of 'progress') said when the gradual phasing out of clerical privileges at Celtic Park ended with their abolition in July 1996, 'The days of priests having no money and relying on hand-outs are long gone.'[13]

Football by the 1980s had become a truly global game, especially as television linked the entire world so that people in the most remote places could tune in and watch the giants of the world game. At the same time as football embraced the world, however, Europe took a stranglehold that concentrated the money being made from the game in that continent. South America still produced some of the world's greatest teams and players, but most of them were playing where the money was: in Europe. Out of Africa came young black stars, a trickle in the 1970s; but now few top-class teams in Europe are without a star African, or player of African origins. The loss of talented players to their homeland is part of the logic and history of the game: beginning with the Scots going south for the money on offer in England from the 1870s; the Argentines being tempted by open cheque books to play in Italy in the 1920s; the stars of the smaller countries of South America who went to Brazil, Uruguay or Argentina . . . Today there are football honey-pots in the Middle East and more recently in Japan, but money is not the only reason why these young men with talent in their feet leave their homelands: they also want to play with the best, and the best want to play with each other. And today, for good or ill, that is in Europe, where the European Cup, now called the European Champions League, is the world's most prized football competition outside the World Cup itself.

Entry to any European competition has to be through the domestic competition, and the peculiar set-up within the FIFA 'family' of the four 'nations' of the United Kingdom being allowed four representatives within the single political nation, has tied Rangers and Celtic to the Scottish game. Souness made it clear when questions were put to him in the wake of publicity after the publication of the centenary history of the Old Firm in 1988 (*Glasgow's Giants*) that his ambitions lay outside Scotland – it was obvious that the vast Rangers expenditure was not to

ensure victory against Raith Rovers or Dunfermline, let alone Celtic or
Aberdeen. A British League was out of the question, as the English
competition had little to gain from a merger with the top two or three
Scottish teams, and such a move would play into the hands of those who
would like to see the British nations reduced to a single entity. A British
Cup was more feasible, or at least opening the FA Cup to the rest of the
United Kingdom, as was the case until the SFA banned the participation
of Scottish clubs in it in 1887. It would have been feasible, but unlikely
as it has little attraction for the English teams, while the SFA would be
concerned about the effect on its own cup competition.

Rangers' entry into Europe was guaranteed every year after Souness
arrived, but they saw themselves as shackled by the domestic game and
tried to blame this for their failures in Europe. Certainly the Scottish
League system was in a state of disarray in 1991 and 1992, as it had been
before and would continue to be afterwards, as the small clubs tried to
survive in the top ranks and the richer tried to get rid of their influence.
This has usually ended in compromise. When Rangers tried to break
away from the Scottish League in May 1964 they were thwarted by the
small clubs and Bob Kelly of Celtic, a constant champion of their rights.
Rangers had then proposed that the League should be wound up and
that whatever assets were left to the League after all its debts had been
settled should be divided up among the clubs in the League at the time.
This was clearly aimed at a breakaway by the bigger clubs, and the
smaller clubs used their numbers to block the Rangers proposal.
Throughout they were backed by Kelly.[14]

The Premier League was in part prompted by Jock Stein's frustration
with the old Scottish League. At the height of his triumphs in the 1970s
he had said: 'It is difficult to stay in an unhealthy house without catching
some of the disease.' But he was calling for its reform, rather than
expressing a wish to leave it, and the Premier League was the result. In
1986, David Hay said in exasperation at the refereeing after the Skol Cup
final of 1986 that if he had had his way an application to join the
Football League would be in the post at the earliest opportunity. In 1993
the most determined attempt until then to form a breakaway Super
League was thwarted again by Celtic.

On 26 June 1992 five of Scotland's top teams announced the
formation of a Scottish Super League (SSL). To comply with the League
regulations, they declared their intention to resign from it so that they
could start their new League in two years' time. The SSL was to be made
up of eight teams, access to which would be available only to one
approved club that beat the bottom team in the SSL in a play-off. In
addition to the League, there would be a Super League Cup and a

British Cup where the top 11 English clubs would be invited to join the
top five in Scotland. Three points for a win would add an attacking
flavour to the game and there would be a four-week winter shut-down.
The five core clubs were Rangers, Celtic, Aberdeen, Dundee United and
Hearts, to which would be added three more to make a SSL of eight
clubs, based on the Premier League in England. It lacked, however, the
wide range of top clubs down south, and one of the factors that made
the FA's hijacking of the biggest clubs in the League so messy was that
the top ten clubs in England in the late 1980s when the issue was being
mooted were not the same as those in the 1970s – a decade when even
Manchester United had been relegated. But an even greater impediment
to the success of the SSL in Scotland, compared to the Premier League
in England, was that the SSL was battling against both the SFA and the
Scottish League, while it was the FA, reversing its traditional role in
English football, that led the richest English clubs in their breakaway
from the Football League.

Apart from the richest clubs ruling in their own interests, it is hard to
see how the rest of Scottish football and its fans would have benefited.
Hibs would have to have been added to the Super Five, but who made
up the lucky two to complete the SSL was going to end up in a terrible
bun fight – Motherwell, Kilmarnock, Dundee, Dunfermline, St Mirren
and other clubs had often been within striking distance of the top. And
to further confuse matters, one of the select five, Dundee United,
managed to get themselves relegated from the Premier League in 1995.
The breakaway was engineered by Rangers and Aberdeen, but it was
Wallace Mercer of Hearts, fresh from trying to get rid of Hibs, who acted
as spokesman for the SSL, claiming that the new streamlined competition was the way forward and all was for the best in the best of all possible
football worlds. Murray's intentions were quite clear: he wanted Rangers
to be freed from the tyranny of the wee clubs that made up the Scottish
League. Above all the big two (or five or eight) would be free to keep
more money to themselves instead of sharing it with those they regarded
as little more than leeches. In the end it was Celtic, along with Partick
Thistle, who scuttled the deal, by which time the proposed new League
had been expanded to 12 teams.

Little was gained from it, but when Murray launched his next attack
on the football authorities three years later, his plans were kept under
wraps, the other nine teams in the Premier League were brought into the
scheme from the beginning and the details were worked out by a private
company before being released to the public, in part at least, in September 1997. Above all he then had Celtic's new owner as a firm ally. From
the moment McCann arrived at Celtic Park in 1994 the Old Firm were

back in business, ready to express their contempt for the underdogs of
Scottish football. In the meantime both Rangers and Celtic continued to
show that they were the underdogs in European football.

THE OLD FIRM IN EUROPE

There was a time in the decade from the mid-1960s when Rangers and
Celtic could reasonably vie for the title of European champions – and
that with home-grown players. In the early 1980s it was Aberdeen and
Dundee United who most proudly carried the Scottish flag into Europe:
Aberdeen beat Real Madrid in the European Cup-Winners' Cup in 1983
and went on to beat Hamburger SV in the Supercup over two legs; and
a gallant Dundee United, who went so close to the final of the European
Cup in 1984, lost in the final of the UEFA Cup in 1987. The glory days
of European football now seem to be lost to Scotland, however, and
neither Celtic before Seville 2003, nor Rangers, a few cherished games in
1993 notwithstanding, have been able to bring them back.

In 1984 both Celtic and Rangers were involved in torrid encounters
in European competition, in one of which Celtic were cheated out of a
hard-earned victory in the Cup-Winners Cup, and in the other Rangers
were plunged into the Irish conflict in a UEFA Cup game in Dublin.
Celtic had lost the away leg of their second-round UEFA Cup game
against Rapid Vienna by 1–3, but in a night of passion at Parkhead on 7
November 1984 they had come back to win 3–0. Or at least they
thought they had. Instead the victory was snatched from them thanks to
weak refereeing, the antics of an Austrian player who claimed to have
been felled by an object thrown by a spectator and whose wound was
quickly bandaged up before anyone could see it, and worst of all by the
complaisance of UEFA who decided that the game had to be replayed at
a ground more than 100 miles from Glasgow. Desmond White decided
to go ahead with the replay, confident of a win and assured of a monster
gate, but the game played at Manchester turned out to be a nightmare as
Celtic lost 0–1 and two fans, one wearing a Celtic jersey, attacked the
Austrian goalkeeper and the Austrian scorer in separate incidents. This
time UEFA's punishment was justified – lenient even – as they fined
Celtic £17,000 and decreed that their next home match be played
behind closed doors.

Celtic and Rangers played in Ireland as representatives of one or other
of the religious communities there, so that when Celtic played in the
south they were welcomed with all the symbols of Ireland and the fans of
both clubs could join together in expressing their hatred of the British
government. The Protestants of Belfast and Ulster regarded Rangers as

their team, and happily followed them when they visited the island. Rangers had played in Dundalk in the Inter-Cities Fairs Cup in November 1968, as the troubles in the North were brewing, without any problems, and in 1975 a Rangers visit to play Bohemians in the European Cup in Dublin passed without serious incident. But when the two teams were drawn to play each other in the first leg of a UEFA Cup first-round game in Dublin on 18 September 1984, the arrival of thousands of Ulster supporters of Rangers in Dublin resulted in a game that was played in virtual riot conditions. Buses coming down from Belfast had to run the gauntlet of missiles both to and from the game. Rangers lost 2–3 in Dublin, but won 2–0 at Ibrox, with both goals coming in the last six minutes, to go through to the next round where they lost to Inter Milan.

The story of Rangers and Celtic in Europe has, with a few exceptions, been a dismal one ever since. In the year before Souness arrived, Rangers were eliminated in the first round of the UEFA Cup by Spain's Osasuna. In Souness's first year Rangers advanced to the third round by beating Finland's Ilves Tampere and then Boavista of Portugal, with 2–1 at Ibrox and 1–0 away respectively. In the third round, however, which was also the quarter-final, they lost on the away goals rule to Borussia Mönchengladbach after two draws, 1–1 at Ibrox and 0–0 away. In his first taste of the European Cup with Rangers, Souness took them to the third round, defeating Dynamo Kiev and Poland's Gornik Zabrze before losing to Steaua Bucharest: they lost 0–2 in the away leg and gave away a first-minute goal at Ibrox to make their task impossible.

Back in the UEFA Cup for the 1988–89 season, Poland's Katowice were dismissed with a 5–2 aggregate, but a 1–1 draw against Cologne in the next round was not enough to overcome a 0–2 loss in the away leg. From then on it was all European Cups for Rangers, but Souness's last two in Scotland saw Rangers eliminated in the first round by Bayern Munich, and in his last European season the minnows of Malta, Valletta were crushed 10–0 over two legs, but Rangers then fell to Red Star Belgrade with a 0–3 away loss and a 1–1 draw at Ibrox. In the summer of 1991 Rangers sold Trevor Steven to Olympique de Marseille for a Scottish record of £5 million, and were bitterly accused in the press and by some of their fans of having given up any European ambition. Walter Smith's Rangers were duly eliminated in the first round of the new manager's first taste of European football as manager, but only on the away goal rule, at Ibrox, after Rangers had recovered from a 0–1 loss to Sparta Prague in the Czech Republic. Rangers took the Czech champions to extra time, and, when they scored twice seemed to be coasting to victory, only to give away a goal in a bizarre defensive mix-up that made the score 3–2, although it was 3–3 on aggregate. The following year, however, Smith was to enjoy his *annus mirabilis* with a clean sweep of the domestic trophies and a great run in Europe.

Rangers won the Scottish League Cup in October 1992 with a 2–1 victory over Aberdeen, and the following May they repeated the same score-line with another victory over the Dons in the Scottish Cup. In the League they coasted clear of Aberdeen to take their fifth successive League title, but it was in Europe that the real glory came, above all when they qualified for the new Champions League with home and away victories over Leeds United, 2–1 on both occasions. It was one of these few occasions when most of Scotland could enjoy a Rangers victory: beating the English is about the only time when some Celtic and Rangers fans can tolerate a victory by their rivals. Rangers in 1992, like Celtic in 1970, won in style, on the latter occasion McCoist and Hateley showing devastating form. Prior to disposing of Leeds, Rangers beat Denmark's Lyngby BK 2–0 at home and 1–0 away. In the Champions League there were two sections of four teams and the winners of each would play each other in the final. In the league section Rangers never lost a game, beating Club Brugge and CSKA Moscow and drawing the other games; against Marseille, they drew twice, 2–2 at Ibrox and 1–1 in France. But it appears that there were other forces at work, as Marseille thrashed a supine CSKA and beat a Brugge team that seemed to have lost all interest in the competition, to pip Rangers for a place in the final when Rangers could manage only a draw with CSKA in the last game of the league section. If Celtic were cheated in their European game against Rapid Vienna, it is highly likely that Rangers were cheated out of reaching the final in 1993, as rumours of the way the French club had bought its way to victory that year became fact and eventually the club was punished when it was convicted of bribing players in the French League to ensure their title. As the investigations got under way there was talk of the final being replayed, with Rangers playing AC Milan, but it was not to be.

Rangers' success served only to heighten the depths into which Celtic had sunk, as they failed in the domestic competition and gave their fans little joy in Europe. In the year after the Rapid Vienna fiasco, Celtic drew 1–1 away to Atlético Madrid in the first round of the European Cup-Winners' Cup then lost 1–2 in the ghostly atmosphere of an empty Celtic Park, courtesy of UEFA's punishment for the excesses of the previous year. Shamrock Rovers were overcome in the first round of the European Cup in 1986, but Dynamo Kiev eliminated Celtic in the second round. They were to have trouble advancing further than the second round thereafter: in the 1990–91 season Celtic failed to make it into Europe for the first time in 12 years. Celtic's return to Europe in Liam Brady's first year in 1991–92 ended in Switzerland after a first-round UEFA Cup victory against Belgium's Germinal Ekeren: their 1–5 defeat at the hands of Neuchâtel Xamax in the next round was the worst in the club's European history, and gave the fans a new word for a thrashing: to be 'xamaxed'.

CELTIC AND THE SOUNESS CHALLENGE

By the time Celtic were being 'xamaxed' in Switzerland, Billy McNeill had left the club. The touch that had inspired Celtic in his first two seasons back in charge seems to have deserted him thereafter, and while he was given more money to spend on players than any previous manager, he was working from a much tighter budget than Souness. If Souness made any bad buys this was soon lost in the merry-go-round of players coming to and from Ibrox – nearly £16 million spent and just over £6 million in sales, but always the Rangers fans were left with the memory of those who had produced some scintillating moments: Trevor Francis, Ray Wilkins, Trevor Steven, Mark Hateley and Pieter Huistra.

McNeill's first buys were shrewd rather than spectacular: Chris Morris from Sheffield Wednesday for £115,000, Andy Walker from Motherwell for £375,000 and Billy Stark for a bargain £75,000 from Aberdeen. The £850,000 to bring Frank McAvennie from West Ham was a club record, and he was joined by a player of great promise in Joe Miller, who came from Aberdeen in November 1987 for £650,000. A cosmopolitan touch was added to the club in the summer of 1989 with the signing of London-born Paul Elliott from Pisa for £600,000 and Dariusz Dziekanowski from Poland for the same amount, while Mike Galloway was bought from Hearts for half a million pounds. Galloway was no success, Elliot had festering contractual disputes with the club, and the Pole 'Jacky' had some great moments but took too fondly to the Glasgow good life. In the following close season McNeill spent over £2 million on three players: £650,000 on Martin Hayes of Arsenal who was given a free transfer 18 months later; Charlie Nicholas, also from Arsenal, for £450,000, but the one-time Celtic hero was past his best and never reached full match fitness; John Collins came from Hibs as Celtic's first million-pound transfer, had a patchy career and left the club for Monaco in 1996 on a free, thanks to the new Bosman ruling on players' contracts.

McNeill's later signings were often expensive failures, and of the £7 million he spent, only McAvennie, Elliot, Walker and Stark could have been said to be big successes. McNeill's purchase of Polish players was said to be because the money the board allocated allowed only bargain-basement buys. However that may be, McNeill was not given the money to match Souness's English signings – apart from anything else, too much was needed to staunch the haemorrhaging bank balance. McNeill's replacement, Liam Brady, was given more money to spend, but it often meant money wasted, especially when players were signed on weekly wages that chased away would-be buyers when they did not fit in. Brady bought Tony Cascarino from Aston Villa for £1.1 million in July 1991, with a £250,000 signing-on fee and a salary of £3,000 a week. As a result his four goals in 30 appearances over seven months works out at about £48,000 per appearance and £360,000 per goal (Celtic did recoup some of this in the shape of Tom Boyd when Cascarino was offloaded to Chelsea in a swap deal). It was all part of the insanity of contemporary financial orthodoxy as reflected on the football field: a frequently injured Gascoigne and a drug-bloated Maradona were costing their clubs on the continent even more for little return, while managers dismissed for lack of success could expect to walk away with a tidy sum in their bank balance. Still, it was no worse than in the business world at large, where directors of newly privatised companies could pay themselves six-figure salaries and directors in other companies rewarded themselves with massive dividends for doing little more than keeping their seat warm, or received massive pay-outs when they were shown to be incompetent.

McNeill had other problems. Like Jock Wallace he was a man brought up at a time when players were paid good but hardly startling wages, and who accepted the discipline of a manager who did not earn much more than they did. He had little time for agents, or players who spoke for themselves, and he lost some of their respect when he criticised them publicly. He was on bad terms with Celtic's chief executive, Terry Cassidy, as indeed everyone was, and resented his expectation that he should discuss team plans with the rest of the staff at Parkhead. But above all he had problems with the board.

McNeill was ultimately sacked for his lack of success, in which poor judgement in buying new players played its part, but if directors were to be sacked for their mistakes then there would have been a clear-out of the board at Celtic Park. The Celtic directors continued to close their eyes to the future, or if they saw it, did not like it and tried to turn their backs on it. They had rejected the offers of Fergus McCann and Paul Green because this would have involved them giving up some of their power. In turn the directors came up with a scheme at the beginning of 1990 in which they suggested that 30 of their wealthiest supporters give an interest-free loan of £1 million pounds to renovate Celtic Park. In return they would receive a few privileges involving wining and dining in the company of the board members, but without the slightest sniff of power-sharing. Perhaps the Celtic directors were even surprised when nobody came to the party, and so they had to come up with other ways of finding money to build a new stadium or have Celtic Park completely renovated. They also had to find more money to spend on players.

FACING UP TO THE FUTURE

Rangers during this time were not without their problems, but success on the field and a superb stadium served to silence the critics. Alan Montgomery, appointed as business manager to work alongside Souness, was quietly removed when Souness found that he could not work with him. When Terry Cassidy, in a similar position at Parkhead, fell foul of Liam Brady, the air remained poisoned for a long time before the unpopular Cassidy was finally removed. Even Murray's disagreements with Hugh Adam, manager of the Rangers Pools that had done so much to bring extra money to the club in its earlier days, and Jack Gillespie, whose share deal with Marlborough allowed the latter to take the club over in 1985, and who had also entered into an agreement with Murray regarding shares when he took over in 1988, were resolved with minimum adverse publicity. When Adam was removed from the board in late June 1992, he attacked Murray with a fulsome array of derogatory terms along the lines that Murray was little more than a 'football carpetbagger'.[15] Murray, however, had no jurisdiction over Adam's position as chairman of Rangers Development Fund and managing director of Rangers Pools, the most successful in the country. These were kept independent of the club in order that its contributions, given as 'donations', would not be subject to tax. According to Adam, Murray resented his independence, although he could not have been too enamoured, either, of Adam's contempt for his business sense; whatever, the two had been at loggerheads since Murray took over, although eventually Adam was restored to the board. Gillespie sorted out his problems with Murray in private a year later, but not before a few pounds had been spent in the courts. And compared to the controversy surrounding the slightest contretemps out Parkhead way at this time, it was all little more than a tiff in a tea cup.

Rangers had a paper debt of £7 million when Murray took over in November 1988, and in 1992 he faced some financial stringency when the club, and Murray International Holdings that largely owned it, was hit by the property slump and recorded a loss of £5 million. The income from attendances at home games at Ibrox in the early 1990s, at least half a million pounds, was still a major source of income, but increasingly, as with most big clubs throughout Britain, profits were coming from other sources: corporate hospitality, sponsorship, advertising and merchandising. Fans were encouraged to buy replica strips and parents forced to change them regularly as the clubs deliberately altered the design to ensure that they quickly went out of fashion, and so-called 'away' strips were often invented that had little to do with the traditions of the club – in this Celtic and Rangers were no better than other clubs. Fans were encouraged to ring special numbers to talk to their heroes, or at least listen to their recorded messages, giving them news about what was going on at the club. None of this was forced on the fans, but their commitment to the club was an increasing strain on their budget. When costs of entry to European games was raised to what some saw as extortionate levels the fans did see that there were limits, and crowds for some major European games at Ibrox were attended by anything up to 10,000 less than those who would come to an irrelevant League game. Now, as the money from sources outside attendance continues to multiply there is no reason why admission prices should not be reduced; already Berlusconi had said that in his aim of a mid-week TV league the fans could get in for nothing just to ensure the atmosphere.

However, Rangers still tried to keep in touch with their fans, to reach out beyond their 5,000 existing shareholders and 27,000 season-ticket-holders. This was the float by Murray, in August 1991, of 34,560,000 shares at 10p each – in effect existing shareholders found their shares, then selling at £70, increased by a factor of 100 but revalued at 70p. The intention was to increase the capital of the club by nearly £3.5 million and allow the less impecunious fans to buy a small share in the club. The move was passed at the September 1991 AGM and within a couple of years the value of these shares had increased by over 500 per cent.

While Rangers tried to involve their fans in the club, the Celtic board continued to keep them at bay, whether it was wealthy fans trying to buy into the board or others calling for it to be opened up to the public. In May 1990, however, the Celtic board made an inspired move that seemed to be setting the club in a more progressive direction when it appointed two new men to the board. A few months later it all turned to ashes when one of them was sacked and a club teetering on the brink was plunged into civil war.

The two new directors appointed to take Celtic into the new world of cash-driven football were Brian Dempsey and Michael Kelly. Dempsey was a wealthy, self-made property developer and builder, the son of a Labour MP for Airdrie and Coatbridge whose safe Labour seat had almost been lost in 1959 when he, a Catholic, was opposed by a candidate whose main claim to fame was that she was the sister of Rangers' Alan Morton. Dempsey was a Celtic man and chairman of two major building companies, earning enough to spend £350,000 on the club (although Celtic claimed when he withdrew his 'Skybox' in May

1991 that in the previous season he had spent only about a third of that)[16] in corporate entertainment, as well as £25,000 at Ibrox. He was a popular man and it was expected that his expertise would be used to establish a new home for Celtic.

The other was Michael Kelly, well known throughout Scotland, and a man whose name and well-publicised beliefs made him the ideal person to brighten the image of the club he had grown up with. With this appointment it seemed as though Celtic had secured a man of vision who had the name and the interests of the club at heart. It was Michael Kelly, after all, who had performed wonders while a Labour Lord Provost of Glasgow between 1980 and 1984, presiding over the transformation of the city under the slogan 'Glasgow's miles better'. He was criticised during this time for refusing to visit Ibrox, and made no secret of his sympathies for Celtic. He was also the grandson of the great James Kelly whose name went back to the origins of the club and nephew of his successor, Robert Kelly. But Kelly was also an academic, with a doctorate in economics, and perhaps not very comfortable with the idea of young men who expected to be treated like kings and rewarded with gifts beyond the dreams of Croesus for occasionally kicking a ball around.

The hopes aroused by the new blood on the board were crushed when Dempsey was sacked on 26 October 1990 when his name came up for what was expected to be the formality of his ratification. This roused the Celtic faithful to an even greater pitch of anger than that which would greet McNeill's dismissal a few months later – whatever the manner of McNeill's passing, he had had little success on the field. Dempsey's dismissal was a demonstration of the power that two men with the names and shares of Kelly and White could wield, and with that other name so long associated with the club, Grant, the 'families' set about ensuring that they remained in complete control of the club. Above all they refused to go public or accept money from outside sources that would threaten their power. Fans who could not earn in a year what some players were paying in tax increasingly vented their frustration on a board that tried hard to ignore them. With Rangers continuing to lead the way, from players and stadium to the collection of the fabled silverware, the board found itself assailed from all sides. Such was the wondrous power of success that Murray could even admit, without losing any popularity, that he wanted to set up a family dynasty at Ibrox, with his sons taking over when he left.[17] At Celtic Park the cries mounted for an end to the ruling dynasties, so much so that there were times when it seemed that the only support for the Celtic board came from joyous Bluenoses, as Rangers fans, in response to Celtic supporters' cries of 'Sack the board!', gleefully chanted 'Keep the board!'.

5. Uncivil War at Celtic Park

The optimism that greeted the appointments of businessman Brian Dempsey and public relations consultant Michael Kelly to the Celtic board in May 1990 was well warranted at the time. All it needed was for them to work together and the team to get back on the winning track and Celtic would be once more in pursuit of their great rivals. It all came crashing down at the AGM of that year, on 26 October, when Dempsey's ratification to the board was blocked, two days before Celtic were due to play Rangers in a crucial Skol League Cup final. The majority on the Celtic board wanted to ratify Dempsey's appointment, but this was opposed by Chris White and Michael Kelly, ostensibly because of Dempsey's determination to proceed with a new stadium project at Robroyston. The majority on the board was defeated by the votes wielded from the floor by Kelly and White, and greeted with dismay by the fans. The popular Dempsey made a dignified exit, but he had every reason to be seething, and while he did not show his anger, the fans did, especially when Celtic lost the final 2–1.

The defeat on the Sunday could not be directly attributed to the wrangling on the board, but squabbling among the directors did not make for a happy atmosphere at the club, and Celtic manager McNeill was probably being more diplomatic than honest when, in reply to a question by Michael Kelly before Dempsey's board ratification was blocked, he said that the players did not even know who the directors were. The fans did, and they were beginning to mobilise their discontent. Dempsey went home to nurse his wrath and had no difficulty in keeping it warm over the next three years. A young business consultant, David Low, wrote a letter to *The Herald* congratulating the board for getting rid of Dempsey, but soon he would become Dempsey's right-hand man in a scheme to buy up enough shares from small shareholders to bring about a revolution from within. Low, a business associate of Kelly before the two fell out, was the first to realise not only that Celtic shares were grossly undervalued, but that they were not invulnerable to outside interests, as the board believed, and this was the major factor in their ridiculously low valuation.

In Canada, Fergus McCann kept his eye on events with a calm and resolute detachment, increasingly determined that he would put up the money to see Celtic through its problems, so long as he got a controlling interest and part of the new funding came from the fans. Another millionaire who would come into the act, Gerald Weisfeld, had still not been converted by his stepson to become a Bhoy.

At Celtic Park the money to buy new players and renovate or relocate the stadium was not forthcoming, the players faltered on the field and the directors firmly averted their gaze from the future. In March 1992 a few of them committed themselves to each other in a self-preservation pact which, when it was made public, added more fuel to a fraternal bloodletting as bitter as all family quarrels, known when played out in the wider world by that grotesque misnomer, a 'civil war'. It all ended at Parkhead with the ousting of the old board in March 1994, to make way for a new regime under Fergus McCann.

SOME LESSONS FROM HISTORY

At the same time as the Celtic directors were retiring to their bunkers, two of the world's most odious regimes were opening up to the world at large: in the Soviet Union the reforms of Mikhail Gorbachev had led to the collapse of communism in Eastern Europe, while in South Africa apartheid was being dissolved without the anticipated bloodshed, thanks in large measure to Nelson Mandela, whose forgiveness of his former tormentors is without equivalent since the founding of Christianity. And it was nearly three decades since even the Catholic Church had brought itself into the modern age. None of this seems to have affected the Celtic board, who continued to live in another age, the traditional families clinging to power like the privileged elites of France at the time of Louis XVI. No more than the Bourbons before them were the offspring of the Kellys and the Whites and the Grants able to assure the worth of their descendants through some hereditary divine right passed on to their children and their children's children.

Of this offspring, clearly the most talented was Michael Kelly, but in his absorbing inside account of the events at Parkhead, *Paradise Lost: The Struggle for Celtic's Soul*,[1] he shows that the lessons of history are not read by all people in the same way. Kelly quotes appositely from Milton in his book, and criticises David Low for his use of 'one of the lesser' works of Niccolo Machiavelli, *The Prince*, as his bible in planning the destruction of the Celtic board. But he himself, if he was not to learn from some of the great individuals of his own time who were dealing with problems of power on a scale somewhat greater than that of the Celtic board, could have learned more from others who have written about the problems of coming to terms with inevitable change. Giuseppe di Lampedusa's *The Leopard*, for instance, where the wily old Sicilian aristocrat, faced by the intrusions of the money men in mid-nineteenth-century Italy, learned how to change to remain the same. Better might he have pondered over de Tocqueville and his analysis of the events that led up to the great French Revolution of 1789, where families intent on retaining their power and privileges, albeit in the name of God and His social order, refused to recognise the power of the moneyed and educated classes who would not submit to feudal subservience. The king, the prelates and the aristocrats, instead of losing some of their power and privileges, ended up by losing them all. Faced by opening up their ranks to the men with the money to build a new stadium, or a public issue that would have involved ordinary fans in running the club, the 'traditional families' of the Celtic board shut themselves up inside their own Bastille and waited until it was battered down by the force of public opinion. And financial reality.

In the final analysis, it is Kelly's book more than any other that shows just how effete the old board was, an indictment if ever one was needed, of the nonsense of nepotism and the futility of determining worth by birth rather than by merit. The sadness is that someone of Kelly's abilities should not only find himself embroiled with such narrow views, but become the leader of what he called 'the old guard who had run Celtic down remorselessly over the years . . .'[2] Kelly's is a tale of a board that was motivated by self-interest under the guise of 'family' or 'Celtic' tradition, of incompetence on a grand scale, and deviousness that Machiavelli would have criticised only for its amateurism.

THE DUMPING OF DEMPSEY

Dempsey's removal from the board was opposed by a majority of the board members: Kevin Kelly, Tom Grant, Jim Farrell and chairman Jack McGinn. However, on the basis of votes held by shareholders, White and Michael Kelly carried the motion, a shareholding power that they would use in subsequent meetings. The reasons given for Dempsey's removal was his insistence that the club should build a new ground at Robroyston, where Dempsey had several business interests. There were no doubt problems attached to Robroyston, in terms not only of planning approval but also of the emotional issue of taking Celtic fans away from the club's spiritual home. The concept of the new ground being part of a wider commercial, retail and leisure development was bold, but there were major questions about where the Celtic Football Club would stand in terms of the ownership of its own ground. Rumours surfaced about Dempsey standing to profit from the move to Robroyston, rumours that Michael Kelly still insists were well founded, but it was far from unusual and certainly not illegal for a football club director to benefit in his business from his position in the club.

The scale of Dempsey's proposals was huge, and consequently intimidating, but even more fear was felt by some directors about his popularity with the fans: it was the insensitive way in which Dempsey was removed that most appalled the Celtic faithful. And its timing. The fans of 1990 were much more aware of what was going on behind the scenes than those of their father's generation, and less willing to put up with it. The players who went out to play Rangers two days later could well have been spared a controversy that was eventually to cost the board much more than the Skol Cup they lost that Sunday in October.

Celtic supporters have generally been more critical of their board than Rangers supporters, whose frustration about what happened on the field was more likely to be taken out on the players. In the 1980s fans were better educated than in the past – and better organised. With the changes in computer technology they were able to put out cheap publications to express their own opinions. On the broader front, and in reaction to the Heysel disaster and the debate on hooliganism that accompanied it, fans in England concerned about the game's image got together to defend it against those who would destroy it, be they the hooligans on the terracing or the vultures in the boardrooms. Out of this came the Football Supporters Association in 1986, bringing in the fans of clubs from all over Britain. Unlike the traditional supporters associations, in which Rangers and Celtic had been well to the fore over the years, and which were essentially support bodies for the clubs in return for a few privileges in regard to season tickets, travel to away games and the appearance at their socials of representatives from the club, the FSA was concerned about the future of the game and not just the welfare of a particular club.

At the same time fanzines started to appear, giving voice to those followers of the club who felt they were overlooked in the daily press and patronised in the bland club magazines. By 1990 what had started out as photocopied sheets held roughly together by hand-held staplers had become glossy publications showing all the expertise of the new desktop publishing. One of the best was Celtic's *Not the View*, an early arrival on the fanzine scene, in early November 1987, its name inspired by the club's official publication, the *Celtic View*. The first editorial in *Not the View* squarely set the board in its sights:

> We can all have a good laugh at the Huns as they go through the
> annual ritual of the shareholders meeting, which at times
> resembles the Nuremberg rallies with fat loonies in Rangers strips

demanding that no 'Tim' ever be allowed to darken the doorstep of Ibrox. But at least they can make their views, however bigoted or stupid they may be, known to the directors face to face. The Rangers board must attend these meetings. Who are the Celtic directors accountable to?

Celtic should go public and float a large number of shares. Not only would this provide a massive injection of cash, but with any luck we might end up with a chairman with a bit of style and charisma . . . at least they should be more accountable to the people who make the club what it is – you and me, the supporters. If we didn't go along every Saturday then these Mr Magoos wouldn't have a club to run.[3]

The new fanzine found favour with the fans, and was soon selling more than 10,000 copies, while its plans for modernising the club were taken up by a broader spectrum of Celtic supporters, whose hopes came to rest with a single director, vaguely echoed in that first editorial.

Among the other fanzines that started to proliferate, several devoted to Rangers and Celtic, was one that emerged directly out of the Dempsey sacking: *Once a Tim, Always a Tim*, founded by Matt McGlone. McGlone became one of the main leaders in organising fan discontent, not just through his fanzine, but through public meetings and well-organised publicity campaigns and demonstrations, ending with a successful boycott of a game at Celtic Park as the old board was in its death throes.[4]

Having lost Dempsey, the board decided to advertise for an Executive Director to make full commercial advantage of the club name. They chose Terry Cassidy, a man keenly supported by Michael Kelly, who saw in him 'a brilliant choice' but went on to make what was an error in English that perhaps revealed a more significant Freudian slip, when he wondered whether Cassidy understood the 'enormity' of the job.[5] 'Enormity', not to be confused with great size, has to do with outrageous or excessive wickedness – but this is perhaps going too far; Basil Fawlty and the Keystone Cops were images more appropriate to the board than Attila the Hun or any of the Renaissance popes.

Cassidy was duly appointed and wasted no time in making himself the most unpopular man at Parkhead, surpassing even the unpopularity of Hood at Ibrox because Cassidy upset not only the fans, but soon put the board off, alienated himself from McNeill and his successor, Liam Brady, and by a full and wholesome expression of his contempt for the media in all its forms, ensured that all of this would be picked up and amplified to his disadvantage. If managers get crucified for the mistakes they make in the players they buy, then directors can scarcely complain when the finger of incompetence is pointed at them for their dud appointments.

Cassidy was English, and while this is not something to boast about in Scotland, he was also happy to say that he was not a Celtic fan and thought Rangers were stupid for not employing him first.[6] He came with an impressive CV, but he never measured up to his own opinion of himself. And yet among his mind-boggling 'embarrassment of stupidities', the stupidity for which he is best remembered, his plan for the sacking of Billy McNeill, was in fact a reasonable attempt to set before the board a series of options, one of which included retaining the legendary 'Caesar'. The leaked document was manna to the press and *The Sun* made the most of it, especially when Cassidy claimed that there was no such document and challenged them to publish it. They did.

Cassidy's time at Parkhead was up when David Smith was appointed to the board in February 1992; thereafter his requests to be made a director were passed over and on 24 October 1992 he was duly sacked, with 14 months of his three-year contract, worth £60,000 per year, still to run. This led to a long and drawn-out legal case over the terms of his pay-out, in which claim and counter-claim were met in court before being settled in a private arrangement.

David Dallas Smith was a lifelong Celtic supporter, who lived in London but still made regular trips to Scotland to see his team play. Born in Brechin into a Celtic supporting family, he trained as an accountant in Glasgow and went on to make a name for himself in the field of liquidation and takeovers, most notably the £2.2 billion takeover of the Gateway supermarket chain by his own Isosceles company. He was a long-term friend of Chris White and he and Michael Kelly spent a great deal of effort trying to convince him to join the board. He was also a Protestant, which not surprisingly was mentioned in the press: indeed if there hadn't been so much else going on at the time it probably would have been a major splash – he was, after all, Celtic's first Protestant to be appointed to the board. His religion was irrelevant in the opposition by certain members of the board to his appointment, and as in the case of Dempsey's dismissal, Michael Kelly and White steam-rollered their choice through against the wishes of their recalcitrant colleagues. They were helped this time by the casting vote of chairman Kevin Kelly, who had replaced Jack McGinn in that position the previous October.

THE NON-APPEASEMENT PACT

It was Smith who concocted the 'shareholders' agreement' that brought some relief to a beleaguered board, but in the end it was to help destroy them. By this agreement, drawn up on the eve of an EGM called for 30 March 1992 (although the full details of its contents were not revealed to the public until June of that year) five of the directors agreed never to sell their shares without first offering them to the others. This was to bind the Kellys, White, Grant and David Smith together for the next ten years. By doing so they claimed to be achieving stability, safeguarding the soul of the club as Michael Kelly would have it, protecting it from the 'crusade of revenge'[7] being launched against it by Dempsey and his acolytes.

Before the pact was entered into, Kevin Kelly and Tom Grant had been in contact with the 'rebels' to come to some arrangement with them – but by agreeing to the pact they had thrown in their lot with the old regime. Grant was a troubled soul: shortly after his appointment to the board, Tom Grant had told *Celtic View* on 18 November 1987 of his fears about a public issue of shares, claiming that 'there are many for whom a public share offer would present an opportunity to destroy Celtic. We do not want to dilute what the club's founders envisaged.' By contacting the 'rebels' he showed his concern for the direction the club was taking, but by entering into the pact he demonstrated the dilemma he faced concerning what was best for the club and what was best for himself: a dilemma that would beset him for a long time to come. Smith, appointed to the board without any shareholding in the club, soon acquired the necessary shares to legalise his appointment. When the naked self-interest in the pact was revealed, it was immediately denounced in a variety of images bestriding the world from Beijing (the 'Gang of Five') and Munich (the 'Non-aggression Pact' – Hugh Drake, a shareholder), to Hollywood (the 'rat-pact' – Gerry McNee, the journalist).

Behind the pact was the knowledge that a group was at work buying shares in the club with the intention of challenging the board from within. In *Scotland on Sunday* on 19 January 1992, Kevin McCarra and Francis Shennan wrote an article entitled 'Secret bid to stir up Celtic' in which they revealed that a group of businessmen had got together to overhaul Celtic Football Club by bringing in £16 million to dilute the control of the White and Kelly families; this had involved meetings since the previous October in North America, Ireland and Scotland with the target of attaining a 51 per cent holding in Celtic shares. Low and Dempsey refused to confirm the story, and Low even denied it outright to the *Sunday Mail*. Shennan, a business journalist, had been in possession of the information for some time, and would go on, with Low, to write a book about it all,[8] but much of his information had come from privileged sources. McCarra on the other hand, one of Scotland's few journalists with an academic background, showed that this was no disadvantage as he ferreted out information through his own sources, so that the story had to break some time sooner rather than later.

One of those in on the secret was Matt McGlone. He met Low for the first time in November 1991 at a Glasgow University Celtic Supporters Club 20th Anniversary Night where he told the astonished schemer that he was about to reveal the story of his trafficking in Celtic shares in his fanzine. Low managed to persuade McGlone, with whom he was later to team up, to keep quiet. In the meantime Low continued his travels that took him, as the blurb to his book tells us, from 'secret meetings in luxury apartments in Montreal, Phoenix and the Caribbean to Belfast graveyards and Fermanagh cowsheds'. Low, financed by Dempsey, was playing on the feelings of a widely scattered family of Celtic shareholders who felt that they had been neglected by the club or did not like the direction it was taking. Some were even happy to accept the attractive price that they were being offered for the shares: as much as £350 for shares valued by the board at £3.

Under the articles of association all Celtic shares had to be ratified by the board, and so the sales were obtained with a proxy that allowed the would-be buyer to vote at the AGM. It needed 10 per cent of shareholders to call an EGM, and it was at such an EGM that the 'Rebels', as they came to be called and were happy to call themselves, hoped to topple the board. In a trip to North America in mid-November 1991, to secure Celtic shares from the Grant inheritance, Low went to Montreal in an attempt to win McCann over to his cause. McCann had returned to Scotland in 1990 to make a further offer to Celtic, similar to the previous ones, and was again repulsed. McCann also met Dempsey and Weisfeld on that trip, but neither then nor after his accession to power, could the three wealthy men get on with each other. Low failed to win McCann over to his scheme, and while McCann greeted him with typical bluntness, he congratulated him on his plan, but preferred to stick by his own scheme: to set up a public limited company, called Celtic's Future plc, into which he would put millions of his own money to gain a controlling interest and raise extra cash through a share issue to the public. McCann and the Low group, however, agreed on the need to remove the reigning board.

Low, who would later become a disciple of McCann, then flew to Toronto to meet Jim Doherty, a wealthy yacht broker and cousin of Tom Grant. Doherty was easily won over, as he, like the other shareholding Canadians, felt he had been neglected by the board. It also helped that he had caught the soccer bug on a visit to Scotland earlier in the year, during which he saw the towsy Old Firm game of 17 March 1991. Doherty was unwilling to sell his shares, but acting as spokesman for his

relatives in Canada he promised to give Low his full backing in the battle
against the board. Doherty also helped blow their cover when he told
Gerry McNee in a television interview on 13 February 1992 that the aim
of the rebels was to get rid of White and Michael Kelly.

The rebels had been winning the public opinion war, but to strike a
serious blow they needed to use their accumulated sales purchases to call
an EGM and to use their voting strength to unseat the board. In fact the
board acted first: in February 1992 they called for an EGM with the
purpose of confirming Smith's co-option to the board. They also asked
for the removal of Tom Grant and Jim Farrell who were deemed to have
been openly disloyal to the board. The meeting was set for 30 March
1992 and like those before and those to come was preceded by deals: in
this case that Grant's removal would be taken from the agenda if he
joined the pact, and he in turn could vote for Farrell to have him retained
on the board. This transpired and despite all going according to the plans
of the pact, the rebels were declared to have won a great victory in saving
Farrell and Grant. Their cause for celebration was that they were now out
in the open and could be seen as a legitimate source of opposition to the
board.

But it was clear that Grant had switched sides, and this led to
suspicions about the secret deal. In the meantime the board had to show
that they were worthy custodians of the Celtic soul; above all they had to
come up with something concrete to convince the fans of their ambitions
for the club.

BOARD AT BAY

And so it came to pass that the hitherto modest suburb of Cambuslang,
a healthy jog up the road from Parkhead, became imbued with all the
attributes of a modern Brigadoon. This was to be the chosen spot for a
new stadium as part of a vast commercial centre which would trade off
the club's name and take it, as the saying goes 'well into the twenty-first
century'. The result of a feasibility study carried out over the previous
year by a firm called Stadivarius, it was launched in April 1992 by Kevin
Kelly. Revealed was a plan for a 52,000 all-seated stadium with what was
described as a 'space-age roof', two railway stations, a 200-bed hotel, a
Celtic heritage museum, cinemas and shops. There would also be a 30-
lane bowling alley, fast-food restaurants and parking for 4,500 cars. It
was along the same lines as Dempsey's plans for Robroyston, but as
Michael Kelly insisted, this time the basic problems in regard to licences
and funding for the £100–£120 million project were well under control.

In fact most of the projections were over-optimistic and even if things had worked according to plan, football would have brought in only a third of the stadium's income, with the rest having to come from American football, rugby, boxing, rock concerts and the like. Celtic would have only been a minority shareholder in the stadium, which would have been owned by a separate stadium company. Some might have wondered where the Celtic soul would have been in all this, and the public was sceptical, the media more so – even before stories surfaced of noxious gases that would have made the site impracticable. Worst of all there were no hard and fast offers of money to finance it all.

In the midst of this turmoil the team struggled on the park and Celtic finished another trophyless season in May 1993, third in the League behind Aberdeen and Rangers, who cleaned up with the treble. Since winning the League in 1988, Celtic had not even managed to come second behind Rangers, finishing fifth in 1990 and third in the next three years. After winning the Cup in 1989 Celtic failed to make it a treble of Cup victories in 1990 when they lost to Aberdeen in the final on penalties. They reached the semi-final in 1990, beating Rangers on the way, but fell to Motherwell after a drawn first game. In the following year they again reached the semi-final, but on 31 March 1992, on a rain-drenched Hampden pitch, they were unable to beat a Rangers team without Hateley and reduced to ten men from the sixth minute when David Robertson was sent off. McCoist scored Rangers' only goal, but Celtic were unable to equalise. Walter Smith claimed that his team came of age that Tuesday night with a dour struggle against the odds. Celtic thought they had no luck, what with hitting the woodwork three times and coming up against an in-form Andy Goram who was displaying the qualities that confirmed him as one of Rangers' best buys. Celtic were also denied a strong penalty claim in the last few minutes, which the conspiracy theorists will no doubt have engraved on their memories, while overlooking the offence that got Robertson sent off; Rangers fans and James Traynor of the *The Herald* thought the offence warranted a yellow rather than red card. It was a heart-breaking night for Brady's team, who had been playing some classy football in previous weeks.

Celtic failed miserably in the Cup in the following season, scrambling home to lowly Clyde over two games then falling 2–0 to Falkirk at Brockville. In the Skol Cup the story was no better: after losing to Rangers in the final in 1990, Celtic were eliminated on penalties by Airdrie in the quarter-final in 1991 and the following year lost to Aberdeen in the semi-final. Brady and the divided spirits at Celtic Park had little to look forward to in the troubled summer of 1993. Meanwhile, Rangers celebrated their greatest season in recent memory.

Brady entered his third season at Celtic Park with little to show for the money he had spent, and after a poor start to the new season and a loss to St Johnstone in Perth, he offered his resignation on 6 October 1993. This was the signal for the rebels and the malcontents to regalvanise their forces.

In late June 1993 Michael Kelly and Fergus McCann had exchanged a fruitless series of faxes across the Atlantic, following which McCann issued a statement saying that he was finished with the negotiations. In fact Low was at work to bring him and Dempsey together again. Low also tried to get McCann and Weisfeld to work together, but no sooner had they met than they split up. On 24 September Dempsey, McCann and Dominic Keane told a packed press conference that they had come up with a package of £20 million to save Celtic, £12.5 million of which had been promised by McCann. They forced the calling of another EGM on 26 November 1993, joined this time by Weisfeld. Weisfeld, who with his Scottish wife had built up the immensely successful What Everyone Wants chain and had sold it for an estimated £40 million, was assisted by Willie Haughey and his stepson, Michael McDonald, who was a fanatical Celtic supporter. The pact used its power to reject the McCann proposals, but this time they were also met by an offer from Weisfeld through Haughey to buy up all of the directors' shares for £350 each, a total outlay of £3.6 million. This too was rejected, but it was an offer that set some of the pact members thinking about personal compensation should the unthinkable happen.

In the meantime, the rebels retired once more, again with some bitterness, but the fans were infuriated that the board had once more turned down an injection of funds, and were determined to do something about it. A couple of months after the Dempsey sacking, on 25 February 1991, Willie Wilson, an ordinary supporter from Clydebank, had invited 300 Celtic fans to a meeting at Shettleston Town Hall where a group calling themselves Save Our Celts was formed. The meeting was chaired by the prominent Glasgow lawyer, Joe Beltrami, and attended by Brian Dempsey, as well as Celtic directors Grant and Farrell. Christopher White turned down the invitation saying that the meeting could only serve to embarrass the club. George Delaney of the official Celtic Supporters Club went even further and dismissed it as 'a nonsense'. Lisbon Lion Jim Craig was there, the one who gave away the penalty on that day in 1967, as Michael Kelly reminds us. He was also the son-in-law of Jim Farrell, the longest-serving member of the Celtic board, but a director at odds with 'the families'. He spoke passionately, and a few days after the meeting was dismissed from his job as a commentator at Radio Scotland. No Freemasons to blame for that one!

Save Our Celts had a few more rallies, but there were always problems

BHOYS, BEARS AND BIGOTRY

in maintaining a rage against the object of your affection, and it was difficult, if not impossible, to clearly distinguish attacks on the board from attacks on the club. The board liked to attribute the anger of the fans to conspiracies by their enemies, a standard fall-back for bankrupt regimes, and dismissed the fans as 'malcontents' fed by the lies of their enemies and subsidised by the finances of the unscrupulous. In fact the opposition to the board came from fans at all levels, including the sponsors of the executive boxes. One of these was Harry Hynds of Harry Hynds Travel, and in April 1991, in response to a gibe by Cassidy, he had formed with other sponsors a Celtic Fair Weather Supporters club. They spent £2,000 to sponsor a match at Dunfermline, where Celtic were the visitors, so that as well as sharing the corporate facilities with the visiting Celtic directors, they listened in amusement as the tannoy, to the confusion of the fans and the embarrassment of the Celtic directors, announced several times that the game that day was being sponsored by the Celtic Fair Weather Supporters. Cassidy replied by ending Celtic's relations with Harry Hynds Travel, a company in which Dempsey had a 75 per cent stake.[9]

The disillusion among Celtic fans was spread right through the ranks, from the Jungle – finally closed down to install seating in the summer of 1993 – all the way to the executive boxes. Even *The Celt*, a precursor to the fanzines, but more a mild-mannered recorder of the club's affairs than an uninhibited critic, gave new words to the 'Celtic Song':

> *They are Celtic directors,*
> *Useless through and through*
> *Always and always*
> *They haven't got a clue*[10]

The departure of Brady sparked renewed activity by Celtic fans, leading to the formation of 'Celts For Change' in October 1993. Brendan Sweeney and Matt McGlone were the instigators, helped by Dempsey and Low, but ultimately inspired by the energy and contribution of fans who had had enough of the old board. A first general meeting, advertised in the press to be held in Glasgow's City Hall in the Candleriggs, was attended by 30 people in a room that held 50. But then came the board rejection of the rebels' offer of cash injections and the next meeting, held on 2 December 1993, had to be shifted to a much larger room to hold the 450 who crushed inside, leaving another 500 outside. A week later 850 people attended a meeting in the Govan Town Hall.

Out of this came a campaign of advertising, banner-waving, picketing of the Celtic shops and even the Bank of Scotland, Celtic's bankers –

with the ultimate weapon, a boycott of games at Parkhead, held as a last resort. The board, naturally enough, refused to allow the banners and other signs of organised protest inside the ground, but the ingenuity in overcoming this resulted in the CFC's most spectacular success. This came when various individuals went to the home game against Hibernian on 18 December 1993 dressed in jeans and white T-Shirts which sported a single, innocent letter. They had arranged that an area around the Jungle be kept free of spectators and it was there that those sporting the T-shirts lined up in prearranged order to spell out in perfect view of the assembled fans, the photographers and the television cameras, the words: 'BACK THE TEAM; SACK THE BOARD'. The official Celtic Supporters Association had refused to back the 'malcontents', but many of their members were sympathetic, and they formed an Independent Celtic Supporters Association. Then the official Celtic Supporters Association turned on the board: on 3 October 1993 they passed a vote of no confidence in it, and at another meeting on 30 January 1994 a delegates' meeting representing 150 clubs demanded that the directors quit immediately.

The pressure was telling on the board, but the main pressure came from its own internal contradictions. No stadium was emerging, the team was still falling behind on the field, and the overdraft at the Bank of Scotland was growing beyond that which any self-respecting business could allow. Income was declining because of the poor attendances and the drop in commercial dealings within the club. On all fronts the prospects were getting more dismal by the day, and on 1 March 1994 the Celts For Change group finally went ahead with its threat of a boycott. It was another success, as little more than 10,000 (according to the group's independently contracted invigilators) turned up for a home game against Kilmarnock, including a fox that mysteriously streaked across the pitch and offered the only moment of light relief when the fans there took up the chant: 'There's only one Michael Kelly!'

THE END OF THE OLD REGIME

The 'Gang of Five' began to crumble, and members of the board were forced to admit that outside money was needed to save the club. But before that they played their last desperate card with the presentation to a packed media conference of their latest plans for the new stadium at Cambuslang. The plan proposed by David Smith on 25 February 1994 was indeed a thing of wonder, a magnificent vision of the future along the lines set out so optimistically by Kevin Kelly two years before. The sceptical journalists were no more impressed this time than they had

been before by this 'Field of Dreams' (mark II), a sarcastic reference to
the 20-carat corn of the American movie of that name, but thought by
the Celtic directors to be an apt allusion.

The meeting was told that a Swiss company called Gefinor had put up
cornerstone funding of £20 million, and this time the board allowed
provision for public funding. The final blow to the board's ambition to
keep themselves in power was delivered by Allan Caldwell, a freelance
journalist whose articles for the *Evening Times* had brought the board
many times to curse the existence of a free press (and who in turn would
also write a book about the affair, entitled *Sack the Board*). Working
away with terrier-like tenacity he discovered that Gefinor knew little
about the deal, and had hardly even heard of the Celtic Football Club.

Now the board fell apart as Kevin Kelly made overtures to the rebels
and Tom Grant appeared to side with the coming strength. Even Michael
Kelly seemed to be cutting his losses as he stood out for a decent return
on his shares, defending at the same time the families whose interests he
was protecting. On offer was the £350 per share from Weisfeld that was
still on the table, and Weisfeld was so confident of taking over that he
went on a holiday to Australia – a fatal mistake so far as his own
ambitions were concerned. Dempsey and McCann prepared to move in
for the kill as the Bank of Scotland put pressure on Celtic to decrease its
overdraft or come up with increased security, terrifying the directors by
saying that they would have to pledge their personal property. Weisfeld,
who several times thought that his offer to buy the club out had been
successful, returned from Australia to push his claims, but in the end it
was the unprepossessing figure of Fergus McCann who strode through
the doors of Celtic Park on 4 March 1994 as the new owner.

Much has been made of the dramatic last hours, with newspaper
headlines screaming that the club had been saved with only eight
minutes to spare. It is doubtful if millions of pounds are going to be
rejected because they come in late – this was not a student essay coming
in after the deadline after all. And if McCann and company had been real
sharks instead of individuals concerned about the club they would have
done better to let it go into receivership and to pick up the pieces at a
much reduced price later. But despite what everyone says, football is not
a business, especially not where Celtic – and Rangers – are concerned,
and this was recognised by the bank. Indeed, banks throughout Britain
have recognised this, dealing with football clubs on different terms from
normal business companies. The nature of a football club was also at the
heart of all the discussions concerning the rival groups. The families of
the old board, however, believed that they alone should hold the key of
succession in unbroken line, that they alone could interpret and speak on

behalf of Celtic traditions, that they were the keepers of the Celtic soul. By the 1990s, however, infallibility was a long discredited doctrine.

It is a characteristic of revolutions that those who gain power soon start to squabble among themselves. The conditions that create revolutions and the character of the men needed to carry them out mean that life for the new regime will not be easy: they often end up in dictatorship. McCann, however, helped by the retreat, once more, of Dempsey, soon established a firm authority over the new board. Of the old board, Michael Kelly, Chris White and David Smith retired to their private affairs, but Kevin Kelly, Grant and McGinn held on until they resigned in the autumn of 1994. James Farrell fought to stay on the new board, but he was removed at an EGM in September 1994. McGinn and Kevin Kelly were given titular appointments: McGinn as legislative adviser, Kelly as chairman emeritus and president of the boys club. Tom Grant was offered a position as stadium manager, but this became a rather empty title and when he had to report to Celtic's capital projects manager, Charles Martin, and became derisively known as the 'janitor', he resigned in July 1996. The last link with the old board was effectively gone, as Kevin Kelly and McGinn were seldom to be seen in the official corridors of Celtic Park.

McCann would have preferred to have made a clean sweep of the old board and to have carried out his pledge not to give any of them 'a thin dime'. In retaining the services of four of the old board, McCann recognised the role they had played in bringing him to power, while he had no choice but to pay out on the shares of the departing directors. He was then involved in claims for compensation by Superstadia for their work on the Cambuslang project and faced another problem in the form of manager Lou Macari, a bizarre appointment of the old regime to succeed Brady. He was sacked in June 1994, leading to a bitter court battle in which he claimed £431,000 for wrongful dismissal, McCann counter-claimed for breach of contract and compensation of £250,000. The final judgement in February 1998 found against Macari, but McCann failed to win compensation and had the embarrassment of being described by the judge in her 82-page report as 'an uncompromising and somewhat arrogant employer'.[11]

On to the new board McCann brought Eric Riley as financial director, Patrick Ferrell as marketing director, and three men who had played a role in the ousting of the old board: Willie Haughey, John Keane, the Edinburgh builder, and Gerald Weisfeld's stepson, Michael McDonald. It was not the new board that would be controlling the club, however, and a couple of years down the track McCann started to emerge as a new Napoleon. He created a public liability company, with men of proven reputations in the business world and prepared to sink some of their own money into the club. McCann was the first Celtic official to invest a substantial sum of his own money in the club, and with Celtic plc he brought in three other major investors: Patrick Sheehy, a former BAT chief; Brian Quinn, formerly of the Bank of England; and Dermot Desmond, a property investor said to be one of Ireland's leading stock-brokers, who was also a close friend of the Irish Prime Minister Charles Haughey. And all were men with names that chimed in tunefully with the Irish image of the club, even if only one of them was actually Irish. Above all they were businessmen with a knowledge of finance, held in respect by the new mystical god of the football world: 'the City'.

In Fergus McCann, David Murray at Ibrox now had a man closer to his own mettle at Celtic Park, but the gap between the two clubs was still enormous. On the field Celtic came to the end of the 1993–94 season without any joy on the field. Off the field they were faced with a huge debt, a crumbling stadium, a disappearing business reputation and a dwindling number of season-ticket-holders, now as low as 7,100. Under McCann, however, there was to be a resurrection on all but one front (unhappily the most important) with a new manager, a magnificent new stadium and a response to the share issue from the Celtic supporters that surpassed all expectation. The Old Firm was back in business, even if it might have been more appropriate to call it the 'New Corporation'.

There were some who feared that the Old Firm was now under a 'New Firm' of two men whose interests were not so much in upholding a tradition or safeguarding a soul, as in capitalising on the products they had bought in order to maximise their profits. This was a foreign language to most of the Bhoys and Bears who followed the two clubs. According to the jargon of the day, fans did not watch football, follow it or get involved with it, but consumed it, while the clubs were not so much objects of their devotion, outlets for their passion, but commodities at the disposal of those with their hearts in their hip pockets. In the eyes of the business world, the loyalty of countless thousands of Celtic and Rangers fans had nothing to do with the hopes and dreams of whole communities, but were brand names whose loyalty could be milked for millions. This was the language emerging out of the moral chaos of the postmodern world, but behind it lurked a reality that was in some ways as ugly as the bigotry of bygone days. McCann and Murray had no time for bigotry, but there were fears harboured by some as to whether they could save their clubs from the corporate raiders.

6. A New Firm: Murray and McCann

As McCann started going through the accounts at Celtic Park to find out just how big a hole he had been left, Rangers proceeded to complete the 1993–94 season with their sixth League Championship in a row. Earlier in the season Smith's team had wrapped up the Skol Cup with a 2–1 victory over Hibs in the final, but had lost 0–1 to Dundee United in the final of the Scottish Cup. Celtic's interest in the Cup ended on 29 January when they were eliminated by Motherwell by the only goal of the game, and staggered on to finish fourth in the League. Under the new regime, however, high hopes were held for the coming season, as Celtic fans waited over the summer break to see what plans the new manager had.

The close season break was the time for fans to take off for their various holiday retreats, now spread well beyond Saltcoats and Troon to take in the delights of the Mediterranean and points closer to the sun. For Rangers fans the summer break was also the time to wait and wonder in eager anticipation about which new foreign stars would arrive in Scotland to don the once light blue jersey, but now a regularly changing combination of colours and design to please the marketing men, the only constant being the name of the brewers who had paid to have their name emblazoned across it. In Smith's first year in charge he had to cope with the 'three foreigners' rule that meant he had to sign Scottish talent. Two of these were in fact born in England: Andy Goram who signed on from Hibs and after some spectacular blunders went on to make enough saves to break the hearts of many team managers, and Stuart McCall from Everton. Also signed that year was David Robertson from Aberdeen. Among the more exotic imports was the Ukrainian Alexei Mikhailichenko who joined from Sampdoria. But it was with established players, the Friesian Pieter Huistra and the partnership of McCoist and Hateley that Rangers surged ahead. The summer of 1993 saw the arrival at Ibrox of another home-based talent, the tall striker from Dundee United, Duncan Ferguson, for a record Scottish fee of £4 million. Ferguson had a stormy time before moving south to Everton, at first on loan, then permanently, while he became the first professional Scottish player to be jailed for an incident on the field, when he was convicted of head-butting John

McStay of Raith Rovers during a League match at Ibrox in April 1994.

In the summer of 1994 Rangers signed Basile Boli from Marseille for £2.7 million, an African-born French national who was a republican and a Catholic, but worse, an outspoken critic of Rangers' training methods and the abilities of their manager, so that when he left a year later it had nothing to do with his politics and religion. Signed along with Boli in the summer of 1994 was the man who became revered as the 'Prince of Denmark', Brian Laudrup from Italy's Fiorentina, and he was joined the following summer by the English wonder-boy Paul Gascoigne, from Lazio in Rome. Contrasting characters off the field, the Dane and the Geordie shared a range of skills on it that elevated them to a class above most of those with whom and against whom they played. Between them, but above all Gascoigne in his first season, they accounted for Rangers' eighth League flag in a row and set the club up for its tumultuous struggle for the much coveted ninth.

McCann's summer of 1994 saw the return to Celtic, as manager, of Tommy Burns, a former Celtic player of great skill and popularity whose private life fulfilled the most demanding code of the most traditional followers of the club. However, his lifetime devotion to Celtic, as a supporter, a player and then as manager, was to prove of no avail when he failed to build a team that could halt the Rangers juggernaut. To get him Celtic engaged in practices that did not meet the approval of Kilmarnock FC to whom Burns was contracted, and in addition to the bitterness this caused, the SFA upheld Kilmarnock's grievances and hit Celtic with a whopping £100,000 fine. It was the first of several incidents that set McCann against the SFA, in the course of which he found an ally in David Murray. Whatever differences the two millionaire club owners had, they could agree on the need to do something about the pettiness of the Lilliputians in Scottish football trying to tie down the giants who should have been ruling the game.

FROM GAPS TO GULFS

Celtic would never quite catch up with the expensive signings of Rangers, but they did begin to attract players of international class. Pierre van Hooijdonk came from the modest Dutch club NAC Breda for £1.25 million in January 1995, and it was with Celtic that he blossomed into a star striker. This caused some problems when his enhanced status encouraged him to try to renegotiate his contract and force more money out of the club, especially when later arrivals were on conditions much better than his. On the issue of payment to players, Celtic still had echoes from the past coming to haunt them as several players were linked with the club but for one reason or another did not sign, with hints that they did not like the financial terms. McCann himself expressed a few pertinent remarks about over-paid players, which, however justified, could hardly have helped the situation. Shortly before winning the Scottish Cup in May 1995, Burns made the acid comment that while his vision for the club consisted of 'hopes and dreams', the managing director saw only 'profit and loss'. Burns was forced to back down, but the two continued to be at odds over expenditure on players, leading almost to an explosion with the negotiations over the signing of Andreas Thom from Bayern Leverkusen in August 1995.

This was a problem at the heart of the contemporary game. Burns was angry at McCann's reluctance to spend the money to buy the players he wanted, but McCann had every reason to baulk at Thom's financial demands on top of his transfer fee of £2.2 million. Celtic fans, however, had seen too many star foreigners unsuccessfully associated with the club and the effect on their overwrought emotions of having to bear more taunts from their rivals about failed transfers finally decided the issue. The personal terms thus won by Thom provided fuel for future dressing-room squabbles when other players earning less, but performing better, reacted jealously to what Thom was being paid.

Of the foreigners Celtic had failed to sign, the most notable were David Ginola from Paris St-Germain, Marc Degryse from Anderlecht, and the Russian, Dimitri Radchenko. Worst of all they had Gordan Petric of Dundee United stolen from under their noses by Rangers, attracted by the higher wages on offer. Celtic's failure to sign these players was not always their fault: Degryse never really sounded serious about coming to Scotland, while Ginola allegedly used the club to negotiate a better deal from Barcelona, although it was Newcastle who signed him in the end. When he was abused by Celtic fans at a pre-season friendly, however, Ginola claimed his interest had been genuine, but that he had been advised not to go to Celtic by his compatriot, Basile Boli – prompting one sardonic Bear to declare that this was the only good thing Boli ever did for Rangers.

Another delayed transfer had nothing to do with McCann, and had the Celtic owner fuming: this was over the Portuguese striker Jorge Cadete from Sporting Lisbon towards the end of the 1995–96 season. McCann accused the SFA of deliberately holding up the transfer, which meant that for five crucial weeks, three of which were taken up by Cadete arranging to buy out his own contract with his club (or getting Celtic to buy it out) Celtic were without a player who could have made all the difference as they chased Rangers to the penultimate game of Rangers' eighth successive League flag.

Celtic's frustration in regard to signing big-name players was afforded little sympathy in some sections of the press, and in February 1997, Ian McGarry of the *Evening Times* claimed, on the strength of one Italian agent, that Celtic were regarded by some as a joke in Europe, making offers but never concluding any deals.[1] McGarry was referring to the hold-up in the signing of the defender Enrico Annoni from Roma. Despite McGarry's allegations, Celtic went on to sign the Italian. He joined the other foreigners who had come to grace the Parkhead turf – Thom, van Hooijdonk and Cadete, and the forward Paolo di Canio who had come from AC Milan in the summer of 1996 and was an immediate hit. Di Canio became a close friend of Burns and adapted wholeheartedly to the atmosphere at Celtic Park, adding his voice to the chorus that cried out bias against Celtic. He broke the long run of Rangers players winning the Scottish Players' Player of the Year award when he won that honour in 1997. Perhaps less fortuitously, Celtic paid a record £5.5 million to bring Alan Stubbs from Bolton on a five-year contract. With players of the calibre of Cadete and di Canio, Celtic were well and truly into the big time, but despite this, Rangers with Gascoigne and Laudrup were just that extra class ahead.

With the fortune spent on bringing in these foreign players, Rangers and Celtic left the rest of the Scottish League clubs in the rear, and the climactic 1996–97 season had all the features of a two-team shoot-out. The gulf between the two Old Firm teams and the rest of Scottish football was further emphasised as an impressive new oval-shaped stadium arose at Celtic Park on the site of the old, financed, as McCann had promised, by some of his own money and a share float among the fans.

McCann wasted no time in tackling the stadium issue shortly after he arrived at Parkhead, opting for what some had always seen as the natural one: building a new stadium at Paradise. This he did by injecting several millions of his own funds and then putting the club on the open market. The Celtic fans responded eagerly, and soon 10,000 of them were in possession of shares sold at £60 each and which would soon reach a market value of £300 and going as high as £425 at the beginning of 1997. It was the most successful share offer in British football, and no other club had such a wide fan involvement. At the end of McCann's second season with the club, Celtic had 37,000 season-ticket-holders, as against Rangers' 36,000, and the stadium was well on its way to completion with a projected capacity of 60,000, all seated. McCann turned a loss of £180,000 into a profit of £2.74 million for the financial year ending 1995, on a turnover that increased from £10 million to £16 million. Average crowds were up to more than double what they had been in the last season of the old regime, from over 25,000 in 1994–95 to over 34,000 the following year. With the increased seating capacity for the 1996–97 season, the average at over 48,000 was as good as the attendances at Ibrox.

With the biscuit tin a distant memory, Celtic embarked on a series of commercial developments that fully exploited a brand name that could be bettered for customer loyalty only by Manchester United, Liverpool and Rangers in Britain. A new mail order scheme doubled Celtic's income from merchandising for the 1996 Christmas period over that of 1995. The array of goods on offer from the Celtic Merchandise mail order scheme could be pored over in the colourful brochure itself on sale for £1. Set out in this catalogue is a range of goods in green and white from children's wear to adult leisure wear and full dress tartan for the special night out: clothes for all occasions, from the cradle to the Celtic Ceilidh or the Caledonian Ball. On offer are beer and wine, specially coloured to suit the Celtic palate with matching containers to drink from; trinkets of various shapes and sizes, and wallets and pennants and key-rings, all with the club's logo or colours. There is even the odd book or video on football, to remind you of what it is all supposed to be about. And for any Celtic fan concerned about the prices, there was the consolation of knowing that the profits would go towards bringing some millionaire to Glasgow and helping him to get by on his £10,000 a week for wearing the green and white hoops (or whatever other colour or design then in fashion).

Over at Ibrox it was all much the same, with only the colours being changed to protect the sensitivities of the buyer: red, white and blue instead of green and white, and a tartan of a more distinctly blue shading. And lots more of it! In 1996 Rangers added to their shops sprinkled around the city with a new superstore at the ground itself, crammed on match days with a procession of people adding to their stock of ways in which they could be associated with the club (and none of them in any way concerned that the foundation date that dominates the decor outside is one year out). And if some of the eager buyers had to make economies in the domestic budget to subsidise their loyalty, at least they knew Walter Smith was going to have even more money to bring even richer players on even bigger weekly salaries than those being paid at Celtic Park.

The bulk of the income of football teams throughout Britain at this time was now coming from sources other than admissions to the grounds. By 1997, the commercial side of Rangers' income, made up of corporate hospitality, sponsorship, advertising and merchandising, was claimed to account for 43p in every pound.[2] Since 'turnstile' admission accounted for about 35p in every pound, this left 22p from other sources, mainly television. For the rich clubs, television and merchandising seemed to offer ever-expanding pots of gold. Rangers did have some anxious moments in 1992, but they soon recovered from them and by January 1995 they had returned a net profit for the first time in three years.[3] Despite this, the club still felt it necessary to ask its fans to dig deeper into their financial resources to help realise the club's vision of a 'blue heaven'.

By this scheme, called 'Ready for the Future' and launched in mid-April 1995, Rangers fans were asked to fork out £399 to buy the right to season tickets for the next 25 years. This was expected to bring in £5 million, and would help pay for the £4 million to fill in the corners at Ibrox and bring the capacity of the ground up to 51,000. At the same time the club took the opportunity to paint all its seats blue, removing the anomaly of having brightly coloured seats spanning the entire spectrum with the solitary omission of green. In return the purchaser had the right to his name on the seat, transferable to family members, and a 10 per cent discount on Rangers goods, as well as a free weekend ticket to Rangers' pre-season international tournament.

While the ordinary fan pondered the £400 outlay, selected wealthier fans were asked to pay an estimated £1 million to achieve the honorary title of associate director, a means of raising money that had been popular with French monarchs feeling the financial pinch in the years before the Revolution, by creating positions at court that could be bought complete with a title to go with it, and a bit extra to make it heritable. Rangers, of course, were not plugging a hole to prevent a deluge, but were building for the future set just a few years off, in this case the year 2000.

Murray still resisted floating the club on the open market, and claimed to be comfortable with his 82 per cent holding. His April 1991 share-issue had aimed at involving a wider range of fans in the club, but it was clear that the gulf between the club and its fans was getting wider. In *Follow, Follow*, the faithful showed their alarm at the way they were being treated like dollar signs and were incensed at what they called the 'extortion racket' in prices for European Cup games, while unflattering comparisons were made with Manchester United in the way they treated their fans. Always, however, there was the consolation of the victories against the Tims and the pleasure of being part of the cathedral that was Ibrox. And at least until January 1997 it all seemed to stay inside the family.

KEEPING IT IN THE FAMILY?

Money has been part of football since its earliest days, when *Scottish Umpire*, *Scottish Sport* and the *Scottish Referee* constantly denounced its commercial aspects, in editorials, outraged articles and pungent cartoons – it was indeed disgust at such involvement that led to Rangers and Celtic being called the 'Old Firm'. In more recent times, however, football seems to have been engulfed by talk of deals and profits and the effect on the stock market of failing to make it into Europe or a defeat there after qualifying. There have always been individuals ready to use football for their own personal gain, but most directors, however fatuous or incompetent, have usually had a basic love of the game: until recently most of the people involved in the financial deals also had an involvement with the club. David Murray was bereft of Rangers credentials before he became a high-class Bear, but since then he has directed all his energies into the club, taking no salary or fees and ploughing profits on shares back into it. Fergus McCann was an avid Bhoy in his youth, a social convener for the Croy Celtic Supporters Association and he never missed a game in the 1962–63 season, the one before he left for Canada.

Nevertheless, McCann and Murray could expect to leave football with a massive profit on their investment, a shining example of the new age in which those with millions can walk off with even more millions. There was a time, not so long ago, when the involvement of the rich in football was a way to pay back rather than cash in on the passion of a misspent youth: among the football lovers prepared to plunge their personal fortune into a club was Elton John at Watford, while Jack Hayward at Wolves, Jack Walker at Blackburn and John Hall at Newcastle are millionaires for whom money expended on a mere hobby was to prove immensely profitable in the 1990s. Alan Sugar at Spurs had no interest in football nor indeed, it would appear, in anything that had no obvious profit outcome, until he saw the dollar signs flashing in English football with the imminent arrival of a Super League;[4] David Dein, football lover as a kid, had a foot in both camps, while Robert Maxwell had a finger in several clubs, none of which suffered for the criminal activities for which others among his employees have had to pay. Probably no one has made more out of sport than Rupert Murdoch, although unlike his one-time compatriot, Kerry Packer, the Australian by birth but American by commercial choice is not renowned for any particular interest in many things beyond making money, which has not prevented this scion of good Presbyterian stock being awarded a papal knighthood in 1998, like all such dubious awards a reflection on the giver as much as the receiver. Martin Edwards inherited his role as director and chairman of the legendary Manchester United, a legend which many followers of the club with memories of Matt Busby, the Babes and a time when the club was concerned above all about football, believe has long been betrayed.

The Celtic board before 1994 tried to keep at bay millionaires wanting to invest in Celtic, but despite their expressed fears, all of these millionaires, even Weisfeld, had an interest in the club beyond profit. Then Rangers allowed a certain Joe Lewis to stake a massive £40 million in the club, a man who is neither Scottish nor with any great interest in football, although he was said to love the sports more traditionally associated with men of money – tennis, golf, horse-racing and sailing. It is just possible that he was the first man to join the club with the explicit intention of making money from it. As the *Daily Mail* reported: 'It is understood Mr Lewis sees the deal purely as a money-making scheme to make a big profit when Rangers is eventually floated on the Stock Market.'[5] Since then he has investigated the money-making potential of other football clubs.

Towards the end of 1996 David Murray had let it be known that he was considering diluting his holding at Rangers by issuing new shares that would still give him a majority holding, but reduced to about 61 per cent. After a few whispers as to who this might be, the headline news on 23 January 1997 was a variation on the theme of the 'Mystery Midas' or 'Bahamas Billionaire'.[6] Lewis was reported to be a recluse, who refused to give interviews or to be photographed, but all agreed that he was one of the wealthiest individuals in Britain, a man who had made his billions by various theme ventures, including investment in the immensely successful Hard Rock cafés and Planet Hollywood restaurants, and even a chain of banqueting suites 'often used by Freemasons'.[7] Above all, however, his profits had come from speculation on the international money market.[8] He became a tax exile in 1979. A neighbour of Sean Connery in the Bahamas, it was thought to be through the former Agent 007 and alleged one-time Celtic supporter later with Rangers, who had once been linked to a takeover of the club, that Lewis came to offer Murray the £40 million that gave him a 25.1 per cent stake in Rangers. Then again he was a friend of Dermot Desmond, the non-executive director of Celtic who had invested £4 million in Celtic shares in 1995 and would eventually become chief executive, and it could have been he who had told him about the money that was there for the making. Whatever the case, there was no talk of him entering the club in any custodial capacity. As reported by *The Scotsman*, the deal was made by Albany Inc, a holding company set up by Lewis's English National Investment Company (ENIC).[9] Some of Murray's money was invested in ENIC and two of the English company's employees were appointed to the Ibrox board, one of whom, Daniel Levy, declared that football was merely a financial concern for the company. The proportion of the small shareholders in Rangers fell as a result of the deal, from 19 per cent to 14 per cent.

In the meantime Daniel Levy, using the Rangers brand name to help gain entry, bought into three long-established European teams: close to 30 per cent in Italy's Vicenza for £2.4 million with an option to buy a controlling interest for £2.6 million; a controlling interest in Slavia Prague, former great of Central European football, now fallen on hard times; and AEK of Athens. With these teams and Rangers, Levy and ENIC could run a European mini-league of their own teams.[10] Levy, like Lewis, made no pretence about having any interest in football: it is to be hoped that UEFA and FIFA, who surely do, keep a close eye on those intent on using the game purely for their own interests.

Half of Lewis's money was said to be immediately put aside to buy more players, while the rest would be used towards the building of a 150-bed hotel at Ibrox and a nearby multi-purpose leisure centre. Murray told the Rangers supporters to go and enjoy themselves over a few beers, but for the more thoughtful Bears there was little to cheer about. Rangers might have further distanced themselves from Celtic, but even further were they distancing themselves from their own natural fans. Shortly after the Lewis share deal was completed, more sober columns in the press passed on the news that the company that had started the Rangers revolution, John Lawrence (Glasgow) Ltd, had gone into receivership.

At the same time as Lewis sought to advance his millions by speculating on Rangers shares, Brian Dempsey reappeared on the Celtic scene like a blast from Celtic's past – not so much the recent past, the memorable moment when he had stood outside Celtic Park on 4 March 1994 and announced that 'The rebels have won', but rather to the days before John H. McLaughlin and company took over almost exactly a century before, when the club had been run by enthusiastic volunteers. There could be little doubt about his sincerity, and his emphasis on youthful players to eliminate the need for an influx of foreign players has much to recommend it. Above all it would be reassuring to have football finance in the hands of people who love the game, as he would like to see it: but it seems impossible in the present financial climate for anyone to keep shares in Celtic out of corporate hands, as Dempsey said he wanted to, by gaining control so that he could then 'give the club back to the people who support it by selling them shares at a price they could afford'.[11]

In December 1997 Fergus McCann confirmed that he would adhere to the promise made in 1994 that his commitment to the club would be for five years, and that as from the summer of 1999 he would return to a life no doubt less stressful than kicking against the pricks of petty authority and having to justify himself before fans who thought they owned the club he had bought. The charms of bringing up a young family and relaxing with a few rounds of golf bears no comparison with suffering fools less than gladly and putting up with the abuse and ingratitude of outraged football fans. In line with his commitment to the club as a custodian of its essential values, he promised that he would try to ensure that his shareholding would be made available to the Celtic faithful.

Unlike Murray, McCann seemed more willing to involve Celtic fans in a broad ownership in the club, which did not prevent Murray from criticising Rangers fans for having had it too easy, never having to put their hands in their own pockets to finance all the wonders he had achieved at Ibrox. McCann, more than Murray, seemed to have a better understanding of what it is like to be a fan, with all the irrational devotion this involves. Both men, however, have dedicated their life to commercial success and see football through the eyes of businessmen, and in the amoral commercial climate of the new football, as in the wider world of the economic so-called rationalists, there is no place for those who cannot defend or look after themselves, be it football teams that cannot attract supporters and the sponsors' dollars, or children in Asia working on slave wages to supply leisurewear for the world's rich and footballs for the giants of the world game. If football was ruled from the heart and not the marketplace, Partick Thistle would not have had to be fighting for their very life, yet football in Glasgow without the Jags is unthinkable, and not just from the standpoint of the masochists and the light relief of those who do not follow the Old Firm. That said, and there must always be a place for the wee teams of Scotland, rich in their own particular histories, the future of the game lies beyond the borders of Scotland, where only Rangers and Celtic have a realistic chance of competing at the highest levels.

A LEAGUE OF THEIR OWN

Celtic and Rangers have been called the giants of Scottish football, but they have now virtually outgrown it. Effectively they are in another league compared to the other teams – and literally wish that they were. In the lopsided Scottish game there continued to be upsets in Cup games and the odd league reversal, but it is hard to see how even Aberdeen or the Edinburgh teams can match the spending of the big two, Rangers could still tower over Celtic in this regard, but since the McCann takeover the Parkhead club has managed to stay within the financial orbit of its main rival.

As Rangers and Celtic outdistanced the other clubs in Scottish football, so they increasingly came to treat with contempt its ruling bodies,

unfortunately often with good reason. Rangers fans even found themselves, by their accusations of bias against their club in the media and by
the men who ruled the game, joining in harmonious counterpoint with
the paranoia chorus of their rivals. At the highest levels the two clubs
came ever closer together, and as the two teams fought it out on the park,
Murray and McCann, in the spirit that gave the Old Firm its name in
the first place, joined forces to ensure that the power and wealth they
represented was reflected in the running of the game in Scotland.

McCann showed no reticence in pointing out what was rotten in the
running of Scottish football, beginning with the SFA and the League
itself: in his estimation both were overstaffed and overpaid, Hampden
was a white elephant as far as football was concerned, 30 clubs needed to
be wiped off the League's playing-fields, and clubs that loaned players for
national duty had to be paid for this service. Such sentiments would have
sounded as music to Murray's ears, and so it was little surprise when the
Ibrox supremo sympathised with McCann in his battles with the
authorities.

McCann's first confrontation with the SFA and the League was over
the fine he received for poaching Burns, followed by a tribunal order to
pay Kilmarnock £200,000 for inducing the manager and his assistant
Billy Stark away from the club. Appeals proved fruitless as the League
and the SFA backed each other up, ignoring that the fine against Celtic
was so much greater than for any previous similar offence, namely the
£5,000 Rangers had been fined for poaching Ferguson from Dundee
United. Certainly payments to players were rocketing at an astronomical
rate, but this fine still seemed excessive. Above all, Celtic had no recourse
to legal opinion outside the football authorities, and this brought
Rangers to their side.

At the SFA's AGM in May 1995 Celtic moved, seconded by Rangers,
that clubs in the League have recourse to law should they disagree with
the rulings of the SFA. The motion was clearly defeated: there had been
occasions enough in the past when Rangers in particular had been
angered at 'outside' interference in the game, as after the notorious Old
Firm game of 1987 or the prosecution of Duncan Ferguson, but this was
different. The small clubs were telling them what to do, and since they
had recourse neither to the laws of the land nor entry to another football
league, Rangers and Celtic would have to remould the game in Scotland
so that it more accurately reflected their interests.

Murray had been involved in a few battles with the old Celtic board,
most notably when he banned Celtic fans from Ibrox after the Parkhead
club refused to pay for damage to seats in the Broomloan Stand following
an Old Firm game in October 1993. He claimed £7,800 compensation

for this, although up to £20,000 damage had allegedly been done at previous games. Murray was equally upset that Celtic supporters did not buy the club's programme or sample the fine Bluenose catering on offer: a Broomloan stand full of Bears was obviously a much more profitable concern. Michael Kelly had little time for Murray and his ways, and McCann and Murray were hardly bosom buddies, but they were businessmen and they shared a disdain for those who made the laws and carried them out, McCann with the added suspicion that the SFA and the League looked on Celtic with a malevolence that had its origins deep in Scotland's past. A series of what appeared to be bad refereeing decisions fuelled Celtic's anger, and in January 1997 rumours circulated about the club's plans to buy English Premiership club Wimbledon as a means of entering the English Premier League. Wimbledon had themselves thought of relocating to Dublin, but no one seems to have asked them, at a time when they were still in line for a UEFA Cup place and doing well in the two English cup competitions, what they thought of going out of existence in Scotland. The issue was given serious treatment in the *Evening Times*,[12] which 'revealed' the story, but most serious commentators treated it as pie in the sky. McCann was no doubt serious about his earlier idea of bringing a Dublin team into the Scottish League, but talk of Celtic joining the English Premiership had to be seen as little more than a broadside at the Scottish football authorities.

Murray was equally contemptuous of the Scottish league system, controlled as it was by 40 clubs, many of which he could have bought with his pocket money and thrown away – if League rules had permitted it. Yet these were the teams whose numbers could frustrate the ambitions of the bigger clubs, and whose instincts for survival refused to recognise the need for rationalisation, a favourite buzz-word of those ruled by the economic imperative. Murray saw the small-team mentality reflected in the SFA and the League, and in this he could have found many to agree with him – and outside the Old Firm. The SFA's Think Tank, dreamed up at the beginning of the 1996–97 season to set out guidelines for the future of Scottish football, was seen as a joke by some observers, especially when Murray and McCann were not invited to be part of it.

The two men called their own summit meetings instead, the first of which took place over a private lunch at Celtic Park on 13 November 1996. As was later revealed, part of the discussion at that meeting was over the fate of young players and how to introduce a standardised youth training scheme, a particular concern following the Bosman judgement laid down earlier that year, which gave players freedom of contract and, in the case of a youth player, the right to walk away from a club that might have invested a great deal of money and time in his development.

Out of this discussion, carried on between Smith and Burns, it was suggested that the reserve leagues be scrapped and that young players instead be 'farmed out' to First Division clubs. A similar scheme had once existed in Scotland with 'Junior' teams acting as the nursery club, and in Germany, Italy and Spain it was common practice. The proposed scheme would allow the big clubs to reduce expenditure on youth training, while the lower-division clubs would have the use of an up-and-coming youngster at no expense. There were obvious difficulties to be overcome, one of which would be convincing the League that this scheme would be in the best interests of Scottish football and not just of Celtic and Rangers.

The next meeting of the two tycoons in mid-December resulted in an open avowal of their intentions to go it alone if need be. In mid-December Murray made the peculiar declaration that the other teams in the League had lived off the big two for long enough and it was time for the Old Firm to patch up their differences: 'In the past Scottish football has lived off the split between Rangers and Celtic. That will not happen any longer. Fergus and I have a mutual respect for each other and we want to work together for the good of the game.'[13]

The Scottish authorities were unimpressed, but still seemed intent on driving them closer together. In addition to the League refusing to allow Rangers to postpone a game against Hibs despite having medical certificates for 28(!) players, the chief executive of the SFA, Jim Farry, made remarks that deeply irritated both McCann and Murray. On 7 January 1997 Farry allegedly told *The Herald* that there were too many foreigners in the Scottish game, and less than two weeks later he was reported to have said in *Scotland on Sunday* that there were too many entrepreneurs in the game. He specifically referred to McCann as one of those whose investment in Scottish football had been to its 'detriment'. Armed with these accusations, to which he added his continuing resentment over the delayed Cadete signing, McCann 'went to war' against the SFA with a letter of 27 January for discussion at its Executive Committee meeting the following day.[14] He demanded that Farry be called to account for his behaviour and demanded an explanation for the delay in the Cadete signing and compensation for two weeks of the player's salary. Two years later, in March 1999, Farry was sacked by the SFA for 'gross misconduct', when that organisation – which had previously exonerated Farry after two internal investigations into the matter – was advised to make an out-of-court settlement with Celtic following an independent inquiry.[15]

At the same time as McCann battled with the SFA, Clydebank chairman Jack Steedman called a meeting of all the First Division clubs and five from the Premier League to seek approval for a reorganisation of the four leagues of ten teams into three of 16 in the top division and 12 in each of the two lower ones. When the plan was put to a League meeting in April, it was rejected. It was then that the plans for an elite breakaway league of ten teams, an idea that had been mooted throughout the season, was brought into the open. On 9 April 1997 a meeting of the chairmen of the ten Premier League clubs announced that they had taken steps for the creation of a new league system, run by themselves, and that as a consequence they would be retiring from the Scottish League. Aware of the mistake he had made in 1992 by telegraphing his intentions, Murray, who had never dropped the idea of a Super League, kept a low profile while consultation went on with the other Premier League chairmen. In the outcome they agreed to hire an independent professional adviser to prepare plans for a new league to be in place by the beginning of the 1998–99 season. This would be an autonomous body, independent of the League, and so it would be able to work out the most lucrative television contracts and keep the revenue to themselves: a copy, more or less, of the English Premiership, albeit without the support of the game's ruling body, and a microcosm in comparison. For Rangers and Celtic it would be their preparation for the European Super League.

Some details of the plan being cooked up by the existing ten Premier League clubs (plus Raith Rovers) were revealed to the public in September 1997. Among its ironies was that the top ten clubs already hogged so much of the wealth in Scottish football (85 per cent) that it would cost very little to compensate the 30 other clubs in the League. More than money was at stake, however, and the more ambitious of the excluded clubs were not at first prepared to let the breakaway Premiership ten (plus one, later two) have it all their own way, insisting that they have more information before they approved the plans and allowed the others to retire and set up the new league before the statutory two-year period. They were particularly concerned about access to the new league and whether it was worth their while investing in ground improvements, such as all-seated stadiums for a minimum number of spectators. The main aim of the top ten (plus whoever else hoped to be part of it) was to run their own affairs in their own interests, but they also claimed that they were acting in the best interests of the game, since they would attract more money to Scottish football than the SFA and the Scottish League had done. They tried to back this up by making the always spurious comparison with the English Premiership, and offered inducements to those they would exclude from their private league, smaller slices of what would be a much larger cake, enough to keep the noses at the windows of the rich clubs' banquet harmlessly on the outside. The would-be benefactors of Scottish football also made the obligatory comments about being concerned about youth development in the Scottish game, although this never excited the same enthusiasm as the dollars expected to come rolling in to pay for the wages and other expenses of the elite clubs.

As the debate dragged on, the exclusiveness of the new league was breeched to suggest that 12 and then even 16 teams might be included. By December 1997, faced by the ingratitude of the sulky malcontents who refused to accept the offerings from the rich clubs' table, Murray took out the big stick and warned them that if they did not accept what was on offer they would get nothing and the deserving rich would go their own way in any case. The wrangling ended in 1998 when the split between the Premier Division (the aforementioned ten Premier League clubs) formally resigned from membership of the Scottish League, bringing into operation from season 1998–99 a four-division set-up comprising the Premier League – with its own organisation – and three other divisions run by the Scottish Football League. In all the claims and counter-claims it was hard for the ordinary fans to see how their enjoyment of the game was going to improve, and there was very little talk of money going back to what had once been the bedrock of the Scottish game: the schools, churches and other grassroots competitions, now struggling to survive in the dog-eat-dog world of municipal competition and savage cutbacks. The proponents of the new set-up were concerned about the game only at the elite level, and from this point of view it is true that in a country with a population as small as Scotland's, 40 professional clubs claiming equal access to power is unrealistic. These clubs all have their place in Scottish football, albeit for some of them perhaps in a regional league, but they also have the right, however unrealistic such an ambition may seem, to aim for promotion to the top ranks, whether it be a single Premiership of 10 or 12 or 16 clubs, or a two-division league of 10, 12 or 14 in whatever combination. Increasingly for the Old Firm, however, the first priority is how to escape from Scotland.

THE OLD FIRM, SCOTLAND AND THE WORLD

The imbalance in Scottish football has been with the game for well over a century. Rangers and Celtic have consistently attracted crowds for home and away games that no other club could match: even in the early 1980s when Aberdeen and Dundee United were playing the best football in Scotland the crowds who came to see them were small in comparison with those who turned up to see the Glasgow clubs. And when either Celtic or Rangers were playing poorly and fewer fans came to their games, witness the resurgence after Souness at Ibrox and at Celtic Park after the civil war, it would appear that these fans occupied their Old Firm-free time in pursuits other than watching football in Scotland. It was a sad fact, but a fact nevertheless, that the Celtic and Rangers fans coming from all over Scotland and Northern Ireland every other week in the season had at best only a secondary interest in their local team. Whether or not this has been good or bad for Scottish football is a perennial matter of debate.

For some, Rangers and Celtic have kept Scottish football alive in the way they have provided a gravy train, a milch cow or whatever metaphor you wish to choose to picture the weak living off the strong, the poor surviving on the hand-outs of the rich. Others might compare the Old Firm to the legendary Upas Tree that was believed to have the power to destroy other growth within a radius of 15 miles, an image used in the title of a history of Glasgow that saw its heavy industries as having a detrimental domination of the city's economy and society.[16] However that may be, the Old Firm and the Scottish League have been stuck with each other, knowing that a breakaway needed the approval of the SFA, who could call on support from UEFA and ultimately FIFA to back them against recalcitrant clubs. And the world body has never lost a battle with nations that have bucked its authority, whether it was Colombia in the early 1950s or Australia a few years later. But that was all in the past; above all it was pre-Bosman.

There is little doubt that if Rangers and Celtic were playing regularly in a competition such as the English Premier League they could hold their own and would soon be challenging for the top spot. But a British League or an expanded Premier League to include them is a pipe dream – the only way the Old Firm could be brought into a British League would be if the greed of the richest clubs in England encouraged them to break away from the merely wealthy clubs to form a smaller league which included the two Glasgow clubs. This reduced league programme would allow them at the same time to take part in a European league. This would also require the approval of UEFA and FIFA, but as the Bosman judgement has shown, there is an appeal beyond the courts of the gods who run the world game: a Bosman-type appeal on behalf of the rich clubs could smash all the existing rules and allow them to play in whatever league they wanted. More likely, FIFA would intervene and give its approval: either way it would be in the logic of the game's history: a Super League of the world's best teams.

In the meantime, the Old Firm, with their eyes on Europe and the Scottish game merely an entry point for the more lucrative leagues to come, are in a contradictory situation. The more successful Rangers and

Celtic are in Europe, the more money they earn and so the further they find themselves adrift of the other Scottish teams. And yet without a strong competition in Scotland they have inadequate preparation for their European encounters. And the more unattractive the Scottish League becomes, the more difficult it is to persuade top international stars to play there: there is little attraction for a Vialli or a Zola playing against Aberdeen, Hearts or Dundee United four times a year, let alone Dunfermline or Kilmarnock, all teams that once held their heads high in Europe. According to Fernando Couto when he rejected a Rangers offer, Scottish football was 'rubbish'. Ronaldo was much more polite when he rejected what must surely have been the most attractive offer ever made to any footballer until then. Rangers' offer to the brilliant Brazilian – one which the cynics say was made because they knew it would not be accepted, or was made after he had signed for Inter Milan, but which was in any case a mere publicity stunt – was mindboggling not just in its payments to the player (a salary of more than £4.2 million and a percentage of his transfer fee if he left before the end of his four-year contract), but in Ronaldo's right to choose the games he wanted to play in, thus excusing him from having to go through the motions against the majority of the Scottish teams Rangers had to play against each week. All this in addition to the £20 million transfer fee to be paid to his club, Barcelona.

For many in Scotland, above all the fans of the Old Firm, primeval passions were centred more on home turf than the baubles to be gained on foreign soil, and for them as the 1996–97 season got under way and the bitter memories of early departures from Europe were pushed into the background, there was only one question that bore serious consideration: whether or not the resurgent Celtic could stop Smith's Rangers from equalling the record set by Jock Stein's team back in 1974, a record that several commentators said at the time, and for well over a decade later, would never be beaten.

7. The Chase for Ten: End of an Era

Rangers, despite a shaky start, won their seventh consecutive League flag in 1995 at a canter, with Celtic finishing in fourth place. Standing between a revitalised Celtic and Rangers' eighth successive League flag were Gascoigne and Laudrup, above all the former, as Celtic fought their main rivals to a finish only to come in second, four points behind the winners. With the magic nine-in-a-row approaching, the other trophies seemed inconsequential to Rangers. They fell to Hearts 2–4 in the fourth round of the Scottish Cup in 1995, but had their revenge in the final the following year with a 5–1 hammering of the Edinburgh club. In the League Cup Rangers were beaten by Falkirk (1–2) in the third round of the 1994–95 season and by Aberdeen (1–2) in the semi-final the next year. By then the momentum begun by McCann off the field at Parkhead was showing results on the field, as Celtic dramatically cut the gap between the two clubs.

In McCann's first year at Celtic Park, Burns's team got off to a spark-ling start to the season, taking Rangers apart in a 2–0 victory at Ibrox on 27 August 1994. To add to their natural joy at triumphing over the Huns, the Celtic fans could also take a perverse pleasure in seeing Rangers supporters turn on Walter Smith and the team as Rangers' crushing defeat came just three days after their elimination from the preliminary rounds of the European Cup by AEK Athens; then on the last day of August Rangers were beaten 2–1 in the League Cup by Falkirk, their third successive defeat at home, and all in key games. But the gods must have been teasing the men from Paradise, as Rangers soon found form and outstripped their rivals. Celtic reached the final of the League Cup that season, but lost to Raith Rovers in a penalty shoot-out, leaving the good folk of Raith to dance in the streets while the Bhoys tore their hair out in anguish. In May 1995 Celtic won the Scottish Cup, but even this first touch of silverware in any form since 1989 was greeted more with relief than celebration. It was a lacklustre victory, 1–0 against Airdrie, but it was a trophy nevertheless.

In McCann's second full year, Celtic won nothing, and yet there was an air of expectation, even euphoria, at the club, as the fans were buoyed with dreams of what lay ahead. This, they hoped, would be the year they stopped Rangers matching the Stein record. It was a year as tense as the pundits predicted, with controversies on and off the field, but with a climax that proved to be more of a whimper than a bang.

SHOWDOWN SEASON

Rangers won the first trophy of the 1996–97 season with a 4–3 victory over Hearts in the League Cup final after Celtic had been eliminated by the Edinburgh side (1–0) in the quarter-finals. Celtic made up for this in the Scottish Cup, where they went through to the semi-final on a wave of delirium after eliminating Rangers with a classy 2–0 quarter-final victory on 6 March. Again the promised joy turned to torment as they were brought down to earth with a thud by lower-division Falkirk, who beat them 1–0 in a replay after a 1–1 draw and went on to lose to Kilmarnock in the final. Celtic's defeat was more devastating than the League Cup loss to Raith Rovers, as this time they were beaten without recourse to penalties and in a replay, which would normally have been a formality for either of the Old Firm teams when held by a minnow in the first game. Disaster in the league chase also cut short the optimism that accompanied the elimination of Rangers from the Cup.

That Cup victory over Rangers on 6 March 1997 had ended a long drought in Old Firm encounters going back ten games to 6 May 1995, but hopes of a turn-around in Old Firm fortunes ended in a crunch league game just over a week later, on 16 March, when the championship was all but decided after Rangers beat Celtic 1-0 at Celtic Park. At one stage in the league race, towards the end of October with 11 games played, Celtic were at the top of the table on goal difference; two games later they were five points behind. One of these games was against Rangers, who won 1–0 at Ibrox, the second of Rangers' four Old Firm league victories in the only season when one team whitewashed the other in Premier League games. Rangers charged ahead in the league after the Ibrox victory, but a win for Celtic in the Ne'erday game at home would have kept them in the race. Instead, Rangers won a controversial encounter with a 3–1 scoreline that flattered the visitors, who benefited from a disputed refereeing decision when a late goal by Cadete, which would have equalised the score at 2–2, was disallowed. At that stage Celtic were applying all the pressure, having regained the initiative after the daftest of defensive errors had cost them their second goal. Eric Bo Anderson sealed it for Rangers in the last minute. The Ibrox side were now 14 points ahead, although Celtic had two games in hand. Celtic then won five games in succession, and Rangers, suffering from a string of injuries which had plagued them for much of the season, including a broken ankle for Gascoigne in a pointless tournament in Amsterdam, meant that they dropped some vital points. Celtic somehow managed to do the same, but by the time the two clubs met for their last league game against each other, Celtic had cut the gap to five points.

Played on 16 March 1997, the last Old Firm game of the showdown season turned out to be a spiteful encounter. Mark Hateley, temporarily back with the club he had left against his own wishes, was sent off for a gentle head-butt on Stewart Kerr, while Malky Mackay of Celtic was also red-carded. Paolo di Canio and Ian Ferguson carried on their own personal feud, but boiling point came at the end of the game when Rangers, having won 1–0, celebrated with a mockery of the Celtic huddle. This was a ritual that Celtic had introduced into the game, usually before matches, but in the recent Cup game they had used it to celebrate victory. Throughout the tensions, the supporters kept their cool, showing a discipline that they certainly had not learned from the players or even the manager. Burns denounced the manner of the Rangers victory, prompting Walter Smith to speak out in defence of his players when he returned from a scouting trip to Italy. He pointed out how Rangers had congratulated Celtic after their defeat in the Cup game, which his players had accepted without recriminations. The signs were there that tensions were building up at Paradise and it all burst into the open when Celtic were knocked out of the Cup by Falkirk.

In the meantime Rangers tormented their fans as they failed to kill off the league race in the style they craved. It all seemed to be falling into place on 15 April when they thrashed Raith Rovers 6–0 at Kirkcaldy and were all but mathematical certainties to win the flag. They could even have won it without playing another game after that, but Celtic delayed the popping of the champagne corks with two victories, against Aberdeen and Hibernian, while Rangers themselves held up the celebrations when they failed to beat Motherwell in a Monday game at Ibrox on 5 May. The giant party planned for Ibrox on the Monday night, including a 20,000-fan congo line all the way to George Square, had to be postponed. Celebrations took place two nights later, on the east coast, or in pubs and private homes and public places throughout the country, as Rangers duly wrapped up their ninth consecutive flag when they went to Tannadice and Brian Laudrup scored the game's only goal. As if to give a special touch to the magic he had been producing all season, it was Laudrup's first-ever headed goal for the club.

Rangers fans were even deprived of a proper celebration at their final game, against Hearts. They lost 3–1 at Tynecastle, with 30,000 fans at Ibrox that day decked out in party gear to watch the last match of the historic season relayed direct from Edinburgh and projected on the new giant television screens. However disappointed by the result that day, Celtic's record had been equalled and there was every chance that the chant of 'Ten-in-a-Row' would become a reality the following season – especially when Celtic appeared to be disintegrating as the hectic season came to an end and Rangers went in for ever more fantastic buying sprees over the summer.

SUMMER OF HOPE AND HEARTBREAK

When Motherwell beat Rangers that Monday, some of the more optimistic Celtic fans were still hoping for a miracle, that Dundee United might repeat Motherwell's feat on the Wednesday. It all became irrelevant when, that same night, Celtic could only draw 0–0 against Kilmarnock, so that Rangers did not even have to take a point at Dundee to win the trophy. Celtic by then were managerless, Burns having left the club a few days before. In reality, Celtic's season and Burns's career as the club's manager ended after the Falkirk defeat. After another long, drawn-out saga about his future, during which Burns is said to have demanded that McCann back him or sack him, the chairman ended the speculation when he refused to renew the manager's contract and effectively forced Burns to resign on 2 May 1997 by offering him a new position at Celtic Park as head of youth development, an offer Burns was not expected to accept.

It had been a stormy partnership from the outset, and there was speculation that Burns had not even been McCann's first choice as manager. Ivan Golac of Dundee United and Bobby Robson, then in charge of Porto, had been linked with the position. And Kenny Dalglish. But if Dalglish were to come back to Glasgow, it seemed more likely then that it would have been not to his former club, but rather to the team he had supported as a boy. Dalglish's 1996 autobiography reads in places like an application for a job at Ibrox,[1] and indeed he looked all set to go there on an outrageous salary as some sort of roaming ambassador and public-relations man for David Murray's other leisure concerns, when Newcastle United intervened and Dalglish joined the Geordies instead, replacing Kevin Keegan as manager. His eventual return to Parkhead in 2000 made many Celtic supporters wish he had fulfilled his earlier ambition and gone to Ibrox.

Over the summer of 1997, with Burns off to contemplate his future and find some way to let the world know of the wrongs that had been done to him at Celtic Park, Keegan and Robson were back among the names being touted as the club's new manager, while the *Daily Record*, which seemed to be running a campaign on behalf of Bobby Robson, announced in an exclusive that the former England coach would definitely be joining Celtic. McCann refused to show any sign of being rattled by the rumour-mongers as he embarked on his plan to restructure the club around the model of that of the best of such continental teams as Ajax and Juventus, with a head coach and a general manager to run the team and its business affairs. It took an agonisingly long time before McCann, ignoring the clamour in the press to accept one of their candidates, finally, in July, settled on the Dutchman Wim Jansen as coach. Jansen, whose only previous connection with Celtic was as a player in the Feyenoord team which beat the Glasgow side in the European Cup in 1970, was not the big-name signing the fans had hoped for. The new man, six months out of work after a spell coaching in Japan, was signed on a three-year contract to work with the general manager, who would deal with the legal and administrative affairs of the team. If Celtic's choice of coach caused some dismay, the appointment of Jock Brown as general manager on 20 June had provoked a few agonised protests, and not for the reputation for arrogance that he brought with him from his previous job, and which would allegedly lead to serious conflict with the head coach. Of more concern to some Celtic supporters, including a spokesman for the Celtic Supporters Association, spouting a religious purity so recently the preserve of the Protestants, the club was in danger of betraying its origins. Such suspicions were reinforced with the departures under a cloud of Burns and later Davie Hay, the latter muttering darkly about Celtic straying too far from their traditional roots, while Burns warned McCann that 'Celtic have to be wary of mixing up bigotry and tradition'.[2] In an amazing response, and without naming the two former managers, McCann denounced the accusations of people he branded 'Catholic bigots'.

Brown was the son of a Hamilton Accies man; his brother Craig, the Scotland coach, had once played for Rangers; and another brother was a Church of Scotland minister in Aberdeen. And while Brown was a fully qualified lawyer, he was best known as a football commentator and was widely thought to be a Rangers supporter. The new man spared the public protestations about how his life-long ambition had been to manage Celtic, but with his signature came his commitment and a reminder that two of Celtic's greatest ever signings, Jock Stein and Kenny Dalglish, came from non-Catholic backgrounds.

It was his skills as a lawyer which had brought Brown to the attention of the Celtic board, but it would have needed more than a genius from Philadelphia to sort out the sea of troubles that faced the new manager. Above all there was the running sore of Celtic's two outstanding players, Cadete and di Canio, who openly expressed their dislike of McCann, their love of the Celtic fans and a desire to play elsewhere. When eventually they left the club – Cadete following his wife back to Portugal and di Canio heading to Sheffield Wednesday – the two former idols, like Van Hooijdonk before them, had used up the last ounce of goodwill that the fans had so bounteously lavished on them. There was a time, before the retain-and-transfer system was abolished, when players were often treated abominably; now the boot seems to be on the other foot, and players on what some would describe as obscene wages are not even prepared to stick by the contract they signed of their own (and their agent's) free will. But these were not the only problems facing Brown.

In the week before Burns left Celtic, Willie Haughey, one of the front-runners when McCann won his battle with the old board, left the club in acrimonious circumstances, to be followed a few days later by Dominic Keane, apparently out of sympathy with Haughey. In the game against Hibs, shortly after Burns's resignation, Paolo di Canio, professing anger at what had happened, threw his jersey into the crowd and told the press that he had lost faith in McCann. Burns had been Celtic's fourth manager in six years. As a player he had often lost his temper and even with his millionaire employer he could not keep his tongue or his feelings in check, at times seeming to be deliberately provocative. McCann was not a man easily provoked, more and more a Napoleonic figure as he restored order after the civil war and revolution, but in danger, like Napoleon, of alienating his support by too authoritarian an approach.

The departure of Haughey and Keane, prominent in the unseating of the old board, and the re-emergence of Brian Dempsey with his plans to save the club from corporate control and return it to the fans, had all the makings of a challenge to McCann. There were rumblings of a new civil war, with some of the same faces in similar roles but with changed allegiances. This time McCann had complete control through his share-holding, but also the support of the bulk of the fans among whom the general feeling was that if Burns had done his job as well as McCann had done his, Celtic would not have trailed Rangers in the climactic season.

All this faced Brown when he took on the job at Parkhead, and no magic wand came with the job description. In contrast to the star players, it is unlikely that Brown was being overpaid, but despite his friendship with McCann he was never able to get on with Jansen and had to leave the club in November 1998. Much of this was kept from public view as the more important business of blocking Rangers' race to Ten-in-a-Row heated up.

Over at Ibrox the only news during the summer of 1997, give or take the odd bid to secure the world's best footballer, or the signing of a new coach, Tommy Moller Nielsen, to relieve Walter Smith and prepare for his move upstairs, was on those days when Rangers were not linked with the transfer of some multi-million-pound foreign star. At the end of June Murray's expenditure on players since he arrived at the club passed the £45 million mark. Several of the new players were Italian, presumably Catholic, and, with those Catholics already at the club, threatened to make up the majority of the first team.

Despite the excitement surrounding the new arrivals at Ibrox, it was the retention of the two reigning stars, Gascoigne and Laudrup, that most cheered the Rangers faithful. Not that the newcomers were not looked upon with some wonderment: above all, the four Italians – the youngster Gennaro (Rino) Gattuso, secured on freedom of contract from Perugia; Marco Negri, also from Perugia, a striker who would set up an amazing goalscoring streak in his first dozen games, for £3.7 million; Sergio Porrini from Juventus (£3.2 million); and Lorenzo Amoruso from Fiorentina (£4 million). Amoruso, like the recently signed Chilean, Sebastian Rozental, looked like being an expensive buy, living the life of a millionaire footballer on the dole, unlike Rozental not even having kicked a ball in serious competition. He arrived with an injury that was not properly diagnosed by the club doctor and so cost the club (and the fans) a fortune while he underwent expensive surgery. From his first blundering appearance, in the Old Firm semi-final in April 1998, and despite some erratic performances in the six seasons to come, the genial Italian giant went on to become Rangers' first Catholic captain. It was Celtic, however, who would set new standards in blind signing when John Barnes paid over £4 million for the Brazilian, Rafael Scheidt, whose brief appearances in Scotland at least offered some amusement about the unavoidable pronunciation of his family name. In addition to the Italians there was the Swede Jonas Thern, the Norwegian Stale Stensaas, and some other more minor signings, including the Australian Tony Vidmar, out of contract with NAC Breda. Their arrival was waited with cautious optimism, but the re-signing of Gascoigne was greeted with delight tempered with foreboding, while the retention of Laudrup when he seemed set to leave the club was received with unalloyed joy.

Gascoigne, even by his own standards, had had a troubled time both on and off the field in the last half of the 1996–97 season, and although Smith allowed his inner thoughts to be transformed into press headlines about the nightmares the player had caused him, he still put his paternal trust in the troubled Geordie, and Murray persuaded him to stay with the club. Brilliant displays for England brought Gazza back to the attention of English clubs, and Glenn Hoddle caused a stir when he said that Gazza needed the keener competition in England to bring out his best. But, to the surprise of some and at a substantial financial cost to the

club, Gazza chose to stay in Scotland. He was also repaying a debt, to
Walter Smith for his understanding and to the club in general for all it
did to help him overcome his demons by occupying his mind when not
playing football, engaging him in commercial deals and any other work
that kept him from wandering along the empty corridors of his mind.

One player who had openly expressed his disgust for Gascoigne's
behaviour was Brian Laudrup, and in the summer of 1997 it looked as
though he was set to leave Rangers, to join his brother Michael at Ajax,
with one year of his contract still to run. Murray seems to have been at
first prepared to cash in on his prime asset, but a stream of abusive phone
calls and faxes that blocked the daily routine of Murray International
Holdings is said to have persuaded him otherwise. Murray flew the
unsettled Dane by private jet to his holiday home in Jersey, and in
addition to outlining his plans for the future and showing him the long
list of players he intended to buy, introduced Laudrup, a wine connois-
seur, to his collection of fine wines. As the story goes, Laudrup fully
appreciated the tasting, while Murray, for whom the wine was more an
investment than a complement to fine eating, enthusiastically agreed
with Laudrup's judgements of the bottles on offer. Retaining Laudrup
might have cost Murray a few bottles from his cellar, but he was also
giving up the minimum £4 million the club would have earned from his
transfer. It would all be money well spent, however, if Rangers finally laid
to rest the ghost of European ignominy and secured the success on the
continent that had eluded them until then.

FOREIGN FIELDS

Before the start of the showdown season, the performances of the two Old
Firm teams in Europe had been embarrassingly poor. Despite a cheque
book that allowed Rangers to compete with the richest clubs in Europe,
they failed to come anywhere near the *annus mirabilis* of 1992–93. They
did not even make it to the European Champions League the following
year, being eliminated in the preliminary round by Levski-Sofia, whose
two away goals in a 3–2 defeat at Ibrox saw them through when they won
2–1 in the Bulgarian capital. Worse followed the next season when AEK
Athens knocked them out at the same stage, winning 2–0 at home and
1–0 at Ibrox. Rangers did qualify for the league section in 1995, but only
by the odd goal after 180 minutes of football against Cyprus's Anorthosis
Famagusta. In the league section they failed to win a game in six matches
against Juventus, Steaua Bucharest and Borussia Dortmund, although
they did manage three draws. Despite Laudrup, who seemed unable to
lord it over opponents in Europe as he did in Scotland, and Gascoigne,

who did not enjoy the favour of the referees on the continent as he did in Scotland, Rangers were outclassed. In their games with Juventus (minus Laudrup in both games and Gascoigne for the home game), they lost 4–1 in Italy and 4–0 at home.

It was to be the same story the following year. Rangers went through to the league section after magnificent wins both home and away to Alania Vladikavkaz of Georgia, but then the promise disappeared. Gascoigne once more let his teammates down by being sent off: in his first season he was red-carded against Borussia Dortmund, and in 1996 he was dismissed for a petulant foul on Winston Bogarde of Ajax. Beaten in their first game against Grasshopper of Switzerland, Rangers then lost to Auxerre, the team from a town in France which, with a population of 40,000, is not much bigger than Largs. Rangers' only victory came when it no longer mattered, a 2–1 win over Grasshopper at Ibrox. Rangers had an inordinate number of injured players in these games, but as suggested elsewhere, a few injuries can be bad luck, a whole coach-load smacks of more than carelessness.

Celtic were equally unable to revive their glory days of European competition. In the 1992–93 season they did well to recover from a 2–0 defeat against Cologne in Germany by winning 3–0 in Glasgow, but then went down home and away to Borussia Dortmund in the UEFA Cup. In Lou Macari's only taste of European football as a manager (1993–94), Celtic beat BSC Young Boys of Switzerland with a 1–0 aggregate, but in the next round took a one-goal home lead to Portugal, only to be eliminated on a 2–1 aggregate by Sporting Lisbon. They failed to qualify the following year, but then Burns led his team into the 1995–96 Cup-winners' Cup, losing both legs to Paris St-Germain after beating Dynamo Batumi of Georgia in the first round, 7–2 on aggregate. In Paris the score was 1–0, at Parkhead it was 3–0, the visitors leaving the field to a standing ovation. In the qualifying round for the UEFA Cup in 1996–97, Celtic survived the first round with a 1–0 aggregate against FC Kosice of Slovakia, Cadete scoring the only goal in the first leg in Glasgow in the 88th minute. Against Hamburg, though, Celtic were easily eliminated, 2–0 in both legs.

Freed from the tyranny of 'nine-in-a-row' and filled with hope by Walter Smith's summer spending, Rangers fans had every right to look forward to their club's progress in the European competition of the 1997–98 season. There was the small matter of qualifying for the league section. GI Gotu of the Faroe Islands were eliminated 11–0 on aggregate in the first qualifying round, but beating their second-round opponents proved a more difficult proposition. Rangers found themselves 3–0 down against IFK Göteborg and with a mammoth task to face in the return leg.

It turned out to be too much, and the Swedish minnows went through instead of the Glasgow giants after a 1–1 draw at Ibrox. Having been knocked out of the Champions League, Rangers were allowed into the UEFA Cup which, if it did not have the prestige of the European Cup, was still a major competition and promised a compensatory financial bonanza. They were drawn against Strasbourg, struggling at the wrong end of the French first division, but no more than against the Swedish part-timers were the millionaires of Rangers able to assert any supremacy, falling 2–1 both home and away.

It was a disaster in no way mitigated by Celtic's elimination in the same competition; worse, in fact, in that Celtic at least departed from Europe with some honour. In the early rounds, they dismissed Inter Cable-Tel of the Welsh League, 8–0 over the two legs. They came back from Austria having been beaten 2–1 by FC Tirol and, despite losing three goals in an amazing game at Celtic Park in the return leg, scored six to win 7–5 on aggregate. The reward was another Battle of Britain encounter, Celtic against Liverpool. The Merseyside club may no longer have been the great Liverpool team of the days before Souness became their manager, but they were a side bristling with individual talent nevertheless. Memories of Leeds in 1970 (or even 1992) were fresh in many minds, but it was the defeat of 1966 that was repeated, the result hanging on a brilliant Steve McManaman last-minute equaliser at Celtic Park to make the score 2–2, and a Simon Donnelly miss at Anfield that failed to break the 0–0 deadlock. Liverpool went through on the away-goals rule.

LOST ILLUSIONS

The two Old Firm teams were back to domestic competition, and the Rangers fans had to face up to the reality that the millions spent on players had been wasted: nine-in-a-row salved the souls of the narrower spirits, but the real goal was as far off as ever. Walter Smith realised this and, at the AGM on 28 October 1997, said he would resign at the end of the season. His dignified recognition of reality was not met with the same detachment among the contributors to *Follow, Follow*, who, angered by the European disasters, launched into vitriolic attacks on those running the club. The Govanhill Gub denounced, and on the face of it not without some justification, the 'shoddy work practices, poor coaching, non-existent shambolic medical care and financial incompetence on a horrendous scale'; his solution was for Murray to go, taking 'the manager, assistant manager, Mutton Chops [Donald Findlay], Mr SFA Ogilvie, Hood and the rest of the hangers-on Rangers entourage with him'.[3]

Shortly after the defeats by Strasbourg, Murray further annoyed the Rangers fans in an interview he gave to Graham Spiers in *Scotland on Sunday* of 21 September 1997, where he expressed his dislike of some of the citizens of Glasgow whom he characterised as 'very loud and vociferous' with 'an awful lot to say'; more specifically, he castigated the 'incredible arrogance about some Rangers fans', whom he chided for not even knowing how to spell some of their favourite swear words. Murray's sin was compounded by giving the interview to what *Follow, Follow* saw as the Edinburgh-based enemy of the club, especially its Rangers-hating chief sports columnist, known in some quarters for his neutrality as the 'Fenian baptist'.

As if to prove Murray's assertions about the citizens of Glasgow correct, *Follow, Follow* savaged the dictatorship of Mr Mint and made at least three references to Bill Struth 'turning in his grave' at the direction the club was taking. Not for the first time, John Greig was lambasted for his failure as public-relations officer to present the club in a better light, although this, coming from a fanzine that gives every impression of regarding PR as a dirty word, sounds particularly rich – or more appropriately in this case, rancid.

Among the Celtic faithful, there was little in the appointments of Jock Brown and Wim Jansen to get terribly excited about, but the Dutchman soon assembled a team with international talent which he moulded into a skilful unit. None of his imports could match Gascoigne or Laudrup, or the goalscoring feats of Negri, but they had impressive credentials – or, as has happened in the past with Celtic, promised to emerge from comparative mediocrity to star status: to foreigners like the Dutch star Regi Blinker, the Swedish striker Henrik Larsson, the Dane Marc Rieper, the Frenchman Stéphane Mahe and, later, the Norwegian Harald Brattbakk, Jansen added Scottish internationals Craig Burley, Paul Lambert and Darren Jackson. They joined the Dane Morten Wieghorst and the Italian Enrico Annoni who had been signed by Burns. Jansen's team, after a faltering start, put together a string of victories, but the real test was delayed until November when the Old Firm faced each other for the first time.

The first Old Firm game of the 1997–98 season was to have been played on the Monday evening of 1 September 1997. Events in Paris, namely the tragic death in a car accident of Diana, Princess of Wales, the previous day, determined that it be postponed until a future date. Games were played in England that night, but to have allowed the Old Firm game to proceed would have been to invite trouble. Among the Celtic support would have been the handful of cretins prepared to express their contempt for royalty, and enough outraged royalists among the Rangers support to see the need to exact honourable retribution.

There were no Premier League games in Scotland the following Saturday because of the Scotland–Belarus World Cup qualifier, and none in England because Princess Diana's funeral was taking place that day. Jim Farry of the SFA, showing a not unusual insensitivity to public feeling, gave every sign of going ahead with the Scotland–Belarus game, but it was left to three Rangers players in the squad, McCoist, Goram and Gordon Durie, to protest and let him know that they would not play on that day. For this they were warmly applauded, but for those who could not overlook the fact that Diana's death had been caused in part by a drunken driver, the moral stance of two of these players lost some of its impact.

As a result of this, there were two Old Firm games in November. Rangers won 1–0 at Ibrox, thanks to two crucial saves from Goram and a goal from the newly returned Richard Gough, who slotted home an inch-perfect Laudrup pass, to ensure justice for their superiority on the day. In the game at Celtic Park it was the home side who dominated, but until the 90th minute Rangers had the only goal, Negri scoring in the 71st minute. Rangers played with ten men for most of the second half after Gascoigne was finally red-carded in a domestic game. It was Stubbs who came to his side's rescue with a last-gasp header, saving Celtic not only from falling a further three points behind Rangers, but also from a psychological blow that would have been difficult to survive.

At the end of the year Celtic were in a better position than at the same time in 1996. Rangers were knocked out of the League Cup by Dundee United, who in turn lost to Celtic in the final, to give Jansen his first trophy. For a while Hearts looked as though they might have rewritten the script to upset the 'ten-in-a-row' season, but a 5–2 thrashing by Rangers at Ibrox, followed by a 1–0 defeat by Celtic the following week, seemed to betoken an end to their hopes. Celtic, however, managed to lose games while Rangers dropped points in draws, so that if Hearts had beaten Hibs at the derby game on New Year's day, instead of drawing 2–2, they would have begun 1998 at the top of the table. Celtic won the New Year derby at home 2–0 after a brilliant spell in an otherwise scrappy affair, so that the title race remained wide open. The result was almost overshadowed by the political fall-out (discussed later), Gascoigne's flute gesture to the Celtic fans and Goram's black armband, claimed by some against the protestations of Goram himself, to be worn out of respect for murdered Protestant terrorist, Billy Wright, in the Maze prison.

As Rangers and Celtic continued into 1998, fighting to gain or frustrate Ten-in-a Row, the battle did not have the same desperation as equalling the Stein record. The defeats in Europe at the start of the season had brought a sense of reality to most Rangers fans, where only a fanatical minority could convince themselves that there was something of global significance in ten successive league flags. In the Scottish situation the importance of the pursuit by Rangers of Celtic's nine successive titles was understandable, just as a tenth successive flag would have been cause for rejoicing by Rangers fans. But to claim that this has any relevance outside Scotland is ludicrous. To try and place such a domestic success on a world scale is an embarrassment rather than something to be proud of. The health of a sporting competition is not in the stranglehold of its two top teams, but in the competition as a whole, as can be seen in the contrasting examples of the English league with its multitude of contenders for top honours and the now thankfully defunct East German league and its domination by Dynamo Berlin.

As it was, Rangers' assault on the Stein record was a rather lacklustre affair, despite the outcome being in doubt until the last game of the season with Celtic's 2–0 win over St Johnstone at home. In Old Firm encounters, Rangers lost only once in their five games, but despite the conventional wisdom this was no consolation for losing the flag which would have silenced for ever the Celtic fans and their triumphal gloating over the 7–1 victory at Hampden in the Sun. Rangers lost in the final of the Scottish Cup to Hearts, finishing the season empty-handed. For the Celtic fans it was a desperate season, ending as much with relief as joy, a roller-coaster ride that had even the more balanced supporters allowing signs of paranoia to creep into their judgment of why Celtic were losing some key games. Nowhere was this brought into more vivid focus than in the anonymous and self-published *10* by 'The Andy Thom Experience', where, in the language of a terracing fanatic, the author tells 'The story of Jansen's Celtic and the exorcism of the curse of the ten'.

THE WAY TO THE FUTURE

Television technology has dominated the finances of football in the last decade and more, and for the first time the game seems to be coming second to outside interests. Since the first ball was kicked in serious competition over a hundred years ago, the media have established a symbiotic relationship with football: first the press, then the radio, which grew with the game and helped promote it without ever threatening to take it over, although this is not how the football authorities saw it in the early days. The fears with regard to television seemed more rationally based, and through to the 1980s football clubs imposed restrictions on live coverage of matches, afraid that spectators would prefer the comfort of an armchair to the real thing. In the last decade or so, television technology has leapt ahead and there is more to be gained by the richest clubs from television exposure than there is from live spectators.

In the days before TV coverage, a shirt logo or an advertisement on a perimeter fence meant little when the only people who saw them were at the ground. Now the original black-and-white television with limited viewpoints has been replaced by colour, instant-replays and multiple camera angles so that every aspect of the game can be analysed in the minutest detail; from a commercial point of view the smallest detail on a player's shirt, shorts or socks, as well his boots and the ball, can now be blown up and flashed instantaneously throughout a world united around a single television event. It is brand exposure undreamt of even a couple of decades ago, with all the riches that this conjures up.

Cable and satellite television, and the break-up of the state monopolies in favour of privatised television channels, were behind the revolution in the organisation of the European game in the late 1980s, Silvio Berlusconi in Italy leading the way by buying up television channels and AC Milan (along with a few supermarket chains and multifarious other enterprises) so that he could have it all to himself. His main aim, apart from becoming prime minister of Italy, has always been a midweek televised European League, run through his TV station. Neither Murray nor McCann were likely to buy an entire television company, but they could buy interests in one, or present their own programmes, such as the weekly shows on the satellite/cable company, Sky Scottish, during season 1997–98: *The Ibrox Club Hour* and *The Celtic Park Hour.*

With the development of digital television viewing, club owners could claim the rights to any game in which their team appeared, with the right to charge individual homes on a pay-per-view basis. Rangers and Celtic were looking for the market, ever increasing with the continuous expansion of global technology, of the fanatics outside Scotland: in the rest of the UK and Ireland, North America, South Africa, Australia and New Zealand. For the big clubs, not only was their revenue multiplied by an astronomical factor, but their beady-eyed owners could rest assured that no one was watching the team for nothing or the price of a few bevvies. No longer did David Murray need to worry in the late 1990s, as he watched his multi-million pound players perform in his multi-million pound stadium, that the general public could 'just switch on for nothing'.[4] No longer being ripped off by the non-paying public, the club would have even more cash to spend on players and luxury facilities – eventually even a decent training ground. All this before even more markets would be opened by the marvels of the World Wide Web, of 'on-line premium content' channels whereby the clubs delivered, to monthly subscribers, selected highlights of key matches, live audio and video programmes, transmitted on the club's website as well as on a pay-per-view basis. And so it goes, greed without end from one point of view, supplying a voracious appetite on the other. Club websites and fads like text messaging also helped maintain a healthy (and happy) supporter base – in the first few years of the new millennium reaching out to nearly every country in the world.

Those who claim to hold the key to reality will tell you how there is no alternative to paying ever more money to preserve the lifestyles of ever more extravagant football stars. As well as managers walking off with a fortune after being sacked for incompetence, the testimonials for millionaire players is an echo of the vacuous values of today's economic irrationalists. In the old days a testimonial was a just reward for a player who had devoted his career to a club which paid him a modest salary. Now players on thousands of pounds a week still expect the windfall of a game paid for by fans who have helped to make them millionaires, even in the case of Ally McCoist in one of his less humorous moments showing them an empty wallet as a symbol of the need to give to the deserving rich. Or Richard Gough, who admitted that if the Bosman ruling had come in earlier he might have left Ibrox for a better deal instead of staying on for the nine-in-a-row. Despite the money raining in on the rich clubs from sources other than spectators at the game, admittance charges continue to rise. The fans are told to put up with it, otherwise they cannot expect all these foreign stars to come to Glasgow to entertain them. Yet who would seriously suggest that any Rangers team since Souness has given the supporters more pleasure than Greig's European triumph in 1972 or the team he played for as a youngster in the early 1960s, or that any Celtic team since McCann has given supporters more pleasure than the Celtic teams of the Stein years. Certainly Brian Laudrup brought an unprecedented class both on and off the field to the Ibrox club, while Gascoigne for Rangers and di Canio for Celtic, whatever their inanities off the park, produced magic with the ball: but even these exceptional talents did not surpass the spectacle provided by Jim Baxter or Jimmy Johnstone at the height of their careers – and at a fraction of the cost.

The big money might have been in Europe, and until 2003 this continued to be an elusive pot of gold, but the games between the big two in Scotland and the big names in England still held the greatest interest. And among the big clubs perhaps only Manchester United and Liverpool and the major Italian clubs have such a devoted following outside their own country – even Barcelona in Spain with their massive home following do not have the Rangers and Celtic interest abroad. Games between the Old Firm and the best in England are top priorities for television viewers, and the financial backing and fanatical support of the Glasgow teams is of more importance to the commercial backers of any new league than their performances on the park. The big question when Celtic and Rangers enter Europe on a regular basis is the role they will continue to play in the domestic Scottish game. Where a Scottish league without the two would leave the rest of the country's clubs is a doleful thought. It might also answer in an even more depressing way the question about the importance of the Old Firm to the health of the Scottish game. Most likely they will continue to play in Scotland, and games with each other will continue to be first in the Old Firm fan's sporting priorities.

The peculiar ferocity of the Old Firm clashes is something that foreigners will never be able to understand, especially now that the antagonisms are based more than ever on bygone days of yore than present realities. When Rangers set out to beat the Stein record it was with a team boasting few Scots and at times a majority of Catholics, while the true-blue stalwarts were reduced to a small rump. At the start of that climactic season, while the more thoughtful fans might have mused in the spirit of the (English) bard: 'O brave new team that has such players in it!'; Hearts fans greeted their visitors from Glasgow with the jeering refrain: 'More Tims than Celtic! They've got more Tims than Celtic!' The reaction of the Rangers fans to these changes would show that it was the jersey and not the men who wore it that gives a club its identity. Catholics, mainly foreigners, would come and go at Ibrox, bemused and perplexed at some of the strange rites and forbidden rituals, but for the fans on the terracing the new mercenaries were as welcome on the green, grassy turf of Ibrox as they had been all these years ago at the side of King William on the green, grassy slopes of the Boyne.

8. Battling the Bigots

Fergus McCann, a businessman, looked on the club he had loved as a young man as a source of pride rather than a means of lining his pocket. So it was that he sought to enhance the meaning of the club in the community by launching his 'Bhoys against Bigotry' campaign at the beginning of January 1996. He was perhaps a bit put out when the idea was not taken up wholeheartedly by the Scottish public, while Rangers did not feel prompted to embark on a parallel 'Bears against Bigotry', or even a joint 'Bhoys and Bears against Bigotry' campaign. Perhaps Murray thought that through Alistair Hood and his hard-man tactics he had crushed the problem, and since the club now openly signed and played Catholics, bigotry was no longer Rangers' problem. Just as likely he had no wish to see Rangers tagging along behind an initiative begun by Celtic. For the Rangers fans the whole thing was purely cosmetic, an attempt to create a brighter commercial image – their Pride and Prejudice campaign would have to wait for a few years. They could perhaps even see in Bhoys against Bigotry a concealed barb against Rangers in the Celtic claims that their campaign reaffirmed 'Celtic's pride in its joint Scottish and Irish identity and its charitable and non-sectarian history'. Celtic may have been well aware of Rangers' history with regard to sectarianism, but they were more cloudy on their own origins.

IF YOU KNOW YOUR HISTORY

The 'Mission Statement' that launched the campaign called on history to claim that Celtic had been founded to feed the poor and help integrate young Catholics into Scottish society: specifically that a 'new football club would be a vehicle to bring the communities together . . .' In fact, Celtic were founded, as mentioned earlier and discussed in more detail below, to keep young Catholics in the faith, free from the dangers of Protestant soup kitchens and mixing with Protestants in their leisure time. The aims of Brother Walfrid and such stalwarts as John Glass were soon thwarted when John McLaughlin and the businessmen took over. They realised that a professional football club run on purely Catholic

lines was not a good commercial proposition since an all-Catholic team
might have had difficulties succeeding on the park. Hence the refusal to
limit the club to playing only three Protestants, as was proposed in 1895.
But while McLaughlin and company set out to provide the sound
commercial basis necessary for the success of any professional football
club, the entire ethos of the club remained steeped in its Irish and
Catholic origins, attracting the best Catholic players in Scotland and
Ireland, and retaining its identity with the Catholic Church through its
exclusively Catholic directors until the brief reign of David Dallas Smith
in the 1990s.

By the time the businessmen had taken over at Celtic Park, Walfrid
had left Glasgow, and although he might have had some concerns about
the departures from the club's charitable foundations, he need not have
worried about it being a continuing source of inspiration for young
Catholics. Keeping young men in the faith had always been one of his
principal concerns, and before he conceived the idea of Celtic he had
organised a 'literary society' and other football clubs for boys who had
just left school and who were at the most dangerous time, as he saw it, of
falling into apostasy. This was brought out in a 'Sketch of Brother
Walfrid' presented in the *Glasgow Observer* of 24 November 1900 in the
form of a conversation between two characters speaking in thick Irish
accents. One of them comments on how Walfrid did not want to see
young lads who had just left school:

> . . . stragglin' away an' forgettin' their religious juties; because, as
> he said, 'twas the most dangerous time for the young fellos, jest
> afther they had left school, and begun t'mix up wid Prodestand
> boys in the places where they wor workin'. [And later in the
> conversation, how he was spurred into action in regard to the
> cheap dinners because] . . . there was a hole lot av soup kitchens
> got up thro' the town by the Prodestands, because av the grate
> amount av sufferin' there was in the town; an' 'twas afeerd Bro
> Walfrid was that some av his little wans wud be snared away, an'
> get a 'thract for kitchen wid every plate av soup, the same as they
> used to do in Ireland long ago'.[1]

Had Brother Walfrid seriously tried to *integrate* Catholics into Scottish
society, he would soon have been sent on his way, and the Archbishop's
appeal for subscriptions of January 1888 is concerned only about
'Catholics', with no thoughts of mixing with Protestants: it specifically
refers to the membership of 'several of the leading Catholic footballers of
the West of Scotland', of a team that would 'do credit to the Catholics of

the West of Scotland as the Hibernians have been doing in the East', and that the recreation ground set up would be for 'our Catholic young men . . . to enjoy . . . various sports'. That a Catholic football club was set up for the benefit of Catholics will come as no surprise to those familiar with the history of the early years of football. Church groups were at the forefront in founding football teams in the early years of the game, and several of those in the top ranks of English football today were founded in this way: in the days of Muscular Christianity there was nothing unusual in Catholics adopting the methods of other branches of Christianity to take advantage of the passions of the young. Nor will Catholic fears of apostasy surprise those familiar with the history of the Church, which, through to the reforms of Vatican II, rigorously condemned under pain of condign retribution any compromise with the Truth and insisted that education and marriage had to be within the One True Catholic and Apostolic Church.

This historical detail, even for a club proud 'to know its history', should not detract from what McCann and Celtic set out to do: on the contrary, the club should recognise the way in which it has changed over the years and is now to the forefront in combating bigotry in Scottish society. Certainly, some aspects of the campaign left it open to the barbs of the sceptics: proclaiming that you are in favour of the 'Universal Declaration of Human Rights' is a bit like saying you should love your mother; charity envelopes at Celtic Park for fans already making sacrifices to help pay the wages of the wealthy wearing the hoops has aspects of the widow's mite; and there is something distinctly demeaning in the spectacle of Celtic manager Tommy Burns going out to feed the hungry – a sorry reflection of contemporary society, although it is hardly Celtic's fault if Scotland seems to be heading back to the indignities of the 1890s when all the poor had to rely on was charity. It was good that Celtic players went out to many of Glasgow's schools with their message, but nowhere was it suggested that the very separation of these schools into Catholic and Protestant, so that the one would not become contaminated with the ideas of the other, is in itself a potential source of bigotry, especially through the misunderstanding it could give rise to.

All that aside, there was more to be praised than criticised in the campaign, and this was recognised when the club was awarded the European Commission Scottish Equality Award one year after its launch. In May 1997 both Murray and McCann were offered an anti-bigotry award by the Glasgow City Council. Murray refused on the grounds that he was interested only in sport, although he may well have come to the sensible conclusion that in 1997 employing Catholics to play for his football team was hardly something to warrant a medal. Michael Kelly, quoting Aristotle and aware of a long history of Celtic and Rangers being treated equally even when Rangers had a manifestly bigoted policy, referred to the injustice of treating unequals equally, for even in the post-Souness era, he claimed, Rangers still flaunted the blue and orange, had a director who 'incorporated an Orange Walk around his house as part of the New Year celebrations' and still did not have a Catholic on the board.[2] He also had a few shots at the Celtic supporters, but congratulated McCann as being a worthy recipient of the award.

BHOYS WITHOUT BEARS AGAINST BIGOTRY

McCann had every reason to be proud of what the club had done since issuing the 'Mission Statement'. It offered tickets and hospitality at Celtic Park to vendors of the *Big Issue*, the journal of the city's homeless, and the Celtic Charity Fund set aside £47,000 for donations to local projects to help different groups in the community. It also recruited ex-addicts to warn young people about the dangers of hard drugs. In addition the club continued to support the Northern Ireland Children's Holiday scheme aimed at bringing Catholic and Protestant children together. All very much to be applauded. Celtic cannot solve the problems of feeding the hungry, housing the homeless or healing the sick: only the government, through professionals paid by a taxation system where the rich pay a fair share, can properly deal with this. But they can help ease the pain. Moreover, there are areas that the state cannot reach, and this is where football clubs like Celtic, with their hold over so many of Scotland's young folk, are in a unique position to influence their lives for the better. Celtic have openly recognised this by working with others in the community and through the education authorities, offering alternative leisure pursuits to vandalism and gang violence, helping to give some meaning to otherwise empty lives that lead to drugs and despair – that is to say, meaningless despair as opposed to the despair of following a football team that never quite makes it.

At the time of the Dunblane school tragedy of March 1996, Celtic players and the club did what they could to bring some joy into shattered lives. So too did Rangers, although at the request of the folks of Dunblane this was not given prominent coverage in the media, highlighting perhaps a difference in approach of the two clubs. Defenders of Rangers' refusal to act along with McCann will claim that the Ibrox club do their good work by stealth, eschewing the blowing of trumpets, and certainly under Murray Rangers have contributed to the local community in a way that was unknown before he arrived. Above all, the club sends out coaching staff to more than 40 primary schools in the

Govan area, as part of their Community Coaching Programme, reaching out to more than two thousand boys and girls, regardless of their religious denomination.

There are areas where the good works of the two clubs should be trumpeted, however, so that the message can get through to those who need to hear it: above all it is incumbent on Rangers and Celtic to act together in areas involving the bigotry with which for a host of historical reasons they have become associated. If Rangers and Celtic sent joint delegations to Northern Ireland or other areas where sectarianism is rife, they would show in no uncertain terms that the two clubs have no truck with that aspect of their past. McCann and Murray had shown that they could work together in their own commercial interests; it would have been an immense step forward if Murray had joined McCann in showing their followers that whatever their differences on the field of play, they could work together on that part of the Celtic Social Charter committed to 'projects that develop and promote religious and ethnic harmony'.

It seems, however, that Murray was never comfortable with what he saw as moral posturing by McCann, and this came into the open in January 1998 when he criticised McCann in the *Rangers News* over a letter he had written to the SFA complaining about what was claimed to be a sectarian gesture by Paul Gascoigne at the Old Firm game of 2 January 1998. The letter was also said to contain other examples of a sectarian nature involving Rangers, and this, coming on top of various other incidents that had got under Murray's skin, nettled him into making an unprecedented attack on McCann in which he accused the Celtic chairman of meddling in what should have been a private matter, adding that he wondered 'why Fergus does certain things. Sometimes it's as though there is another agenda'. In the press, some saw McCann's action as being more provocative than Gascoigne's, and there were references to him being a clype, a tell-tale, a dobber, or whatever phrase one chooses to describe the sneak who tries to get his classmates in trouble.

McCann himself was acting in regard to an incident that took place at Celtic Park and the letter was sent at the request of the SFA. Moreover, Rangers had appeared to be brushing the matter under the carpet, using their time-honoured excuse of dealing with their own problems in their own way. Whatever the outcome, and there has been much worse pro-vocation in the past, all that had changed was a rise in the temperature of the moral heat: it was apparent that the commercial closeness of the Old Firm bosses is not reciprocated at the moral level.

Undeterred by the cynics and the absence of reciprocal gestures from Ibrox, McCann went his own way in the battle against bigotry. At Celtic

Park he has pursued with unremitting zeal his campaign to make the new Paradise a bigot-free zone. Inside the stadium the club made regular attacks on those supporters who insisted on singing IRA songs, and asked that the decent supporters drown them out with non-political songs. The Irish tricolour flying above the stadium is no longer the source of irritation it once was, and there is little the club can do about away supporters who add IRA messages to the tricolour banners they wave in support of Celtic. The most notorious incident of this nature came in Germany where Celtic supporters at the away leg of the UEFA Cup in Hamburg, on 24 September 1996, added 'Provos on Tour' to the Irish flag they waved in support of the club. It is also to be applauded in this multicultural age that the club takes pride in its Irish and Catholic origins. To give its endorsement to 'The Fields of Athenry', however, is surely misguided. No song about the Hungry '40s in Ireland, the darkest decade in Anglo-Irish relations, can avoid political overtones. This was a time when millions were forced to leave Ireland or starve to death because of a famine which, if it was not actually caused by the British government, was due in part to its policies and was embittered by the contempt with which the native Irish were treated. The effects of the potato blight were disastrous, but it was all exacerbated by a government committed to economic policies that, over a century later, would be called 'Thatcherism'. Charles Edward Trevelyan, the supervisor in charge of famine relief, was prepared to bring in the corn referred to in the song (unfortunately it was an iron-hard Indian maize which the Irish could not convert into flour) to distribute among those who could prove that they were deserving and so long as this did not interfere with the profits of the merchants. He religiously refused to interfere with the workings of the market, so that in the midst of the starvation caused by the potato blight, boats loaded with other foodstuffs sailed to markets abroad.

When Dublin man Pete St John wrote the song in 1979 he might have seen it as a simple love song, but whatever his intentions the dirge is about an Irish patriot, a hero languishing, as the opening lines of the song tell us, by 'a lonely prison wall', 'cut down' in his prime because he rebelled against 'the famine and the crown' by stealing corn to feed his wife and child. Now she is left to care for the two of them alone, while he waits for a prison ship to take him to Botany Bay, final destination of a host of political prisoners before him. The pro-IRA fanzine *Tiocfaidh Ar La* was 'heartened' by the 'famine ballad', provided its readers with chorus and all the verses, while 'Mick Derrig' discoursed effusively on how British atrocities of the 1840s were comparable to the Holocaust of the Second World War.[3] The British had 'starved Ireland for profit' and now the IRA was fighting back with 'mortars raining in . . . on their nice buildings in London and their poor soldiers'. And also, presumably, bombing pubs in Guildford, discos in Birmingham and other places of innocent assembly. If it was the club's Irish connections Celtic wanted to celebrate – and there is nothing wrong with that – then there are many themes of a less political nature that could have been chosen, as Glen Daly showed when he brought out 'The Celtic Song' in 1961.[4]

Before McCann the club's associations with Irish republicanism were an occasional source of embarrassment, one of which was when the editor of the *Celtic View* was trapped into admitting support for the IRA. This was in August 1989 when Kevin McKenna allegedly told Mark Dingwall, at a freebie dinner to discuss the Old Firm, of his sympathies for IRA terrorism, including the recent killing of 11 innocents at Enniskillen.[5] Some people found Dingwall's use of a secret tape recorder at an off-the-record social evening reprehensible, although this was how Matt McGlone helped bring down the old board at Parkhead when he taped an attempt by Michael Kelly to get him to write a spoof against the press for *Celtic View*. Others criticised Dingwall for taking advantage of McKenna being the worse for drink: the more cynical were reminded of the well-known Glasgow expression about the effect on the tongue when you have had a few bevvies too many: *in vino veritas*. McKenna was sacked when his indiscretions were revealed to the tabloids, although this has not affected his subsequent rise, despite what many Celtic supporters claim is an anti-Catholic media, to become deputy editor of one of Scotland's best newspapers.

The club is always at pains to distinguish what it would see as the culture of Ireland and the politics of terrorism. From this point of view it is happy enough to be seen, as one prominent Catholic in Ireland put it, as 'almost a proxy for Irish football in the European Cup'.[6] The Rangers fanzines might see something sinister in this, as *Follow, Follow* is free in its accusations of Celtic being 'the athletic wing of the IRA' and that its supporters are 'Provo-loving Republican scum'. It is unlikely that the Celtic board, old or new, would take anything the fanzines say seriously, but every now and then it gives them something to feed from.

The old board committed a *faux pas* in late 1990 when it allowed the stadium to be given over to the Irish political folk band, the Wolfe Tones, to make a video advertising their concert and they took the opportunity to express a few sentiments in praise of the IRA. The original Wolfe Tone, of course, was a Protestant and one of the first to take up arms in favour of a united and independent Ireland, but he was defeated ultimately because of the lukewarm nature of the support from the Catholic Church. The group assured the club that they were not sectarian, and in choosing the name of the Protestant hero they could be said to be emphasising this, but in the present climate any support for a united Ireland, to which the Wolfe Tones are committed, has political overtones that can be construed as showing a sympathy for the IRA. A few months later the Pogues, whose song on behalf of the wrongfully jailed Birmingham Six was banned by the British government, were guests of the club. Again anyone with a sense of justice would be outraged by the way the Birmingham Six were framed and fitted up, but the interpretation in terms of more general Irish oppression is open to debate. Since McCann, the club has been more wary of being caught by such groups, and in a 'voice against bigotry' policy, has banned any advertising in the official *Celtic View* that could be construed as sectarian.

BEARS ON SONG

At Ibrox Rangers continued to play over the tannoy a sanitised version of 'Hello! Hello! We are the Billy Boys!' substituting references to the gang of the inter-war period with 'Rangers Boys' and removing references to being up to one's knees in Fenian blood. The fans continued to sing along in the original – or at least the Rangers original, as the tune goes back to the American Civil War and the soldiers' song 'Marching through Georgia'. There have been calls for the club to be more positive in putting out acceptable lyrics for the fans to sing, but as one Celtic fan delicately put it with regard to McCann trying to eliminate IRA chants, this is 'pissing in the wind'. Football is not a game for the faint-hearted, although at Ibrox the clamp-down seems to have been so successful that some games take place as though you were in a morgue, with the greatest activity among the spectators coming from the constant coming and going of fans taking off to buy bluenose burgers or whatever else is on sale below the stands.

To attract sponsors and enter international competition both Rangers and Celtic have had to project an appropriate image. A sectarian Rangers could never have entered the world of multinational business, and since the signing of Mo Johnston they have gone a long way to eliminating the last traces of their anti-Catholic past. But while the excesses of the fans have been crushed or driven out of the stadium, others closely associated with the club have caused it some embarrassment with their over-enthusiastic singing of sectarian songs, allowing the club's detractors to claim that below the surface nothing has changed at Ibrox. Souness saw the Mo Johnston signing as one of his greatest triumphs, but he was well aware that a simple signature would not eliminate the remnants of bigotry at the club. This was one of the reasons he left Rangers in 1991.

In an article on Souness that appeared in *The Independent* of 14 October 1996, Ian Stafford reported Souness's complaints about the obstacles that had been placed in his path at Ibrox. When pushed by Stafford to explain, he said: 'Well, I'll never be comfortable with bigotry, and it will always be at Rangers.' Just over a year later, Stafford interviewed Souness again, this time for *The Scotsman* (1 December 1997), when Souness was manager of Benfica. Whether Stafford got his notes mixed up, or Souness remembered exactly what he had said the previous year, his opinions about his hassles at Rangers were repeated almost word for word, with the difference that the reference to bigotry always being at Ibrox was omitted.

It is clear, too, that Souness was not referring to the bigotry of the fans. There was a time when they were the only ones blamed for the bigotry, and even James Handley, in his otherwise engaging history of Celtic published in 1960, was guilty of talking tripe on the matter: and snobbish tripe at that. In his short discussion of the trouble between the two clubs he claimed that:

> until a Catholic centre-forward in a Rangers blue jersey scores a goal against a Celtic team the tension will persist. If that should ever come to pass then the rabble would be bewildered and all its fire extinguished. The notion that the mob can be ultimately educated to see the folly of its way is a hollow one, for the creatures who compose it are ineducable.[7]

A Catholic player has now scored that historic goal, the 'mob' and the 'rabble' have shown themselves to be more educable than Handley gave them credit for, but the tensions persist. Clearly today as in the past the problem is not just on the terracing.

When Gascoigne performed his famous flute impersonation to celebrate his first goal for the club in July 1995, it was obvious that someone among the players had put him up to it. In 1994 a player was reported to have been seen celebrating the championship of that year wearing a 'Hang IRA Murderers' T-shirt. For new arrivals at the club there has always been someone to teach them about the club's traditions, usually a player who was a supporter in his youth and whose commitment to the club was due to its Protestantism. Among the newcomers who have taken it all very seriously is Andy Goram. Goram was born in England, but part of his bonding with the Rangers supporters has been by letting them know that he is a proud Protestant. In his autobiography, *My Life*, and in other ways, he has made no secret of his sympathies for the Protestant cause in Ulster. Soon after arriving at Ibrox he was keen to learn about the history of the club and what it stood for, and he made more trips to Belfast than any other player. In 1995 he and McCoist went to the Shankill Road in Belfast to switch on the Christmas lights and mix with the community; as he told Roddy Forsyth, 'I suppose it's my way of giving them something back.'[8]

For such reasons it is not surprising that when Goram wore a black armband at the Old Firm game of 2 January 1998, five days after the murder in the Maze prison, near Belfast, of Loyalist terrorist Billy Wright, few people believed his claim that he wore it out of respect for an aunt who had died back in October, an aunt for whom Goram's mother did not remember her son having any overwhelming affection. A sort of delayed shock it would appear, or perhaps Goram, with all his other off-field problems, hadn't been able to find a suitable armband until then. Blarney about this being the first appropriate time to display his familial affection fooled no one, although Rangers chose to believe him. Goram has been arguably the best goalkeeper Rangers (or Scotland) have ever had, and no doubt it was this rather than his role as a paragon of Protestant virtue that saved him from punishment for an action that would have provoked a storm if a Celtic player had dared wear a black armband out of respect for a murdered IRA terrorist.

Goram's black armband display was overshadowed by the controversy that surrounded Gascoigne's flute performance as he warmed up before taking the field at the same game, a fleeting gesture which would have been missed by all but a few but for it being caught on television. It was just one more incident in a litany of musical performances that accompanied the club on its trips around the football grounds of Scotland, as the walls of wherever Rangers players were celebrating reverberated with the songs and chants of the terracing.

When Rangers beat Dundee United at Tannadice on 21 April 1990 to win the Championship, television cameras allowed into the dressing-rooms recorded the vociferous renditions of what were called 'sectarian songs' with 'obscene references to the Pope'.[9] Homes throughout Scotland were thus, according to their persuasions, able to join in with the players, or ring up in protest. We can never know how many sang along, but the BBC is said to have been inundated with calls of protest.

What the cameras were doing in the dressing-room is a question some might want to ask, and others could plead that adults have the right to do what they like in the privacy of their own dressing-room, but at Celtic Park on 24 November 1996, following a Coca-Cola Cup final victory over Hearts, the full-volume renditions of 'The Sash' were so enthusiastic that the police had to be called in to ask that the volume be turned down – apart from annoying any Celtic people in the vicinity, the celebrations threatened to drown out the post-match player interviews. Some of the Rangers top brass were reported to be with the players, but their role in the choir was not specified. One thing that seemed to be quite clear was that being at Celtic Park added a special lustiness to the rendition of the choruses. It was also said that a framed portrait of the Queen was hung up in the dressing-room, although this was apparently a not uncommon practice at away games.[10]

One Rangers player even got into trouble when he was caught in happy harmony with some friends on a day when he was injured and had come along as a spectator. It was the all-seeing eye of the TV cameras at the New Year game of 1996 at Celtic Park that caught the unsuspecting Stuart McCall in this compromising situation, upsetting the Celtic supporters who were near him, and leading to calls for his removal. The police TV monitors picked him out singing some Ibrox favourites with those around him, but the police did not take action at the time, as they did not want to provoke any trouble. The incident was reported to Rangers after the game and McCall was asked to make sure that on any similar occasions in the future he follow the more accepted practice of sitting closer to the directors' box.

Some of the foreign players found it all a bit hard to take in. Most bemused of all was Basile Boli, who arrived from Marseille in the summer of 1994 without a firm grasp of English. He had been born in the Ivory Coast, but came to France aged 13, where his father had been a bodyguard for General de Gaulle. He was also a Catholic and as such used to the adoration of female images, but he could not understand why there were pictures of the Queen all over Ibrox; coming after Souness, however, he was spared the former manager's exhortations to the players in his pre-match build-up to 'think of the Queen'.[11] His nickname, King Boli, the humour of which can be enjoyed only with an appreciation of the Glasgow pronunciation of the French, showed that he was welcomed by the fans, some of whom changed the intonation of their favourite song to 'Hello! Hello! We are the Boli Boys!' The Rangers players did their best to make the newcomer feel at home, Laudrup and Gough in particular going out of their way to welcome him, but their efforts were rebuffed. On the field where it counts, however, Boli was played out of position and had trouble adjusting to the more frivolous approach to the game in Scotland. Reports in French newspapers of him criticising not only the omnipresent images of Her Majesty around Ibrox, but also the Rangers manager himself, led to him being censured. This was a standard response, and not only at Ibrox, to criticism, but Boli was taking things a bit too far when, having expressed his lack of approval for two Ibrox favourites, he went on to declare his admiration for the Pope. Despite this, he left with the best wishes of the fans and suffered neither for his religion nor his colour while he was with Rangers.

Boli had also been annoyed at being told not to cross himself in front of the Ibrox faithful, and this was a warning given to all subsequent Catholic imports. Jörg Albertz, who came to Rangers from Hamburger SV in the summer of 1996, was well aware of this and had no troubles settling in. He claimed in the *Frankfurter Rundschau* that the Glasgow supporters were more disciplined than those in Germany and fought each other only with battle hymns.[12] The young Chilean star, Sebastian Rozental, followed Albertz at the beginning of 1997. His Jewish name would never have been a problem at Ibrox, but there was a time when the very name of his club, Universidad Catolica (Catholic University), would have kept any Rangers scout at a distance. Although Jewish, he had adopted his club-mates' practice of crossing himself before the start of the game; but, like Albertz, he was told to touch his religious parts in private.

Making the sign of the cross, in Scotland at any rate, is not always an innocent gesture: in some situations it can have the same effect as a two-fingered salute or spitting, and it was closer to this spirit that Mo Johnston made his famous departure from Hampden in the Skol Cup final of 1986. Such was clearly not the situation when Partick Thistle's coloured Catholic player from Liverpool, Rod McDonald, was given a yellow card for crossing himself as he left the field in a game against Rangers at Firhill on 3 February 1996. McDonald was reported to the police by two Rangers fans in the main stand, sensitive souls like their equivalents at Celtic Park a year later who reported Gascoigne, claiming to have been offended when he made strange gestures that they interpreted as religious, but which in fact were imaginary pistol shots being fired into the air to celebrate his equaliser. He then did, as was his custom, cross himself as he left the field, and this was reported to the referee by a linesman. The caution was given in the dressing-room during the half-time interval and, unaware that he had been booked, the unfortunate McDonald was astonished when he was ordered off for a tackle on John Brown that earned a second yellow card.

The referee in that particular game, Jim McGilvray, provoked the anger of all neutral observers, above all for his lenient treatment of Gascoigne who was cautioned in the first half for running beyond the advertising boards to celebrate his goal, but went on to commit more serious offences in the second-half that went unpunished. McGilvray did not help his credibility when he retired as a referee soon after, claiming that he felt like a robot obeying SFA instructions for the Gascoigne booking, and unburdening himself to *The Sun* in the 'sports exclusive of the decade'.[13] McGilvray admitted that Gascoigne should have been given a second yellow card, but he did not do so for fear of provoking the Rangers fans into a riot.

For Walter Smith of Rangers it was part of a witch-hunt against their star player. For Celtic supporters it was just one more proof of the way in which referees helped Rangers on their way to nine-in-a-row. For agnostics it was another example of the religious nonsense that made Scotland a laughing stock beyond its borders.

One of the most insidious examples of Rangers pandering to the prejudices of the Prods was largely passed over by the press. This was at the finals of the Scottish Schools Cup played at Ibrox on 28 April 1996, a seven-a-side competition in front of 50,000 people at half-time in the crunch Rangers–Aberdeen League decider where Gascoigne scored a hat-trick. The winning team was Christ the King Primary School from Holytown, but they did not play under their own name, being called 'the red team' instead; even references to where they came from were fudged, with Motherwell being preferred to Holytown. The decision to label the teams by colour rather than by their real names was taken when the finalists became known: in addition to the winning team, the losing semi-finalists were St Bridget's of Baillieston and St Flannan's of Kirkin-tilloch. In explanation, it was pointed out that the organisers wanted the boys to enjoy themselves without a section of the crowd turning against them.[14]

There can be few more damaging judgments by a football team of its supporters than this. It is a judgment that continued on a match-to-match basis while the ban on players blessing themselves on the field was upheld, a ban that would stay in place for nearly a decade after the Mo Johnston signing. In the meantime, Catholic players just had to put up with it: Jörg Albertz, despite fitting the image of a Nordic god, was not allowed to express himself in his own religious way. Marco Negri, closer to the Rangers image of a Latin, and so Catholic, but forbidden from crossing himself on scoring goals, opted for a surly lack of enthusiasm – annoying some fans who sarcastically called him 'Smiler'. If Rangers banned their players from crossing themselves, they could also have banned them from miming a flute performance to incite the opposition, as Gascoigne did while warming up in the New Year Old Firm game of 1998; unlike his debut before an all-Bear audience at his first rendition, this reprise was in front of nearly 50,000 baying bhoys. Rangers claimed this was a private matter, and smacked his wrist with a belated fine of a week's wages and a dictated apology. Nor did they take any public action against Goram's black armband display at the same game, although in both these cases such actions could be seen as provocation that flew in the face of any battle against bigotry.

Opinions vary on these issues, as they always have, the one saying it is all trivia and should not upset rational human beings, the others claiming that it is an incitement to riot. And both are right. It is a trivial matter and in a sane world this is how mimicking a flute would be seen, especially when the player concerned is responding to taunts, however accurate, of him being a wife-beater. But even in 1998, sanity was still not the norm at Old Firm games. Unlike Gazza's flute-playing impersonation, which had a comic touch, wearing a black armband allegedly out of respect for a convicted terrorist is sinister. There is nothing Rangers can do to prevent a player making an ill-advised gesture, but they have complete control over what their players wear on the field of play. And there can be no two opinions on the right of schoolboys playing at half-time in the big games to do so under the name of their school and not a colour, even if this means references to Lourdes, the Blessed Virgin, the Bleeding Heart or other images that are seen as offensive by some Rangers supporters. In the litany of Rangers' sectarian hangovers, this was surely the most reprehensible.

MASONS IN BLACK

Celtic supporters have been obsessed throughout their history by the idea that the SFA and its referees are biased against them. Many have had the famous Quinn/Craig case from early in the century passed down to them from father to son as an example of the suffering the Sons of Erin have had to bear from the Sons of William. As shown in *The Old Firm*, however, the Quinn/Craig incident is one that has become seriously confused in the minds of those who pass it on, and indeed it reflects very poorly on Celtic. In the wider world, Catholics in Scotland have claimed to suffer from the machinations of the Freemasons, and barely an issue of the Catholic press in the days before the Second World War would appear without further examples of their sinister influence. The two have been easily conflated and in the desperation of the defence of the Stein record in particular some Celtic supporters have blamed what they see as their unjust treatment at the hands of referees on a masonic plot.

Some Celtic fans were said to have set a private detective at work to compile a dossier on a particular referee, Jim McCluskey, after the Skol Cup final of 1990, while another has engaged in historical research to prove that there is a conspiracy against Celtic. According to Father Peter Burns, a Jesuit based in Los Angeles in the US, his study of Old Firm games as reported in the *Glasgow Herald* between 1945 and 1996 'clearly' reveals that over the 51 years covered by his investigation Celtic have been denied as many clear penalties as Rangers have been given dodgy ones.[15] Such 'research' obviously raises more questions than it answers, and it is interesting that in the newspaper chosen for the 'study' one of the main sports writers was Cyril Horne, who conducted a virtual one-man campaign against Rangers throughout the 1950s. Horne was a brave reporter, and his employers even had to assign a minder to protect him on his way home from the newspaper office, but any attempt to judge the worth of penalty claims would have to be based on a variety of sources and not just those sympathetic to Celtic, as Burns has admitted.

Celtic even found support for their suspicions in an article published in the Catholic journal, *Flourish*,[16] where the eminent professor of English at Glasgow University, Patrick Reilly, showing that the spirit of Man in the Know was still alive and well in certain Catholic circles, claimed that religious bigotry was behind the series of decisions that went against Celtic, and anyone who thought otherwise was as blind or blinkered as the Holocaust deniers or believers in a flat earth. His article was framed by one on the great truth of the risen Jesus and another on the duties of Catholics as Lent approached, including the fight against 'the astronomical abortion toll'. Never before can a disquisition on disputed goals at a football match have found itself in such exalted company.

More credible evidence of Celtic being on the wrong end of a series of bad decisions came from an article in the Aberdeen *Evening Express* on 26 November 1996, shortly before a visit of Rangers to Pittodrie. Much of it was based on the hearsay of an anonymous referee and one former player, who claimed to have been hounded out of the Scottish game by referees who kept sending him off, something that would not have happened, the ex-Don said, if he had been a Rangers player. But the article also revealed statistics that suggested 'a pro-Ibrox bias among our top referees – and a strong link with the Masons'. The links with the Masons are tenuous to say the least: it is highly likely that many Scottish referees are Masons, but this is irrelevant to their conduct of the game, and even if they have Rangers sympathies this is no proof that they will give them favours. A tally of red and yellow cards distributed to clubs in the Premier Division makes much more interesting reading. According to this, Rangers was the only club where no player had been ordered off in the current or previous season, and more telling, that in this same time they had received 90 yellow cards. This could show that Rangers players had the sense to behave themselves once they had been warned, but that begs the question of why they could not exhibit the same discipline in European games: there Rangers players had accumulated four red cards in less than a dozen games. As for the Masons in black, and given the number of red cards to Rangers in the Souness years, one has to ask whether there has been a sudden influx of Masons among the whistlers in the post-Souness years.

Football would cease to be a game if all elements of luck and refereeing error were eliminated. This is what keeps discussion alive in the space between games, and is the last resort of the disappointed fan who bewails in time-honoured fashion: 'We wuz robbed!' In the New Year game at Ibrox on 2 January 1997 Celtic were deprived of a goal by Jorge Cadete that would have made the score 2–2. In the entire stadium and the viewing audience at home or in pubs around the world, it appears that only the linesman saw an infringement by Cadete, who did not himself protest in case he earned another expulsion.[17]

Reports soon followed claiming that this particular linesman was a well-known Rangers supporter and, inevitably, a Freemason. It would seriously deplete the pool if referees who were Freemasons were banned from officiating at Rangers games, but perhaps in this particular case the SFA could have exercised more caution: an individual who flaunts his sympathies, as this one is said to have done, is different from one who keeps them to himself. The furore that erupted was not helped by the policy of silence that prevents referees from explaining their decisions after the game. Or even during it, as is the case in American football, and indeed as is done by the best referees, by clear hand signals, in British football.

There does seem to be one factor that has influenced these events, however: Paul Gascoigne. Despite Gascoigne's claim that he was picked on by referees in Scotland so that they could boast to their pals about booking him, it would appear that he received preferential treatment from Scottish referees. Given the number of games he won for Rangers almost single-handedly, this could have had a substantial effect on the outcome of key matches. But rather than any sinister influence, it is more likely that he was treated in much the same way as John McEnroe whom umpires were never willing to throw out of the many tennis tournaments where he metaphorically spat in their faces. (Given the money he brought to the game it is the umpire who would have suffered for taking such action.) However that may be, and whatever concessions to genius were made by some referees, however unconsciously, Gascoigne's misdemeanours on the park frequently escaped the severity they deserved.

There have doubtless been several occasions, in their fraught years in particular, where Celtic fans had reason to cry out in despair at the bad luck – and perhaps worse – that went against them, but when bad luck seems to keep on cropping up it ceases to be an excuse. Rangers supporters could give a list of the decisions that helped Celtic on their way to nine-in-a-row in the 1970s – and like Celtic supporters they would on many occasions have been justified. But, unlike Celtic fans, Rangers fans don't have the Masons to blame it on.

SECTARIANISM IN RETREAT

There is little the 'Bhoys against Bigotry' campaign can do to calm the darkest thoughts of those who would believe in a satanic plot against the club, and Murray at Ibrox did as much as he could to erase the club's anti-Catholic image. In addition to Boli and Albertz mentioned above, as well as many other Catholics since, Rangers tried to sign the Italian Gianluca Vialli, the Argentine Gabriel Batistuta, the Portuguese Fernando Couto and the Brazilian Jardel . . . through to Ronaldo and the arrival of a small invasion of Italians who were probably Catholics. For Murray the question of signing Catholics was no longer an issue. In that Rangers is a business committed to maximising its commercial potential by winning football matches, Murray did not need to go any further than this, but for those with a broader view of the club's responsibilities this was not good enough. Above all, Gerry McNee conducted a long campaign against both Old Firm chairmen, ultimately provoking the normally unflappable Murray into a stinging personal attack on the credentials of 'The Voice of Football' and his motives in criticising Rangers, and to a slightly lesser degree Celtic. This was in January 1998 when McNee wrote in the *News of the World* that Rangers were 'rotten to their sectarian core'. Over a year before, McNee had claimed that 'sectarianism is getting worse not better and both clubs are still guilty of encouraging it'.[18] McNee accused Rangers of not signing a local Catholic, but whether or not this was Rangers' fault is another matter, as any young Catholic star was still likely to prefer Celtic, and despite the changes at Ibrox since Souness, there was still an atmosphere there that could make some Catholics feel uncomfortable: especially if they understood the language or could make sense of the accents enough to know what the songs and chants around the ground and in the dressing-room were all about. Paul McStay and Paul Elliott were mentioned as Rangers transfer targets in the summer of 1992,[19] and a year later John Collins claimed that Murray tried to sign him, saying that he 'would have paid me almost anything to sign for Rangers'. This forced Celtic to 'up their own offer for him'.[20] Michael Kelly's criticism of Rangers for not having a Catholic on their board is perhaps misplaced, but the situation has improved from the time when a director (David Hope) was blocked from becoming chairman because he had married a Catholic 30 years before. As much a matter for criticism has been the absence of Protestants on the Celtic board, given the much larger percentage of Protestants in Scotland. Both clubs have their Protestant and Catholic diehards, but this is more a hangover from the past than a matter of policy.

The sectarian situation has been around in Scotland for so long that it is easy to attach the label to any mindless incident. When Duncan Ferguson committed his act of thuggery against John McStay of Raith Rovers, one of the subsequent headlines and stories of the player's life concerned the tears of his girlfriend who knew that he was no longer the 'boy she'd fallen for' when 'Duncan stood on a table and sang "The Sash" '.[21] Rangers seem to have had more success in crushing the overt expression of sectarian outbursts among their fans than they have in curbing the excesses of some of their players. And as a club that has long claimed to be proud of the image it presents to the public, it has on many occasions been let down by the behaviour of its players, off the field as much as on it – with a sterling performance by the vice-chairman still to come.

The most spectacular 'sectarian' incident came at the summer international tournament at Ibrox in July 1995 when Paul Gascoigne made his first appearance for the club. The new player, who had to be reminded that he had signed for Rangers and not Glasgow, showed that he was a quick learner in other ways. When he scored his first goal he demonstrated his delight with a flute-playing mime that was splashed in colour on the pages of the tabloids and beyond. The game was a friendly against Steaua Bucharest, and as such before an audience of Bears who loved the performance. The match was not televised, but the BBC bought the videotape and when they showed the flute incident they were banned by the club. Gazza was treated more lightly, as he would be in the future, although in this instance he was merely engaging in a bit of in-house fun.

Marx said that history repeats itself: the first time as tragedy; the second time as farce. But in Scottish football history farce seems to follow farce. At Ibrox some of the English imports in particular seem to have been intent on giving some historical continuity to the matches where they had distinguished themselves. First there was Gazza following in the footsteps of Graham Roberts, then there were 'The Ibrox Four' of November 1995 following 'The Ibrox Four' of October 1987. This time it was Gascoigne, John Brown and Alan McLaren (with Billy Dodds of Aberdeen) following in the footsteps of Butcher, Woods and Roberts (with Frank McAvennie of Celtic). This came out of an ill-tempered match at Ibrox against Aberdeen on 11 November 1995. As a result the four players were summoned to appear before the SFA disciplinary committee. The case against McLaren and Dodds was deferred, while John Brown and Paul Gascoigne, whose offences were missed by the match official, but reported by the referee's supervisor, each received a one-match suspension. The incidents involved an alleged head-butt by Gascoigne on a Dons player that resulted in him needing stitches in his face; and, according to some sources, another four bookable offences. Duncan Ferguson, then with Everton but out of jail and appealing against his 12-match ban by the SFA, might have looked on rather cynically, although his head-butting incident came at a time when he was already on probation for two previous offences. For Dumbarton, whose goalkeeper, Ian McFarlane, received a five-match ban for 'exceptional misconduct' at the same time, it smacked of one law for the rich and another for the poor. For Rangers, their criticism was not of anything their players had done, but of the powers given to someone acting in effect as a second referee. But they accepted the punishment: before it was handed down they had been preparing a legal defence should Gascoigne have received a lengthy penalty. There would be other times when Rangers' attempts to protect their expensive but temperamental import would show where the club's priorities lay with respect to breaches of common morality off the field and winning matches on it.

At the same time as Gascoigne was amusing the fans in his first game at Ibrox, Celtic fans, or some of their supporters in England, were involved in 'ugly scenes' during a friendly against Birmingham, a city with a large Catholic minority. Offensive flags were confiscated by none other than the Birmingham City managing director, Karren Brady. Trouble was expected before the start of the game from right-wing Birmingham fans and other 'fascist' and British National Party supporters (as well as some Birmingham 'Zulus', a group of black hooligans) who were thought to have targeted Irish pubs in the area and Celtic fans drinking in them. In response, various groups – *Tiocfaidh Ar La*, Anti-Fascist Action, Red Action and Celtic Soccer Crew – overlooked their differences to form a defensive alliance for the day. At the ground, 6,000 Celtic fans were said to have been taunted by a Red Hand of Ulster banner waved by English fans and chants of 'no surrender to the IRA'. Certainly the provocative symbols did not appear from nowhere, but were part of the pre-match preparations. Celtic supporters who complained of the role of the Celtic 'casuals' were told by their defenders that without them they would have been massacred by the 'fascists'.[22]

Two summers before, in 1993, Rangers fans made the headlines as they went 'on the rampage' before and after a pre-season friendly against Sunderland. All the 42 people arrested were Rangers fans, 30 of whom were from Glasgow; up to 10,000 were estimated to have made the trip. Shortly after the Sunderland troubles, when the scarred faces of two brothers involved were graphically portrayed in the tabloids, the *Daily Record* ran an exposé of some Rangers 'casuals', an Inter-city firm of the better-dressed hooligans whose main aim at matches was to cause trouble.[23] Despite the 'mod' image the 'casuals' like to affect, there was something rather passé about it all, reminiscent of an attempt to revive the fashions of another time. Rangers made the obligatory statement that the culprits would be booted out of Ibrox, but a more refreshing response came from other Rangers fans who supported all attempts to get rid of such trouble-makers. Today's Rangers fans are better behaved than those of the days before Souness, and by signing Catholics Murray removed the most obvious stigma of the club's sectarian past: where he has been less successful is in improving the behaviour of his own playing staff.

GUARDING GAZZA

The skills that take young men to the top of their profession in a highly competitive and physically demanding game like football are not those that guarantee a life of peaceful grace and elegance off it. More money than they know what to do with it, a mind-numbing mix of booze and celebrity, and especially in Glasgow the too-close attentions of a public that does not always respect the players' privacy – and players who do not respect the rights of others – are always liable to end in blows. Inevitably the sectarian element crops up, with provocation about being an Orange/Fenian bastard leading to a brawl.

One of the more disgraceful of these was a mere three days after the Dunblane massacre in March 1996, and involved a group of Rangers players and their friends celebrating in a Renfrewshire pub after a St Patrick's Day game against Celtic. At the game that day, the two teams and the packed stadium had joined the rest of the country in a silent tribute to the victims of the recent tragedy, but all of this seemed to have evaporated in what followed. A certain John McKee, sporting a tattoo of the Pope, a tricolour and the date of the Easter Rising on his arm, is alleged to have requested/demanded that the group stop singing sectarian songs and in the outcome was set on by some of them. Appearing in court the following January was Rangers' Charlie Miller and 'Gazza's best pal and former minder Jimmy "Five Bellies" Gardner'.[24] It was alleged that they were to the fore in beating up McKee, by which time the other Rangers players in the pub had left. Very little of this was noticed by the staff, who seem to have been smitten by a severe case of the Three Monkeys' affliction. Of those accused only 'Five Bellies' Gardner was convicted, but the reputed best friend of Scotland's wealthiest footballer was unable to pay the £500 fine.

Drunken excesses are never pretty, are positively ugly when they degenerate into brawls, and potentially criminal when they continue behind the wheel of a car. Several Rangers players were convicted of drink driving offences in the Smith years, as though they did not have enough money to hire a chauffeur, let alone a taxi, or even buy one, or a fleet of them. The club does not tolerate drink driving, but in the Smith years seemed to be more lenient concerning the drunken excesses of its players in other ways, dismissed by one top official as mere 'youthful pranks'. After one particularly vulgar exhibition at the Britannia Intercontinental hotel in London, in February 1996, where Gascoigne led a drink-and-vomit spree while his wife gave birth to his first child (at another venue), Rangers vice-chairman Donald Findlay was reported to have excused it all as a 'harmless weekend break'.[25]

No one at Ibrox seemed to see any relationship between such behaviour and a lack of professionalism that several foreign stars, and not just Boli, commented on, and which could have played some part in the succession of injuries suffered by the club, or the poor performances in Europe. On the contrary, Gascoigne suggested that the club – which reacted angrily to his 'revelation' – encouraged the players to drink and let their hair down after a game. This was in a 'fly-on-the-wall' television documentary for Channel Four, *Gazza's Coming Home*, that came out in the autumn of 1996; later it was admitted that he downed large whiskies before games and even at the half-time interval. Gazza's reputation was highlighted in the opening credits of the TV film where an artistically presented banner draped over the fence at a game (not Ibrox, probably Italy) proclaimed:

GAZZA'S BOYS . . . are here . . .
SHAG women . . . DRINK beer

It was Gascoigne, too, whose off-field behaviour brought more unkindly light on himself and the club when, hard on the heels of having had himself ordered off for a pointless attack on Winston Bogarde of Ajax in a Champions League match in Amsterdam, photographs of his battered and bruised wife appeared in full colour on the front pages of newspapers and television screens throughout the land. It was not the first time that Gascoigne had been accused of assaulting his wife, and not the first time that he had expressed remorse and promised not to do it again. The role of the club as an arbiter in what some saw as a private matter, others as a national disgrace, was delicate. The video on Gascoigne covering his time at Ibrox and which ended, ironically, with his wedding, revealed a somewhat sympathetic figure, a young man with genius in his boots but nothing in his head, no more aware of what to do with the mansions and limousines his millions had given him than how to relate to others who did not appreciate his childish humour: a man more at home with drunken footballers or their hangers-on than with his wife and children.

All of this was reflected in his public and on-field behaviour: the petulant responses to his overworked elbows and flailing arms, the adolescent humour that had him belching at radio journalists in Italy and belting balls at those in the media he did not like in Scotland. There was also the sadness behind the smile, and the genuine humour, such as when he 'yellow-carded' a referee when the cautionary card dropped out of his pocket and Gascoigne returned it to him, but not before he had mimed the caution, a gesture that the referee apparently saw as an insult to his pride so he gave Gascoigne a real booking. And always with the ball at his feet a thing of wonder, of joy to his own supporters and a source of admiration even to his opponents.

Rangers opted to stand by the boy with the ball at his feet, as did England manager Glenn Hoddle, and Gascoigne went unpunished in football terms for a domestic crime that took up more media attention than all the other atrocities that were going on around the world at that time. What Bill Struth would have said about the wife-beating incident we can only guess, but we can be sure that he would have taken it upon himself to do all that he could have to find Gascoigne a decent tailor.

Indeed, Gascoigne's dress sense seemed to be of more importance than his behaviour to the Rangers vice-chairman, Donald Findlay QC, whose image at the club had been growing steadily since he had taken up that position in 1992. Findlay was one of Scotland's most brilliant defence lawyers, and a Rangers fan who was proud to call himself a 'Bluenose', although he rejected any accusation of bigotry. At the 1995 AGM, Findlay showed that he was a worthy representative of some of the older traditions within the club when he not only expressed his delight about going on to eight Championships in a row, but looked forward to nine and then ten, proudly accepted that 'no one likes us, we don't care', and, to wind up the proceedings, led the gathering in one of the fans favourite songs: 'There's not a team like the Glasgow Rangers'.[26]

A man with his own peculiar sense of humour, he was not perhaps entirely kidding when he claimed, in an interview with Anne Simpson of *The Herald* , that if 'Celtic never won another game it would be a source of enormous rejoicing to me'.[27] Tongue in cheek he said that although St Patrick's day was his natural birthday, his 'official birthday is the 12th of July'. For Findlay it was all match-day banter, a 90-minute exchange of hatreds that was forgotten as soon as the game was over.

The quiet man at Rangers, the man who brought Gascoigne to Ibrox, Walter Smith, later admitted that he might have made a mistake in signing the player. This came when Rangers had effectively won their ninth successive flag and after further incidents in which Gascoigne, while recovering from an injury, went on a 'transatlantic bar crawl' in the course of which he wore Celtic scarves in a Manhattan bar and had an alleged altercation with a young woman in a London street after a night out with some showbusiness friends. In April 1997 Walter Smith admitted that his signing of Gascoigne had turned into a nightmare: 'When I signed him I was 100 per cent clear about my judgement, but the percentage drops with every incident that happens. And so does the level of backing at this club.'[28] He was fined a derisory £30,000 for not looking after himself while injured.

It is all a long way from the days when a Rangers player could be sent on his way for falling in love with a Catholic: whether or not this is progress is a more open question, although for those who believe in winning at all costs it is an irrelevance. Certainly if Rangers had dismissed or suspended all the players who had committed serious breaches of discipline in the mid-1990s their playing strength would have been considerably weakened. When it came to the crunch, however, a hat-trick in a key game could make up for any misdemeanours on or off the field. That genius and loutish behaviour need not go together can be found in many examples through football history, from Eusébio and Pelé on the one hand to Bobby Charlton and Franz Beckenbauer on the other, while at Ibrox Brian Laudrup showed class on the field that was matched by the dignity of his behaviour off it.

PROBLEMS AT PARADISE

The Celtic players at this time managed to keep out of the headlines, except when some of their foreign stars spoke to their home press and then had their words translated back into the Scottish tabloids. There was a long history of this, going back before Boli to Jan Bartram who told a Danish newspaper about life under Souness and the violence of the Scottish game. He did not last long at Ibrox (but then neither did several other imports at this time).

Celtic's imports seemed happy to adopt what they saw as the culture of the club and struck up an immediate rapport with the fans. They were also happy to report on life in Scotland. Dutch Catholic Pierre van Hooijdonk, as well as giving the club headaches over his contract before he finally left for Nottingham Forest in March 1997, gave interviews for several Dutch newspapers in January 1996 in which he spoke freely of Scottish football and the 'religious' life of the city, all of which was reported in *Elf, de Volksrant* (6 January 1996) and *Voetbal International* (17 January 1996).[29] Van Hooijdonk commented on the hard nature of the Scottish game, claiming it was 'rugby with a round ball', and that the Ajax–Feyenoord derby was 'kid's play' in comparison to that of the Old Firm. But he was at pains to stress the intense commitment of the fans. He denounced the hatred that being a Celtic player inspired, claiming that he had to go out in disguise when he left his house. He also said that while he had nothing against the Rangers players, he did not like them as a team, but was somewhat out of date when he claimed that Rangers would rather sign a Protestant than a Catholic, even one of the quality of Romario. His attitude to the Old Firm divide was not helped when he was spat at while sitting in his car at the traffic lights.

Inevitably these players would claim to have been misrepresented and the club would either accept this explanation or a mild apology. The local tabloids were all caught up in a circulation war that depended more than ever on exclusives, being first with mostly trivial information, and preferring sensation to analysis. Long gone are the days when reporters had one or more columns to develop their ideas; now they are down to one or two sentences in a paragraph in which lurid adjectives or nouns jump out at the reader in block letters, with inch-thick headlines that take up most of the page, along with a large photograph to save the reader from actually having to read very much.

The silence of the press over Rangers' attitude to Catholics in the days when Rangers ruled had little to pride itself in, while the Catholic press, with 'Man in the Know' through to the 1930s, showed a grotesque bias in the other direction that makes fascinating reading today. There were other aspects of life then that were also kept under wraps by both the Catholic and the Protestant press, issues far from football and then thought to be too delicate to trouble the minds of their readers. The recent exposure of sexual failings by men in positions of trust and authority is no reflection of a sudden increase in such activity, but merely of the media's concern to bring it to light. Scout and choir leaders have often been the subject of lewd gossip or court reporting in the columns of the best-selling *News of the World*; now that notorious Sunday scandal sheet has been surpassed from all points of view by newspapers on daily sale in supermarkets.

It was into this maelstrom of scandal that the Celtic football club found itself drawn, first and indirectly by allegations involving priests and bishops, at times no more than a betrayal of vows by falling in love with a woman, but more seriously when it involved the corruption of a minor. It was all grist to the anti-Catholic mill and the supporters of other clubs on the look-out for something to throw at Celtic. Then in mid-August 1996 the *Daily Record* brought the club right into the middle of it all, with accusations of a paedophilia scandal when it claimed that two people involved in the Celtic Boys Club had taken advantage of their position to harass young boys under their care. In unambiguous language the *Daily Record* accused the two men, on the basis of statements by former players who claimed they were abused, accusations that were denied but which later led to the arrest of the two men. The worst cases were said to have taken place long before McCann came on the scene, and Jock Stein, whose son George had played with the Boys Club, is alleged to have literally kicked one of the men out of his office when he heard of the rumours. McCann ordered an immediate investigation and promised that the club would do all in its power to sort the matter out. In the meantime one of the Rangers fanzines suggested that Rangers should start a 'Bears against Buggery' campaign.

Fergus McCann surely had none of this in mind when he set out to improve the quality of life in Scotland, but even the 'Bhoys against Bigotry' campaign and the Mission Statement that went with it, had reflections of Scotland's biggest historical hangover: for all its admirable intentions and practical application, the Mission Statement of the 'Bhoys against Bigotry' campaign is more in the tradition of Catholic charity than Protestant self-help. At various times McCann and Murray showed surprising ignorance regarding the history of their club, especially McCann with his insistence that Celtic had never been a Catholic or Irish club, while Murray, in rejecting the Lally award from the Glasgow City Council, said that his club was 'in the business of sport, nothing else'. That may be how he wanted to see it, but he was surely not so naïve as to believe that this was the case. Murray came to Ibrox as a businessman, and it was with this in mind that he wanted to clear out the bigotry he found there in regard to the club's employment practices. Somewhere along the way he got caught up in the thrill of the chase, especially when it meant beating Celtic, but the Rangers he wanted to build was one that reflected a modern business organisation rather than outdated traditions. McCann was as much a businessman as Murray, and a devout enemy of bigotry wherever it was to be found. This applied to Celtic Park as much as in the media or the offices of those controlling the Scottish game, and earned for him the enmity of those he had called 'Catholic bigots'. Just as Murray dragged Rangers into the modern world, so McCann saved Celtic from possible bankruptcy, built a stadium and hoped to create a team that would compete with the best in Europe. For such reasons the two men will forever be associated with some of the most dramatic and exciting changes in the history of the Old Firm. What neither mogul could do, however, was close the door on history. Despite their progressive new owners, Rangers and Celtic approached the end of the second millennium as two clubs still linked to two different traditions.

9. No More, the Bygone Days of Yore . . .

In *The Old Firm* I traced the story of how Celtic and Rangers grew in opposition to each other as representatives of the two major communities in Scottish society: Celtic the team of the immigrant underdogs and the paranoia that this encouraged, but inspired by the 'Celtic spirit' and proud to be known as 'the people's club'; Rangers the team of the established Scots, proud of the 'Rangers tradition' and with the touch of arrogance that led them to being seen as the 'we are the people's club'. Celtic's image was more easygoing and rebellious in the way of the Catholic Irish, while Rangers reflected a dignified – some would say dour – image of a more austere Protestantism. Although the origins of these differences were religious, separate cultures had grown around them, developing into a 'cultural apartheid' that lingered on until the 1960s. This was reflected in both clubs: from playing styles, dress and stadiums to the literature associated with them, their supporters and their heroes. The caricature of the Rangers fans was once of aggressive loud-mouths happy to declare that 'no one likes us, we don't care', while Celtic presented themselves as more happy-go-lucky, open and tolerant. In politics Celtic were inevitably involved in Irish affairs, tended to Labour sympathies, while Rangers were more Conservative, Unionist and Protestant, aggressively so in their Orangeism, more subtly in their masonic associations, and innocently in the bulk of the fans who followed the club for purely secular reasons.

By the 1980s much of this was a hangover from the past, but the club itself, with its belief that silence was the best policy in the face of its critics, did not help to remove the more negative aspects of its reputation. It would take more than Souness and the signing of Mo Johnston to change the traditions of generations, and while the troubles in Ulster drag on there will continue to be the echoes of the historical links between two neighbours that one historian has evocatively called 'intimate strangers'.[1]

There is a mystique that attaches to the awesome splendour of Ibrox stadium, dominating as it does the district in which it stands like a cathedral of old, while inside the mystery of what lies beyond the marble staircase has an aura that charges the faithful with a not entirely secular devotion. David Murray has found himself at home in the imposing grandeur of Ibrox, and there are some who say that however innocent of what are usually called West of Scotland prejudices when he arrived at the club, he soon became 'one of us'. Whatever cleansing influence he has been in regard to the moral welfare of the club, his improvements at the ground itself have made a grand stadium even grander. On view to the public he has set the Club Deck on top of the original Leitch-deisgned Main Stand, provided facilities like the Argyle House restaurant in the new Govan Stand, and filled in the corners of the four stands, two of them now with the largest television screens in Britain. Out of view of the general public he has modernised the decor without infringing in any way on the understated opulence that was there before him. For health reasons, Souness replaced with showers the communal bath in which players once disported themselves in post-match frolics; Murray, for aesthetic reasons, has refurbished the furniture and fittings, retaining the rich panelling of the showpiece Blue Room, reminiscent (and not without accident) of the luxury liners that were the pride of Clydeside in the 1930s. The sumptuous leather armchairs have been recovered with a softer fabric and the carpet replaced: all in royal blue and all exquisitely done, while the Senga Murray mural depicting the history of the club looks over it all, no more out of place in its modernism than the Chagall ceiling at the Paris Opéra.

This is Protestant Scotland at its stylish best, and while the new stadium at Celtic Park is one of the best in Britain, and although it is on the site of the Celtic glory days, there is little in concrete terms to remind the faithful of the club's history: the Jungle is gone, as are the floodlights which were for the poet Tom Leonard reassuring symbols that despite the gloom the game would still be played ('dork init/good jobe they've gote thi lights'), while even the entrance to the Main Stand is little more than a decade old. But whatever physical representations of the two clubs remain, they are as tied to their history as ever.

Since the Souness revolution the image of soccer itself has had a face-lift, so it is hardly surprising that the image of the two clubs and their supporters has also changed, much of this reflecting the changed fortunes on the park. More surprising, perhaps, is what has not changed.

POLITICAL COLOURING

Michael Kelly, the man who in name and in his more recent battles can claim to speak on behalf of the club that has been associated with his family since Celtic were founded, has no doubt about what the club stood for. They represented the Irish in Scotland and defended the underdog. They were anti-establishment and stood for 'social justice and

opposed discrimination'. Throughout their history Celtic had fought
'against poverty and discrimination and for social justice'.[2] They were the
victims of an intolerant Protestantism, and so the immigrant Catholics
and their descendants developed a paranoia against the 'establishment',
represented above all in the eyes of Celtic by the Scottish football
authorities. In October 1992, Liam Brady, 15 months into his job as
Celtic manager, said: 'I was told when I joined about Celtic's "paranoia".
Now I know it is true. We are hard done by. Religiously and politically,
there are people against us.'[3]

The reputation of Rangers as being Conservative, royalist and
Unionist has been encouraged by some of their best-known players and
managers, their most outspoken fans, including the bulk of the contributors to *Follow, Follow*, and the official histories of the club, especially
Allan and Allison. Before the publication of his official history, *The Spirit
of Ibrox*, all of this was given a ringing endorsement by Robert McElroy,
who speaks with the authority of a man who has devoted much of his life
to Rangers, recording its deeds in intimate detail, at first through
statistics and a self-edited journal, *The Rangers Historian*, but now in the
best history of the club to date, written with the help of the journalist
Bob Ferrier, son of one of the great players of Scottish football – Bobby
Ferrier of the outstanding Motherwell team of the inter-war years (the
only one to break the Old Firm dominance of the Scottish League
between 1904 and 1948), and who was deprived of a Scottish cap by the
accident of being born in England where he lived for all of three weeks.[4]
McElroy claims that for over 120 years Rangers have become

> institutionalised as the flag carrier of what a majority of Scots
> would consider to be national virtues – Protestant, Monarchist
> tradition [*sic*] and Unionist in the literal sense of the Union of
> Great Britain and Northern Ireland. Red, white and blue are the
> Rangers colours.[5]

Presumably this applies to the directors and management of the club,
which can fairly clearly be established, but also to the supporters, whose
political opinions are harder to ascertain.

A researcher from Caledonian University, Joseph Bradley, set out
through a series of questionnaires distributed at football matches in
1990, to make a profile, among other things, of the political beliefs of the
fans of Scotland's Premier League clubs.[6] The evidence he thus adduced
generally justifies the popular preconceptions. Celtic fans claimed to be
overwhelmingly Labour voters, about 85 per cent, Rangers fans only 33
per cent. A mere 4 per cent of Celtic supporters voted Scottish Nationa-

list, against nearly 14 per cent for Rangers, and while only 3 per cent of
Celtic fans claimed to be Conservatives, a large 32 per cent of Rangers
supporters were proud to call themselves Tories, which is well above the
figure for Scotland as a whole. The only club to match Rangers and its
Tory following was St Johnstone, with just over 29 per cent (only 12.5
per cent of Hearts fans claimed to vote Tory: indeed there is little in
Bradley's findings to justify their being called 'The Wee Huns'). The
closest to Celtic's Labour sympathies was Kilmarnock with nearly 58 per
cent, while Hearts claimed 45 per cent. The highest nationalist support
came from Dundee United (41 per cent), Motherwell (37.5 per cent)
and Aberdeen (33 per cent).

These figures clearly establish Celtic as the team of the Labour Party,
while the Labour Prime Minister, Tony Blair, is said to have expressed a
sympathy for the club while a pupil at Fettes College. Then again, in the
spirit of New Labour, he is said to support Rangers. Few people have seen
him at either ground. A more spontaneous expression of Celtic's political
sympathies came when Prime Minister Thatcher visited Hampden in 1988
to see the Scottish Cup final between Celtic and Dundee United, and was
greeted with a storm of red cards and Irish tricolours. On a three-day trip
to Glasgow in March 1990 the Prime Minister made the draw for the
Scottish Cup and then paid a special visit to Ibrox. She came as a supporter
of the Anglo-Irish agreement that was hated by the Loyalists, and so her
support from the other end of the political spectrum had diminished. Not
so in *The Rangers Historian*, however, which fell over itself in a fit of
forelock-tugging and general obsequiousness, praising the 'finest' Prime
Minister of 'the last 70 years', along with Winston Churchill and Harold
Macmillan, also, and not coincidentally, prime ministers who had
honoured Ibrox with their presence. McElroy duly set out the Conservative
Party credentials of Murray, Butcher and Woods as typical of the club,
while in another part of the publication the editor castigated a 'minority of
Rangers fans who disgrace the Club's colours with extreme Left-wing
propaganda'. He also lambasted the left-wing bias of the anti-Tory press in
the west of Scotland, with particular reference to Labour MP Brian
Wilson. Rangers, he insisted, had always been a 'True Blue Conservative
organisation', a 'vast number' of supporters were Conservative and
Unionist and the club itself had proudly opposed 'the devolution proposals
of the then Labour Government' in 1979. Celtic, on the other hand, were
dismissed as a club to which 'Socialists have always more readily identified
themselves', some of its players (John Colquhoun, Brian McClair and Billy
McNeill) being so wicked as to 'promote their socialist views, using their
prominent positions in Scottish football to influence the youth of today'.[7]
Something the Tory-loving Rangers players never did.

No wonder then, that some Rangers supporters have been driven to near dementia by the reputation people like McElroy have foisted on the club. It also seems clear that in a Scotland that has recently removed the Tories to rump status, and as supporters of the monarchy lose faith in an institution that stands out (the Queen apart) as an insult to decent family values, the majority of Rangers supporters are far from being the Tory lickspittles McElroy likes to portray them as.

One Rangers fan, the historian Graham Walker, author of various works on Scottish and Irish politics, as well as several newspaper and journal articles on Rangers, has tried to show another side to the club. In a more academic discussion, '"There's not a team like the Glasgow Rangers": football and religious identity in Scotland', he sets out to redress the image of Rangers as an institution that 'perpetuates all that is reactionary in Scottish life'.[8] Walker agrees with the editor of *Follow, Follow* that most Rangers fans are right-wing Labour, but unlike the more traditionalist Dingwall, Walker would prefer that Rangers fans were more nationalist and less tied to the narrower aspects of Unionism. He is perhaps a little over-optimistic, however, in his appraisal of the liberal tendencies of Rangers fans, the most vociferous of whom fit only too closely into the stereotype. Rangers still await a history that will emphasise the other side to its more familiar triumphalism, and while most fanzines generally have a left-wing bias, this is not a characteristic of any of the Rangers fanzines – although *Follow, Follow* has included material expressing views at odds with those of the editor. Until such a history and such a fanzine appear, however, Dingwall and McElroy will speak as the voice of the average fan.

Whether Celtic has the 'socialist' sympathies McElroy attributes to the club or not, the Labour Party allegiances of the fans are reflected in some ways at board level. Many directors have expressed Labour sympathies, from McCann on the one hand, to Michael Kelly and Brian Dempsey on the other: Kelly was a prominent Labour Councillor, Dempsey is the son of a well-respected Labour politician. That men of such wealth should retain Labour sympathies is more surprising than that the millionaires at Ibrox have right-wing sympathies. Souness and Butcher were fairly outspoken in their right-wing beliefs, while Celtic heroes like Stein and McNeill did not object to being called socialists. Souness, like club captains Greig before him and Butcher who followed him, is an ardent royalist. One of his gifts to Ibrox was a full-length portrait of the Queen which he had hung up in the dressing-room, and while he is no longer there to urge the players to look on it as an inspiration for victory, the Queen is still there to gaze down on the players in their various states of undress.

Butcher's less imposing portrait of the Queen, a bust only, was placed above the door for players to make their reverences, should they choose to do so, on the way out to the field. One has to wonder what the foreign players thought about it all, and for the Catholics it hardly made up for not being allowed to bless themselves where and when they pleased.

David Murray, although a capitalist, clearly right-wing and a Unionist, fits into no pre-existing caricature. Unionism comes in many varieties, and it is on the Union of the crowns (1603) and the parliaments (1707) of Scotland and England that the material – and in many ways moral – success of Great Britain has been founded. Scots have gained more than they lost from the Union, certainly in colonial ventures, but above all in the end to wars between the two nations that has allowed energies to be used elsewhere. The treatment of the Catholics in Ireland, on the other hand, has been appalling, a permanent blot in the British government's treatment of a subject people through to the creation of Northern Ireland in 1921. Unionists defending Northern Ireland's refusal to be forced out of the United Kingdom today, however, need not be narrow reactionaries, although they often are, and Unionists in Scotland can retain a cultural independence that has nothing to do with politics. Unionism and loyalty to Scotland need not contradict, as is nowhere better represented than in the case of David Murray. He has chosen not to follow the path of the tax exile, give or take a residence in Jersey, but instead has stayed in Scotland and provided work for thousands of Scots.

Like Brian Meek, Scotland's wittiest and most polished Conservative journalist, as well as other Rangers directors whose company Meek was once tipped to join, and manager Walter Smith who exudes good grace and tolerance in the public eye, Murray and the new Ibrox presented an image of Rangers of which any fan could be proud. Unfortunately for Rangers at the official level, the public image of the club was more likely to be associated with the hirsute visage of vice-chairman Donald Findlay QC. Here is a man who openly expressed his contempt for Celtic, proudly conjured up images of 1690, and who is happy to boast that 'no one likes us, we don't care'. Those who know Findlay privately will tell you of his sense of humour and a support for the underdog that does not discriminate between Catholics and Protestants, but while many Scots will have no trouble remembering his defence of one of the most vile Protestant killers, few will be able to recall the last Catholic activist he defended. What Findlay does in his professional and private life is his own affair, whether it be defending alleged criminals or chairing the 'No, No' campaign in the devolution referendum; but rightly or wrongly, his words and actions could not easily be dissociated from his position at

Rangers Football Club. In this regard he was Dingwall with a more polished accent, McElroy with a better education, reminders that for all the good Murray and others did in raising the profile of the club, parts of its past kept resurfacing to tarnish the image.

RANGERS, FREEMASONS AND HEAD-CASE HISTORY

The association of Rangers and its followers with the Freemasons and the Orange Order is unofficial but clearly established, and these serve as the essential links with its anti-Catholic past. It had long been whispered, proudly by insiders and less respectfully by outsiders, that not only were Rangers an all-Protestant club, but that every player was a Freemason: if not one when he joined, he became one soon after. It was in this way that the ban on Catholics was perpetuated. Much of this, in the nature of things, was based on hearsay, as the club, in the best traditions of Freemasonry, maintained what it believed to be a dignified silence. Again Ferrier and McElroy have at last made an open affirmation of links that the club need scarcely have been ashamed of:

> The Union Flag, the 'Union Jack', was inevitably the flag of establishment Rangers, the club of the Protestant faith, of the monarchy and the union, not to mention of the masonic order and the Orange movement.[9]

In the flurry of press activity that followed the signing of Maurice Johnston, one newspaper contacted Don 'The Rhino' Kichenbrand, one of Rangers' two known or suspected Catholics since the First World War. Kichenbrand, from his home in his native South Africa, was happy to reveal how his religion was concealed from the club, and went on to tell how he had been inducted into the Lodge. The *Daily Record* of 12 July 1989 spilled the beans with a banner headline declaring that: 'One of Rangers biggest stars was a SECRET CATHOLIC', before going on to reveal the 'Amazing confession of an Ibrox legend'. For three years from his arrival at Ibrox in 1955, it declared, Kichenbrand 'lived a lie', but kept his promise not to reveal the error the scout had committed by not establishing the young South African's religion before he signed him. All at Ibrox assumed Kichenbrand was a staunch Protestant, but to be on the safe side he accepted without demur the proposal that he become a Freemason. When he left the club it was assumed that he had been kicked out because he had fallen in love with a Catholic, but Kichenbrand claims that this happened after he had left the club. It was only then that he married Josephine, a Catholic, 'in a Dublin chapel'.

Kichenbrand's testimony gives truth to the rumours freely circulating –
proudly by some Rangers fans – that anyone at Ibrox who fell in love
with a Catholic would soon be on his way out of the club.

That Rangers still liked their players to be members of the
Brotherhood can be inferred from one newspaper report concerning the
sometimes drunk and disorderly Duncan Ferguson, whose unruly
behaviour was allegedly so bad that he could not be nominated for
membership of the Lodge. The Freemasons, indeed, pride themselves on
their behaviour and social responsibility. The popular image is of a closed
society whose members help each other, granting promotions to brothers
in the professions and supporting each other in business. This has
certainly happened, but in violation of the strictest code of the
Brotherhood, and like the Rangers Football Club, the Freemasons have
not helped their cause by maintaining a principled silence on the matter.
But the Brotherhood, like Rangers, is no longer the closed body it once
was, emphasising that while it has secrets it is not a secret society. Indeed
in tune with the times that have seen Ibrox opened up to Catholics,
Freemasons have presented themselves to the public and opened up their
lodges for inspection. Part of this is in a drive for new members, but it is
also a reflection of a more open age. The Freemasons still insist on the
moral probity of their members, that they be upright citizens, true to
each other and loyal to the state. Their associations with Rangers are
doubtless still strong, but not complete.

Freemasonry and the Catholic Church have been enemies since the
days of the Enlightenment of the eighteenth century, when the bur-
geoning movement, because of its beliefs in religious tolerance, social
equality and intellectual progress, was banned by the Vatican. Freemasons were blamed by the Church for weakening the moral fibre of the
French people, so that they fell easy victims to the false principles that led
to the French Revolution in 1789: from that time on Catholicism and
Freemasonry became implacable enemies. In Protestant countries, where
Catholics were distrusted for what some saw as their subservience to a
foreign power, and where the confessional was seen as a threat to the
secrets of the Brotherhood, Freemasons often became part of the
Establishment. Freemasonry was originally an essentially aristocratic
body, becoming more middle-class by the end of the nineteenth century
and popular among the small business classes. In Scotland it was more
working-class than in most countries; it was also more anti-Catholic.

In the more liberal atmosphere since the 1960s some Catholics were
inducted into Freemasonry, believing that they could do so without
threatening their mortal soul. Pope John-Paul II, in keeping with his
attempts to undo what he saw as the damage of Vatican II, has reaffirmed

the ban on Catholics who become Freemasons, but has not decreed instant excommunication. In the last two decades some Protestant churches have turned a dyspeptic eye on the Brotherhood: the Methodists condemned it in 1985; the Free Presbyterians then described it as 'anti-Christian and of the works of darkness'; while even the Church of Scotland, after a two-year study, pointed out the incompatibilities of aspects of masonic worship and that of Jesus Christ, but while warning its followers about this, it did not forbid them to be members.[10] The role of Freemasonry in Scotland continues to exert a more powerful influence than in most other Anglo-Saxon countries, and only in Scotland was attention drawn to the alleged masonic links of the Dunblane killer, Thomas Hamilton, with the implication that it was these links that helped him avoid detection in the years leading up to his abominable crime.

The historian John Roberts, in his book *The Mythology of the Secret Societies*, opens with the statement: 'Though sometimes amusing, it is always disturbing when intelligent people seriously talk nonsense.'[11] Among the people Roberts had in mind was Britain's nineteenth-century prime minister, Benjamin Disraeli, a man 'otherwise shrewd and intelligent', but someone who was obsessed with the machinations of Freemasons and secret societies. Indeed Freemasonry, or more accurately anti-Freemasonry, has resulted in a rich tradition of what might generously be called 'head-case history'. In common with best-sellers along the lines of 'I spoke to a Martian', authors like Nesta Webster have sold tens of thousands of copies of books claiming to explain the real reasons for the revolutions from 1789 to the modern age, and for many decades one of the best selling books on the French Revolution was the ravings of the Abbé Barruel, blaming its wickedness on the machinations of Freemasons – along with Jews (inevitably), Protestants and cosmopolitans in general, the common enemies of the Catholic Church. Towards the end of the nineteenth century, the Frenchman Léo Taxil made a fortune out of books and public appearances exposing in lurid detail the secrets of the Freemasons, and when he gathered another oversubscribed audience at the Grand Palais in Paris in 1898 to reveal 'the biggest secret of all', it turned out to be the only one his audience would not believe: namely that everything he had told them up until then was a pack of lies. The Freemasons have also held a fascination for such renowned figures as General Franco in Spain, the dictator Salazar in Portugal and Marshal Pétain and his collaborationist government in wartime France, all of whom, along with Hitler, the Kremlin and the Vatican suppressed the organisation. Any organisation that attracts a swarm of enemies like that cannot be without its virtues.

More recently the works of Stephen Knight and Martin Short 'exposing' the Masons have enjoyed immense popularity. Short's *Inside the Brotherhood: Further Secrets of the Freemasons*, took up in 1989 the work of Knight, who died in July 1985, aged 33, just 18 months after the publication of his exposé, *The Brotherhood*. Obviously to those who know about such things his death was no accident. One of the chapters in Short's book is on the alleged links between Freemasonry and police corruption, and so it was not surprising, despite some of the egregious nonsense that appears in his book, that he was the first witness in the Home Affairs Select Committee inquiry into masonic connections with the police and the judiciary.

It is an old story, and as suggested above, while there are doubtless instances where police have betrayed the force, Masons have higher duties to the laws of the land. In Scotland all of this was brought into proper perspective when Celtic fans, angered by a series of decisions that went against them, took up the claims of a masonic conspiracy among its referees. As suggested earlier, Celtic supporters often had good reasons to challenge the eyesight if not the morality of some referees regarding decisions that have gone against them at various times, but any accusations of a 'masonic conspiracy' have to be regarded in the same light as the ranting of a wide range of empty and discredited visionaries posing as historians for over a century and more.

Masons do have a duty to assist each other, but not in transgression of laws either moral or man-made. Some individuals have broken this code, and critics of the Brotherhood would say that they all do, but a single swallow does not make a summer any more than one bent Mason makes a conspiracy. Nevertheless, there was a tasty titbit to feed the paranoia of the persecuted in the officially sanctioned Rangers audio-tape that came out in July 1993, incorporating the comments and memories of many individuals associated with the club. One of these was Bobby Brown, the golden-haired goalkeeper of the Iron Curtain defence and later a manager of Scotland. He tells the story of a former referee whose proudest boast was that in 18 years of refereeing he had never officiated at a game in which Rangers lost. Brown recalled the case of a Queen of the South game where the referee deliberately disallowed a last-minute goal that would have won the game for the Dumfries club. It was at Palmerston Park, and with the score 1–1 and Rangers facing a corner, Brown asked the referee how long there was to go. He was told not to worry. The home team scored from the corner, but to the mystification of everyone the referee awarded a free-kick to Rangers. No sooner was it taken than the whistle blew for time. It was two years later, at a Lodge presentation, that the now retired referee made the boast claimed by

Brown. Brown's imagination was perhaps working a wee bit overtime on this occasion, certainly so if his reminiscences of the 1948 Scottish Cup final against Morton are anything to go by – and journalists trying to track down the game against Queen of the South were unable to find it.

HELLO! HELLO! CAN YOU STILL HEAR US?

Before Souness came to Ibrox the Orange associations of Rangers were loudly proclaimed in songs, chants and images of King Billy fording the river Boyne in 1690. Ibrox was the regular venue for the annual religious service of the Order, at least until 1987 when the new management at Ibrox turned down its request – although a few years later this was to be regarded more favourably. At the same time steps were taken to clear out the vendors of Orange literature who plied a vigorous trade outside the ground, although this was as much to clear out unwanted commercial competition as undesirable messages.

Rangers' associations with the Orangemen of Ulster are very much a part of the historic past, today most likely to be seen displayed by marchers at The Walk, either openly or under the regalia, where some marchers can be seen to wear a Rangers replica strip. We would not expect Rangers today or even a couple of decades ago, to send a director to Ulster to address an Orange Order social gathering, as James Bowie did in 1930, praising the Order for its 'traditions' and 'principles'[12] or to send a team to Belfast to help raise funds for the Orange Order, as they did on several occasions before the 1960s. One of these benefit matches, played on 10 May 1955, was to help finance extensions to the Sandy Row Orange Hall. In the programme for that game there is a brief history of the Orange Lodge in Belfast which includes this verse from the 'Orange Poet':

> To guard the faith which Luther preached
> The rights which William won
> The Orangeman relies upon
> His Bible and his gun.

No more, of course, would Celtic, whose trips to the South were as frequent as Rangers' to Ulster, today associate itself with the rabid support of Man in the Know for the IRA, and his summary of a 2–0 victory on Ne'erday 1921 by Celtic over Rangers: 'Rebels 2, Black and Tans 0'. Today you would be more likely to see: 'C.R. Smith (or Umbro or whoever else) 2, McEwan's Lager 0'. And certainly no Catholic priest today would openly associate himself with the club and the IRA the way young Father McRory did, an ardent Celtic supporter and Irish nationalist, and who became a hero in his parish of Calton at the time of the 'Duke Street shoot-out' in 1921.[13]

The Orange Order has not been receiving a good press in recent years in Scotland, as no more today than in other times does its members abide by its strictures on drunkenness and bad language. Its followers are more into slogans and mythologising, particularly since the role of Catholics among King Billy's troops at the Boyne is now so well documented, as is the praise showered on him by the Vatican and the goodwill of Catholic Spain. In the more irreverent reporting of recent times his sexual proclivities have found their way into the tabloid press, luridly in headlines proclaiming him to have been a 'rent boy', and more accurately in reports casting doubts on his heterosexuality. None of this reflects on his undisputed valour in battle, and all of it is irrelevant to the man's main claim to fame as the champion of Protestantism. Perhaps the time has come, however, now that Rangers have Catholics helping them to win titles, to acknowledge that Catholics actually played a significant role in the establishment of Protestant hegemony in Britain: moreover, and as befits the multinational Rangers of the present day, that in addition to Catholics and some home-grown talent among King Billy's troops at the Boyne, were the Dutch, French Huguenots, English, Danes, Prussians, Finns and Swiss.

THE BEST FANS IN THE WORLD

In 1984 the reputation of the Rangers supporters was at an all-time low, saddled as they were with a club being berated for its bigotry and performing poorly on the park. Both Rangers and Celtic had their hooligan fans, but over the previous 20 years the worst examples of spectator violence had involved those of Rangers. Since then it has been the Celtic supporters who have been more in the news for the wrong reasons. The civil war at Parkhead showed an admirable commitment to the club by its fans, but it also threw up an unflattering exchange of insults as Celt was pitted against Celt.

Michael Kelly once believed that Celtic supporters were superior in morals and behaviour to the Rangers fans, but when his family was subjected to threats and insults by those who opposed his activities on the board, and articles sent to him through the mail included a box of excrement, he had to revise his opinion. And Kelly himself, a passionate supporter of the club, reveals the terrible hatred that existed between his father and his father's brother, Celtic chairman Bob Kelly: for decades they passed each other in the directors' box at Parkhead without exchanging a single word.

Few clubs have had an entire book devoted to their fans, but Gerry McNee's *And You'll Never Walk Alone*, published in 1972, celebrates the adventures of the Celtic fans who travelled with the club in its triumphal run before and after Lisbon. This is the same McNee who went on to write a history of Celtic and a biography of its legendary centre-forward, Jimmy McGrory, but who has since earned the impartial hatred of both sets of fans. In his later career McNee was assaulted by a Celtic manager, threatened with physical violence by a Rangers manager and now, through his provocative comments in the press, and on radio and television, has set himself up as a safety-valve for the release of the emotional excesses of Bears and Tims alike. To some Celtic people he is seen as a traitor, as he is now prepared to lump some of the Celtic support with the worst of the Rangers, an indication either that the behaviour of the Celtic fans has deteriorated since the 1970s or that McNee has grown wiser with age.

Since the success of Nick Hornby's *Fever Pitch*, a brilliant attempt to unravel the complexities of his life through his obsession with football and Arsenal in particular, a few others have tried their hand at books in a similar style. They have generally found that it is not as easy as Hornby makes it seem. One of these was by a Celtic supporter, David Bennie, whose memoirs of a Celtic fan, *Not Playing for Celtic*,[14] did nothing to enhance the literary reputation of Celtic followers. In addition to his pretentious style, Bennie reveals himself as someone who added little lustre to the image of the club's followers, especially in the two instances he recounts of attacking wee boys: on one occasion he threw a half brick at a couple of youngsters who had mocked him on his way back from a bad day at Parkhead, knocking one of them off a wall; on the other occasion he battered a wee boy's head for annoying him outside his recently deceased father's house. And if Paul Gascoigne is to be believed, a Celtic fan who drew alongside him in his car after the flute-playing incident at Ibrox promised to find out where he lived and to go there and slit his throat if he did it again. Empty threat or real, Gascoigne admitted to nearly soiling his pants at training the next day.[15]

John Cairney, television idol of the 1960s, one of Scotland's great actors and Burns interpreter without equal, in his private life a Celtic fanatic who bears no ill-will towards Rangers, found to his horror when he watched the first Old Firm game of the 1997–98 season at Ibrox, that the Celtic supporters around him made the experience almost unbearable, positioned as he was between 'two hate-filled teenagers who were never seated or quiet throughout' in an atmosphere that was less 'electric . . . than a stressful, obscene tension'.

Rangers fans inside Ibrox seemed to be so successfully tamed by the

club's police liaison officer that Alistair Hood came to rate on a par with
the Pope as the most unpopular icon at Ibrox. The clean-up at Ibrox was
not without its critics, who had not only lost the East Enclosure to
seating and season tickets, but saw their places usurped by the camel-coat
brigade, denounced in the fanzines as fair-weather followers of the club.
Even before the closure of the East Enclosure the class war within Ibrox
was already evident as chants broke out during the more boring episodes
of games where the team was once more toying with a luckless
opposition. This was directed against the season-ticket-holders of the
Copland Stand along the lines of: 'Can you hear the Copland sing . . .
You can't hear a fuckin' thing.' The atmosphere at Ibrox has been
denounced as funereal except for the big games against Celtic or
Aberdeen. Fans who could not afford season tickets were reduced to
being away followers of the club, leading to the claim that there was more
atmosphere at away games where Rangers were playing than at 'iceberg'
Ibrox.

Gone with the atmosphere are serious outbreaks of hooliganism at
Ibrox and Celtic Park – the last notable incident, before the Coin-
Throwing game of May 1999, was at Celtic Park in the days of the civil
war when fans turned on the directors with their Mars attacks in January
1994 after another humiliation by Rangers and, more seriously, one
Celtic fan attacked the Rangers goalkeeper. Hooliganism, like sectarian
or bigoted behaviour, can never be entirely eliminated. To the extent that
the comparative silence at Ibrox is through the elimination of the more
odious anti-Catholic sentiments ('If you hate the fuckin' Fenians, clap
your hands') then this is surely to be applauded. But there is reason to
regret that more than bigotry has been thrown out with the filthier bath
water of the more rabid Bears. Songs about being up to one's knees in
Fenian blood challenge decency, although it has a great tune – witness
the way it has been taken up by many supporters elsewhere. While
sectarian killings in Ireland and England continue, however, songs and
chants in praise of the killers are somewhat sick. 'The Sash' and one-time
favourite, 'No Pope of Rome', on the other hand, have little to do with
present-day realities and as such can be seen as more humorous than
provocative. At least they have more to do with Scotland than such
contemporary Ibrox favourites as 'Rule Britannia' and 'Swing Low, Sweet
Chariot'. They also come from the fans themselves, a form of DIY
entertainment with more to recommend it than canned music
deliberately turned up to drown them out and to direct them in what
some disembodied presence thinks they should be doing.

It is all part of the general cleansing of the game for the benefit of its
new middle-class clientele: seats that must be sat upon, directions that

must be followed by occasionally thuggish stewards, polite applause at the risk of being thrown out if you get too carried away, and respect for the wonderful sponsors without whom you would not be able to see the millionaire foreigners on show on the field. Some clubs have been worried by the loss of atmosphere, and many spectators have reacted against the new authoritarianism, highlighted at Old Trafford where a near civil war broke out between fans who refused to sit down when ordered to do so by the stewards, and whose response to directives over the tannoy was to deliberately disobey them: the whole East Stand standing up when told to sit down.

THE NEW VOICES OF THE FANS

Rangers may have continued since the Souness days to trump Celtic in the signing of new players, and their commercial developments have put Celtic in the shade until recently, but there is one area in which the Parkhead club is still well ahead of its rival, and that is in the various books and other literary expressions of what the two clubs stand for. In works devoted to them, Rangers have continued to come second to Celtic: *The Rangers Historian* first came out in September 1987, four years after the first issue of *The Celt*; *Not the View* first came out at the beginning of November 1987, then Rangers followed at the end of that season with *Follow, Follow*. (*World Shut Your Mouth* was a Rangers fanzine that actually preceded *Follow, Follow*, but it had a mercifully short life.) When Rangers produced the admirable theatrical production of its history, *Follow, Follow*, which played to appreciative audiences in the summer of 1994, they were following in the footsteps of *The Celtic Story*, produced to coincide with the club's centenary. In most of these productions Celtic have projected a more open and good-natured image. The dramatised Celtic history, for instance, begins and ends with the theme of helping the less privileged, the Rangers play ends on a note of worshipful reverence to Bill Struth and David Murray with the message that 'the club is always bigger than the man'.

The Rangers' aural history produced by Roddy Forsyth, however, is a refreshing break from the more usually wooden treatments: it actually admits that the club was founded in 1872, treats the Mo Johnston signing with candour, and, still fresh from the stings of Souness's departure to Liverpool, is remarkably frank on his impact on the club.

In terms of club histories and books about the clubs, however, Rangers are still a long way behind Celtic. Pat Woods in particular, in various combinations with Tom Campbell and Kevin McCarra, has produced several excellent books which can now, with the old board gone, even be

purchased through Celtic outlets. His publication, with California-based
Jesuit priest Peter Burns, bon viveur and top sleuth on the trail of
masonic malevolence, is a celebration of the famous 7–1 League Cup
victory over Rangers in 1957. *Oh, Hampden in the Sun . . .* is not just a
recounting of a treasured triumph, rather it is a living archive of a period
now long gone. Missing among the myriad stories surrounding that
event is Rangers fan Andy Cameron's recollections of how he and a mate
had stuck it out to the end, ever hopeful, at least until there were only a
couple of minutes left, of an equaliser. On their way home from
Hampden and finding themselves surrounded by a triumphal group of
Celtic supporters chanting the score, Andy's mate whispered out of the
corner of his mouth: 'Don't let them see that it annoys you.'[16] *Oh,
Hampden in the Sun . . .* is a reminder of the grave error made by Graeme
Souness back in that otherwise glorious triumph for Rangers over Celtic
in August 1988, when he chose, with the score at 5–1 and half an hour
still to go, to rub in Rangers' superiority with arrogant control of the ball
rather than banging it into the net.

Other Celtic fans have set their thoughts down in print, most notably
David Potter although there are many others, resulting in a minor
industry in books about the club, most of which are of a very good
quality and carry on the tradition of respect without subservience.
Rangers have at last had a book written about them which, once it has
trumpeted its political message in the Introduction, goes on to tell a story
that rises above the more usual hagiography. Because the Ferrier/McElroy
history is based on systematic research, McElroy has been forced to admit
that much of what was published about Rangers by people with no
connection with the club, and which the more inward-looking fans
found hard to take, was correct. The Ferrier/McElroy history is
essentially a statistical work with an account of just about every game
Rangers have played, and it is written for Rangers fans, but it is based on
years of persistent effort at the grass-roots and it does take time off from
the more usual hyperbole in praise of the club to mention a few of its
negative aspects. McElroy was given the honour of being invited by the
club to write a history of Rangers, and with the full cooperation of the
club produced *The Spirit of Ibrox*, where the McElroy view of the
Rangers tradition was given official sanction. With the new century,
however, voices of a slightly more heretical view would appear, as the
club itself adopted a more open interpretation of its role in the
community than it had done in the past.

Criticism of Rangers in the official club newspaper is as non-existent
as ever. *Rangers News* probably claims to sell more copies than the *Celtic
View*, and the quality of its articles has continued to improve – but it is

still aimed at a more juvenile readership. Although it has been attacked by the fanzines as *Pravda*, the *Celtic View* is still more open to the fans and its articles are of a more independent and critical nature. Its worst critics, indeed, are the Celtic fans themselves: the Rangers paper, *Rangers Snooze*, is so bland that there is nothing to criticise.

The most interesting development in football literature in the 1990s was in the fanzines: the voice of the fans increasingly ignored by the clubs as they aim at a more profitable market. Devoted to the club, but independent of it, some fanzines have become profitable in their own right, and even without selling their soul. A written form of the 'phone-ins', the material in the fanzines is generally less bigoted than the opinions of those letting off steam before a radio audience. Amidst their irreverence and foul language the fanzines often come up with more serious discussion of the game than can be found in the tabloids. The daily press itself is renamed according to the bias of the fanzine: the *Daily Record/Rebel/Ranger*, the *Sunday Mail/Mason/Liam*, the *Evening Times/ Tims*, *The Sun/Hun*. It would appear from this, and the shared cries of foul by both Rangers and Celtic fans that the tabloids are at least maintaining a reasonable balance of objectivity.

In the fanzine market, Celtic and Rangers are well to the fore, although Scotland's best fanzine, *The Absolute Game*, now extinct, studiously tried – impossible task – to ignore the 'Awful Firm'. That Rangers have an independent and critical publication at all is an immense step forward from the pre-Souness days. The club to some degree has put itself out of reach of the worst criticism by its continued success on the field and in improving the stadium, but for the fans being squeezed out of Ibrox and made unwelcome by their unsuitable behaviour in the eyes of the new regime, the fanzines are a means of keeping in touch. As the voice of the East Enclosure, *Follow, Follow* has engaged in several campaigns on behalf of the less privileged fan: to save the enclosure from being converted into an all-seated area; for the preservation of the *Wee Blue Book*, and constantly and increasingly so against the greed of the club. But it has all been doomed to failure. For both Rangers and Celtic fanzines, the staple is still slagging each other off. The vituperation in *Not the View* tends to the humorous, that in *Follow, Follow*, more to the vituperative, although it also has its moments of pure humour in the cartoons, drawings, and extracts from other papers and occasional stories. The big guns are the regular contributors, where the Govanhill Gub and the Major (Forza Prod, Forever Orange) are open in their expression of Protestant bias and hatred of Celtic, while the Dowanhill Hack (who claims to be neither a Rangers supporter nor a right-winger) and Rantin' Robert [Burns] provide more balanced abuse.

Grandmaster Suck (Dingwall) provides the editorial comment for *Follow, Follow,* and from the start has vigorously denied all accusations of bigotry. He has been inflexible in his attacks on racism, and whenever he is accused of being bigoted in his attitude to Celtic he claims that it is only the club's IRA sympathies and its support for terrorism that he is attacking; that any bigotry at Ibrox or in his fanzine is of the '90 minutes variety'. He also justifies his attacks on the 'Beggars' at 'Mother Teresa's Pleasuredome' (one of the new names when 'The Piggery' became clearly unsuited to the renovated Paradise) as a sarcastic rejoinder to the constantly reiterated cant about Celtic having 'the best supporters in the world'. Yet this is the fanzine that has opened an article with the claim that Celtic, a club 'steeped in bigotry and support for terrorism', was 'founded by bigots, for bigots, with the purpose of bigotry its main aim'.[17] On another occasion he refers to the 'rotten pus which Glasgow still unfortunately spews forth from time to time under the guise of Celtic Football Club'.[18] In response to the cretins who on its 20th anniversary disrupted the silence in memory of the Ibrox disaster, Dingwall's rage was vented on the press for ignoring what happened and the BBC for turning its cameras away, but the central blame he laid on Celtic for being a club that 'provide and encourage the atmosphere of hatred of Protestants in which such behaviour is accepted as normal'.[19] We do not expect fairness or modest language in fanzines, and with the Gub and the Major we know where we stand, but it would not be out of place now and then for Dingwall to show some restraint in equating every Celtic fan with gun-happy terrorists and to give up the ludicrous notion that the club is in thrall to the IRA. It would also be refreshing if *Follow, Follow* showed more concern for the game beyond Ibrox and Rangers' away matches.

There have been other Rangers fanzines, such as *The Teddy Bear, Hello! Hello!, Aye Ready* and *No.1,* but none of them has achieved the consistency of *Follow, Follow. Aye Ready* makes the odd good point, but on the whole the humour is rather crude. *No.1* is equally crude, but has some excellent drawings. One of these is a spoof on 'Oor Wullie', where a remarkably accurate drawing of 'Oor Billy' has PC Murdoch replaced by Herr Hood and where the up-to-date scamp of Scotland's conservative Sunday paper is allowed more throaty expressions than 'Crivvens', 'Jings' or 'So help ma Boab', at the same time as he is able to run about chanting, in reference to the troubles plaguing Parkhead at the time, 'Who shagged a' the weans?'

Gerry Dunbar's *Not the View* has retained a humour over the years that is in the best of the fanzine traditions. Just as it came out in protest at the official club paper, the *Celtic View,* so Matt McGlone's *Once a Tim,* as mentioned elsewhere, came out in protest against the old board. When the old board was replaced, claims McGlone, much of the purpose of his fanzine was gone, and so in what some Celtic people saw as controversial circumstances, he accepted a position as regular columnist for the *Celtic View*. McGlone claimed that there was no point in continuing to criticise the club under the new regime and that his critical independence was in no way affected. With the departure of McCann the new regime showed itself less sympathetic to a fighter who had helped pave the way for the new regime, eventually forcing McGlone to return to the role that perhaps best suited him, as a voice of the fans and answerable only to them. *Bhoyzone* was a fanzine said to have first appeared on the Internet, with a support for McCann that could well have earned it the title 'McCann's Mouthpiece'. Its editor, John Cole, was given an official position by the post-McCann board as an IT consultant, while *Bhoyzone* was incorporated into the official match programme. Some saw these appointments as a means of blunting if not silencing critical opinion. But just as the desk-top publishing of the 1980s had opened up new ways to support your club as an individual, so in the 1990s came the World Wide Web. This might have brought the heyday of the fanzines to an end, but with the increasing accessibility of the Web, the fans were free to express themselves without any of the restraints of the past.

Another Celtic fanzine, *Tiocfaidh Ar La*, would justify many of Dingwall's criticisms if it had any respectability with the club – but it doesn't. Its ideals are set out in the meaning of its title ('Our day will come', a Provo slogan) and its contents combine cheery chatter about the club and how it is performing on the field with equally cheery chatter about the latest IRA bomb outrages. One of its main aims is to gain political status for IRA prisoners and it regularly donates money to the 'men behind the wire'. It is also anti-fascist and anti-racist, as well as socialxist, ideals that some might think are not altogether in consonance with the goals and methods of the IRA. On the other side of the political fence, the *Blues Brothers* fanzine is a clear indication of the right-wing sympathies that bind Rangers to stablemates, Linfield and Chelsea. In several issues of *Follow, Follow*, the links between some Chelsea fans and Rangers were discussed at length, and generally condemned. At Chelsea itself, the club was split between a strong minority of right-wing racist fans, who sought close links with Rangers fans, and others of a more liberal disposition, who founded the Chelsea Independent Supporters Association. Dingwall's rejection of the Chelsea advances was practicable: the morons were trying to infiltrate Rangers so that they could run amok in Europe under this cover.

OF SCHOLARS AND COMEDIANS

If the growth of the fanzines is a recent development in writing about sport, so too is the intrusion of academics. When *The Old Firm* came out in 1984 the number of consciously serious works on Scottish football could be counted on the fingers of two hands; now you almost need a computer to keep up with them. Among these, the Old Firm has come under some discussion, in particular from the sociologist Bert Moorhouse and the psychologist Gerry Finn, both of whom have poured scorn on my history, albeit from different perspectives: Finn is obsessed with what he sees as the sectarianism that oozes out of every pore of the Scottish body politic and has denounced me for failing to point this out; Moorhouse believes that sectarianism exists only in journalists' headlines and my fevered imagination. Alas, that truth does not lie halfway between extremes!

Moorhouse is so convinced that sectarianism in Scotland is non-existent that he would like to see a moratorium on the use of the term: he is right, of course, that this and other emotive words have been overused or misused, that there are too many glib references to 'wars' and 'bloodbaths', although he does not always distinguish between what the writer is saying and what he is reporting other people as having said. Moorhouse goes on to dismiss all suggestions that Scotland has ever had a population in which Catholic and Protestant differences have played a significant role. Like Margaret Thatcher and her claim that there is no such thing as 'society', that everyone is out for himself or herself and that is the way it should be, Moorhouse would have us believe that there is no such thing as 'community'. Despite holding such beliefs he seems to believe that he is the only person who has ever said anything sensible on the subject. Nevertheless, Moorhouse has written several excellent articles on Scottish football, and even when he discusses the Old Firm he makes many shrewd points, often in an arresting way. He has a tremendous capacity to gather material from all the scraps of the contemporary scene and present them imaginatively – including long extracts from the script of TV interviews complete with the interviewee's stuttering and repetition, even if this has little to do with his argument. But in the final analysis it is hard to take seriously someone who seems to think that the history of Rangers and Celtic, covering a century and more, should be written in terms of 'wine bars, mortgages, bureaucracy, contractual ties, office blocks, isolation, drugs and tourism'.[20] Until recently, these contemporary concerns would not have meant a thing to most Celtic and Rangers fans.

In complete opposition to Moorhouse, Finn denounces all those who do not agree that Scotland is saturated in sectarianism. In his relentless search for all that points to Catholics having suffered terribly at the hands of Scottish society, he tends to fall himself into the paranoia more apparent in less rational critics. In his work outside the Old Firm, Finn has no doubt made significant contributions to scholarship, but in his specific attempt to denigrate my work on the Old Firm he resorts to distortion and misrepresentation that many fanzines would be too ashamed to publish.[21]

Another academic sympathetic to Celtic who has devoted a large part of his work to the Old Firm is Joseph Bradley. In his book *Ethnic and Religious Identity in Modern Scotland: Culture, Politics and Football*,[22] Bradley justifiably points to the sloppy use of the term 'sectarian', and he performs a useful service in showing by assiduous research using questionnaires the responses of interesting cross-sections of the population regarding Protestant and Catholic identity in Scotland. In his analysis of the material, however, Bradley reveals touches of the persecution complex more readily associated with Parkhead. He shows that Celtic supporters are overwhelmingly Catholic, at 93 per cent a much higher figure than I would have thought is the case. He also shows that they identify more readily with Irish symbols and (Catholic) Irish causes. This is fair enough. What Bradley, in his condemnation of Protestant Scotland, fails to appreciate, however, is that while a few Scots might get irritated by this allegiance to foreign symbols, the vast majority might find no interest in them at all. It is one thing to be anti-Irish or anti-Catholic, another to find it all irrelevant – there is, after all, little reason why any Scot should get excited about Padraig Pearse, the harp, the shamrock or St Patrick. And in his anxiety to brand Protestant Scotland with anti-Irish racism, Bradley has at times allowed his wishes to override his scholarly rigour.[23]

The entry of academics into the world of the Old Firm has probably done little harm, and certainly it is good that the world of academe should at last be taking seriously such a superficially trivial subject as football. Academics often seem to make much of little, unlike the great comedians who make profound observations under the guise of humour. However that may be, one of the more hopeful signs that Old Firm antagonisms are not as bad as they once were can be seen in the way in which the subject is now more openly treated in the media, often as a source of humour. It is only in the last decade or so that this has changed.

Rikki Fulton was breaking new ground when he lampooned Rangers' sectarianism in his television show in 1979, and in 1984, Scottish Television took a risk when it allowed Robbie Coltrane as 'Mason Boyne' to poke some wicked fun at the followers of William. In the beginning

Naked Radio had no football content, but after a few years this changed, when Celtic fan Tony Roper and Rangers fan Jonathan Watson showed that the Old Firm was far from being an untouchable source of humour. From 1986 they broke away to perform their best-selling annual tapes, *Only an Excuse*. Their appeal was based on that of the phone-ins and the fanzines. Others have followed where they led.

The Old Firm have even appeared in cartoon strips. 'Mick' and 'Billy' were introduced to *Evening Times* readers on 29 September 1995 by two friends who transferred to comic form their real life attachment to Celtic (Mick Foy) and Rangers (Billy Riddell). One of Scotland's great cartoonists, Malky McCormick, did not spare the Old Firm, even in the pre-Souness days, but it was an exception back in the immediate post-war years when the *Sunday Post*, in celebration of the return of peace, made so bold as to include a reference to the Old Firm in *The Broons*, when the Bairn held up a placard on which is written 'Up the Rangers!' but was careful to add at the same time, 'Up the Celtic!'.[24] (During the war, in an 'Oor Willie' strip about Halloween in November 1940, one of the guisers playing Lord Haw-Haw, sneering about how Britain was falling apart, referred to the 'civil war between two tribes, the Celtic and the Rangers.'[25] The fighting in Europe did nothing to quiet passions at home at this time, and Rangers and Celtic were involved in several nasty incidents; a year later 'Rex' of the *Sunday Mail* departed from his more usually rose-tinted reporting to condemn the management of the two clubs for the 'religious heat' they encouraged to bring crowds to their games.)

Various entertainers have acknowledged their allegiance to one or other club, but generally have not brought this into their public performances. Lex McLean and Glen Daly played before their own, but the more international Andy Stewart generally kept his Rangers sympathies off-stage, the odd song notwithstanding. Andy Cameron, however, has openly used his support for Rangers as part of his comedy routine, always, however, in a non-sectarian way, while off the stage he was one of the few prominent Rangers supporters to oppose the club's stance on religion before 1986. His tongue-in-cheek dream is of an Ibrox heaven in which Rangers beat Celtic 8–0 each week, with the occasional mid-week game where they win 9–0. Rod Stewart's support for Celtic has seen him make the odd transatlantic flight to see them play, while among the other superstars, Sean Connery has angered some Celtic fans by appearing to transfer his allegiance to the directors' box at Ibrox, a presence not at all appreciated by the Rangers diehards. Broxburn-born Michael Caton-Jones has made a name for himself on the other end of the camera, establishing himself as one of the world's top film directors, most recently with *The Jackal*; a hyperactive brain and an overactive social life stood in the way of his football career, but success in Hollywood and the millions that came with it have not taken him away from his socialist leanings and Celtic obsession.[26] Rangers and Celtic have occasionally featured on the small screen, from *Taggart* to *Psychos* and *Life Support*, as well as a rollicking farce called *The Young Person's Guide to Becoming a Rock Star*, which includes a hilarious stereotype of the Celtic fan and the Rangers fan. In most of these television productions it is Celtic who usually come over with a more sympathetic portrayal. The fact that the two clubs are now appearing in media where before they were regarded as too controversial to even mention is surely a sign of progress. It was only later in his career that Billy Connolly introduced jokes about Celtic and Rangers, and while he openly admitted his love for Celtic at the time of the club's centenary, and helped them open the new stand in 1996, football has not been an important part of his repertoire.

Other pop stars have declared their allegiances to one or other club, such as Wet Wet Wet to Rangers, Simple Minds to Celtic, but only Celtic can boast of a star from the other end of the musical scale who has worn his heart on one of his scores. James MacMillan was still in his thirties when he achieved fame as a composer, one of his concertos achieving the unlikely feat for a modern work of being played more than 30 times around the world in the 1995–96 concert season alone. Said to be a 'passionate and life-long adherent of socialism, Catholicism, Scotland and Glasgow's Celtic football team',[27] MacMillan was so furious after another fiercely fought failure by his team that he was inspired to compose a piece called 'The Berserking'. Put to words by Billy Connolly, or better still if Tom Leonard was to give it lyrics along the lines of his splendid voice poems, this would surely offer a welcome replacement for 'The Fields of Athenry'. In fact MacMillan was about to make his debut performance on the Old Firm, when he spoke before an audience at the Edinburgh Festival in August 1999 and waxed vehemently about the vexations of being a Catholic in Scotland. It was a speech that owed little to the genius of the composer and lots to the war cries of the old Jungle at Parkhead. On the other hand, in what could be seen as a change in the wind as regards religious passions, an old warrior against the evils of the false doctrines of Rome seems to have passed into obscurity. This is Pastor Jack Glass, leader of the Church of the Twentieth-Century Reformation, whose fire-and-brimstone denunciations of those who paid no heed to his version of the Truth once commanded widespread media attention. From being relegated to occasional appearances on late-night television he seems to have been completely shut out by the more strident voices of those who used to be his main targets.

The role of Celtic and Rangers at the end of the twentieth-century had changed dramatically since that at the beginning. Or rather society had changed. The two clubs still stood as champions of their respective communities, but the days of 'cultural apartheid' were long gone, replaced by the ideal of a multicultural society in which Catholics and Protestants not only had to get on with each other but also had to live in harmony with people from other ethnic groups and religions. On the pitch the two clubs barely fielded any native-born Scots and as such could have claimed to be living up to the new ideal, but despite the array of ethnic differences in the men wearing the colours of the two teams, the tensions of the old rivalry remain. The greatest challenge for the Old Firm's multicultural future was to treat their traditions, shorn of their ancient hatreds, as an acceptance of difference rather than a challenge to battle.

10. The Old Firm at Century's End

In the early 1980s players of Afro-Caribbean background were coming into prominence in the English leagues, although exotic imports like the Argentines Osvaldo Ardiles and Ricardo Villa, who had played with Tottenham Hotspur since 1978 and starred in the memorable FA Cup final replay of 1981, were rare birds. There had been black players in English football since early in the century, from Walter Daniel Tull who played for Northampton Town in the years before the First World War (in which he lost his life) to Jack Leslie of Plymouth Argyle between the wars and Lindy Delaphena of Middlesbrough after the Second World War. A few blacks appeared in the 1960s, but it was only in the late 1970s that the sons of the West Indian immigration from the post-war period began to make their impression on English football: in 1978 Viv Anderson became the first black to play for England and in that same year Laurie Cunningham went from Nottingham Forest to Real Madrid for £800,000. By the early 1990s black players, although comprising only 1.5 per cent of the population, made up 12 per cent of the players in the top English League, and the proportion keeps getting bigger. By then such famous names as Jamaican-born John Barnes and up and coming Ian Wright, among a host of others, had been joined by blacks from African countries as well as Afro-Caribbeans.

In Scotland there had always been a few foreigners to grace the game, in the case of Rangers mainly South Africans, Scandinavians and Ulstermen, and in the case of Celtic mainly Irish, from both sides of the border. But they were seldom English and rarely black, although Gil Heron for Celtic and Mohammed Latif for Rangers made brief appearances. Rangers signed another black player earlier in the century, but he was killed before he could play for them. This was Walter Tull, mentioned above, who arrived in Scotland to undertake an officer-training course at Gailes, near Irvine in Ayrshire. His brother, living in Glasgow and Britain's first black dentist, persuaded him to sign for Rangers, but he was called to the front before he could play for them and was killed in the last stages of the war, leading his men into battle.[1] With the arrival of Souness, Scotland, better known for exporting star players than importing them, began to reverse the flow. Today players of all colours and nationalities are to be seen in all major English and Scottish teams. This acceptance of players beyond a narrow national base is a reflection of the multiculturalism that has been one of the more positive aspects of the globalisation of culture in this era. Today foreigners, if not in a majority, are often the best players in the top teams in England and Scotland.

Multiculturalism is the acceptance of people of various ethnic backgrounds into the host culture, a celebration of difference and diversity. From the beginning of this century Scotland has had its Italian ice-cream sellers, and for many a visit to the 'Tallies' was a highlight of the weekend walk; Chinese restaurants have been with us almost as long, although it is only more recently that they have become, along with Indian food, as local as fish and chips; and Glasgow's Italian community has come a long way from the tricycles in the park selling ices on a Sunday to regular cafés – now they provide some of the best Italian food in Europe. Lithuanians, Poles and other central Europeans have settled into the population, and like the Italians, their religion is no problem. In Scotland Jews have not had to suffer the overt anti-Semitism that has been their lot in too many other countries. Coming from a wide range of backgrounds, with strong communities in the Gorbals and Garnethill, Glasgow's Jewry, according to Kenneth E. Collins, participated in a 'wider society which it found, on the whole, to be tolerant and welcoming'.[2] The worst trouble the Jews found was from the missionaries of the Church of Scotland and the Roman Catholic Church, who 'poisoned Jewish-Christian relations for many years'.[3]

That the Jewish population of Scotland was never more than 15,000 can account in some measure for the absence of widespread anti-Semitism. This has perhaps also been the case with regard to racism against the small numbers of Scots of Afro-Caribbean or Asian background. There has been prejudice, and there has been violence against Scots from such backgrounds, such as in the cowardly attack on young Stephen Roberts, a black player who scored the winning goal in a penalty shoot-out for Campsie Black Watch in the Golden Goals Under-21 Cup final in June 1997, but historically Scotland's ethnic animosities have been directed mainly against Scots of Irish-Catholic origin. Even the English, Scotland's largest immigrant group, have had little to fear so long as they kept their accents under control.

SECTARIANISM AT THE END OF THE CENTURY

Depending on your sources, the prejudice against Scots of Irish-Catholic origins is a living scar, a figment of paranoiac imagination, or a relic of Scotland's past. For some it is a 90-minute prejudice, alive and screaming for the duration of an Old Firm game, forgotten as soon as it is over as Rangers and Celtic fans share a few pints while they discuss the finer points of the game and then return to work happily alongside each other on the Monday. Even those who have never seen Rangers and Celtic fans share a pint after a game (just about everybody) would claim that serious prejudice ceased somewhere in the 1960s. But there are others, mainly Catholics who have been the victims of prejudice, who believe that prejudice has never ceased to exist and that it has manifested itself in venues other than football: and for those involved in football, for much longer than the 90 minutes of a game.

Two of the foremost scholars on the subject, Steve Bruce and Tom Gallagher, emphasise the decline in sectarianism, but Callum Brown believes that their opinions are rather optimistic. Brown agrees that there has been a decline in the importance of religion in political parties, and that the influence of the old sectarian institutions has lessened, while religiously oriented street gangs have all but disappeared, but he believes that this is to 'underestimate the vibrancy of the popular culture of bigotry'. Prosperity and better education have made the overt expression of bigotry less acceptable, but it reappears in other forms, and is still 'a factor in the day-to-day life of working-class Scots'. Some might wonder whether the bigotry of the working classes is merely more visible than that of the 'hooligans in high places', but it seems, at least on the part of the Protestants, to have lost any serious religious content. Brown's final comment on the issue is to point out that when the Rev. Ian Paisley led some demonstrators in the early 1980s to protest against the admission of 'the Pope – the Protestants' anti-Christ – to the palace of world Presbyterianism in Edinburgh', only one hundred turned up.[4]

Whatever the reality of the situation, sectarianism in Scotland is still a live issue. Whether or not it is a real one or a media beat-up is another matter. Before the 1980s serious discussion of the Old Firm rivalry on radio or television was either scarce, produced by a foreign film company or dutifully careful in its analysis to tot up an evenly balanced number of opinions for and against each side. Failure to do so could evoke pique in the strangest of ways: Archie Macpherson, the television commentator, was once threatened by a Celtic director with dire consequences if he did not do something about his bias, revealed by his more frequent references to Rangers players by their first name than to those of Celtic.[5]

Foreign coverage of the Old Firm rivalry was often merely sensational, as in the *Stern* article of 1981 with its graphic photographs of Old Firm extremism and the claim that the sectarian fighting at these games had resulted in the biggest number of deaths and injuries at European football matches. A home-based film on the subject, shown on Channel Four on

12 November 1995, was more in line with *Stern* than some of the more balanced attempts at discussing the issues on radio and television. *Football, Faith and Flutes* was produced by the Glasgow-based media company Wark Clements, but it is hard not to question the west of Scotland credentials of the producer when he claims that his film about bigotry and football was the 'big untold story about Scotland'. Moreover, in his diary of the events covering the making of the film,[6] Alan Clements seemed to have been more concerned about sensation rather than analysis: he expresses his delight at turning up groups or individuals who would say what he wanted them to say, and thanks Fergus McCann for refusing to enter the discussion programmed to follow the screening, because of the publicity this was sure to provoke. On the other hand, the abuse Clements suffered, including the vandalising of his car, showed that the subject matter had touched a raw nerve.

McCann's initial willingness to participate while Rangers would have nothing to do with it has a familiar ring going back to the days when Ibrox was a Catholic-free zone. It was to be regretted that Murray and McCann did not appear together or make more joint comments when it came to the issue of sectarianism, but this particular programme was perhaps not the place to start. Since the coming of Souness and the signing of Johnston, Rangers had no reason to feel so embarrassed about making public statements in this regard, a task left in the pre-Souness days to the hapless Rev. James Currie, who did his best to deny the obvious. McCann's appraisal of the programme in a statement to the press branded it as 'a gross caricature of the extremist attitudes of two unfortunate individuals and others in a drunken state . . . a manipulated example of tabloid television which responsible people should deplore'. This may well have been a fair judgement of the film, although it might better have been made in the post-viewing discussion; or at least, since Murray had refused from the start to take part, through a representative of Celtic – and preferably one from Rangers.

'Unfortunate' is perhaps a reasonable enough description of the two main football fans referred to, although, as in the rest of the film, the Catholics come over as more civilised than their Protestant counterparts. Sam the Rangers fanatic reveals the UVF initials tattooed on the inside of his lower lip and expresses his hatred of all Fenians. He describes his despair as he wakes up each day in his home in Parkhead and sees Celtic Park, which he claims is a 'breeding ground for Republicanism, Catholicism, Sinn Fein, the IRA and everything I oppose'. Rather than find a house where he won't meet this eyesore on a daily basis, he expresses his hope that one day the stand at Celtic Park would collapse and bury all who were under it. Paddy, Sam's reverse image – at least so

far as the totems are concerned, for he was less rabid in his bigotry –
claims that as a Catholic he had to hate Protestants, and that as a Celtic
supporter he had to hate Rangers. In another segment of the programme,
which includes the respectable side of Orangeism with its members at
prayer before a parade, there are also scenes of some suitably decked out
Orange women singing (to the tune of the 1970s pop song, 'Chirpy,
chirpy, cheep, cheep') such choice ditties as:

> *Last night I saw my daddy makin' a bomb . . .*
> *. . . woke up this mornin' and the chapel was gone . . .*

– and in reference to the 1981 hunger strike, 'Could You Go a Chicken
Supper, Bobby Sands'. (Since much of the footage was out of date, both
clubs having denied Clements access to their grounds, it would have
been little surprise to hear the Celtic fans singing, to the tune of 'The
Farmer Wants a Wife', 'Fagin Shagged the Queen'.) In the film, Catholics
are seen visiting the Carfin grotto, and a father preparing his wee boy for
the Volunteer Billy Reid Republican Flute Band piously tells the cameras
that while he wanted the British removed from Ireland he did not want
to be associated with the 'football hooligans who sing Irish rebel songs at
matches'.

From a footballing point of view there is better insight into the thinking
of fans at Old Firm games in Stephen Walsh's *Voices of the Old Firm*. This
was made into a very good radio programme narrated by David Francey
and presented on Radio Five on 25 and 26 December 1995. Here a whole
range of Celtic and Rangers supporters freely expressed themselves on what
it was like to be a fan of the Glasgow giants over the last four decades: the
bigotry is there and the hatred, and even the downright callous or inane,
but so too is the humour and the simple devotion and the day-to-day cares
of a section of society that has an obsession with football.

Every society has its pathological criminals, and in Scotland this can
occasionally be given a sectarian label. On 7 October 1995, a young man
returning from a Celtic–Partick Thistle game at Parkhead was murdered
in an unprovoked attack near Bridgeton Cross. Mark Scott was wearing
a Celtic jersey under his sweater and had to undergo a barrage of abuse
along with his two friends as they passed a group of youths outside a pub
and betting shop. Uneasy, they walked on, when suddenly one of the
youths, well known for his hatred of Catholics, and whose father and
uncle were in gaol for serious crimes associated with the UVF, came up
from behind and slit the 16-year-old's throat. Despite the defence of
Donald Findlay, the evidence against the unrepentant Jason Campbell
was overwhelming, much of it from witnesses who had looked on in

horror as the crime was committed. Young Mark Scott's funeral was attended by Celtic manager Tommy Burns, chief scout David Hay and several Celtic players. In the meantime Rangers and Celtic scarves carefully entwined and left as a gesture of reconciliation near the scene of the crime were disentangled, while floral tributes in memory of the young victim were scattered by vandals who used them as footballs.[7]

As Campbell's trial came to an end in mid-March 1996 another young Celtic fan was brutally murdered, this time a 15-year-old boy who had signed 'S' forms with Celtic, and having starred for Scotland Under-15s when they had beaten Belgium the previous week, had had hopes of making the big time. Lawrence Haggart was beaten to death in his own home, but suggestions of sectarianism or hatred of Celtic in the way the killers had burned the feet of a young lad with a bright football future proved to be groundless.

Neither of these two acts had anything to do with Rangers or Celtic or football or even religion, and when in October 1997 Henry McLeish, the Scottish home affairs minister, appeared to bestow political status on Campbell's crime by having him transferred to the Maze prison near Belfast, where he would have had an easier time among criminals of the same political persuasion – and released with the amnesty granted with the Good Friday Agreement of 1998 – the shocked response of the Scottish public forced Donald Dewar, the Scottish Secretary, to intervene and reverse the decision. The crimes committed against Mark Scott and Lawrence Haggart were the acts of depraved individuals beyond the ken of any civilised society. But they should give pause to those who boast of their sectarian hatred and make it felt in the worst of their songs and chants. And in that mad month of March 1996, just a few days after the Dunblane massacre, and on the same day as Lawrence Haggart died, Celtic and Rangers fans battled in the streets of Thornliebank, while a Rangers footballer was involved in the infamous 'Five Bellies brawl' inside a pub in Renfrewshire.

Scotland has been spared the Ulster violence, and some would claim that the concentration of Ireland's sectarian hatreds around a football match in Glasgow has served as a safety-valve in this regard. However that may be, the Ulster violence has been restricted to the arrest of the occasional gun-runner from Scotland, although in December 1995, one Ulsterman and two Scots were convicted of being part of a terror ring supplying guns to the Ulster Volunteer Force: photos of the convicted men showed them defiantly trumpeting their contempt for the verdict. And every now and then you would hear the story of an Ulster terrorist in Glasgow, where he would attend a match at Ibrox.

There had been a time when IRA and UVF supporters used Celtic

Park or Ibrox as cover for their illegal activities, but that is well in the past
and this never had the support of either club. In colour photos for
weekend magazine supplements or television interviews or trials,
spokesmen for the IRA or the UVF have often been happy to be seen
wearing the colours of Celtic or Rangers, and through to the present day,
demonstrators for either cause in Glasgow, Belfast or Derry proclaim
their allegiance by wearing Rangers or Celtic tops. It is in Ulster, too, that
the most extreme reactions to the internal affairs of Parkhead and Ibrox
have been voiced. Scotland, however, has been spared the bombings that
have scarred the lives of too many people in certain parts of England. The
London government is the main target for the IRA terrorists, even if
hundreds of innocent individuals in England have had their lives ruined
by the bombs and bomb threats; to bring a bombing campaign to Scotland would only further convince the vast majority of Scots, Catholics
and Protestants alike, that they want none of Northern Ireland's violence
transported to Scottish soil.

THE MONKLANDS MAFIA

The issue of sectarianism with regard to Protestants and Catholics in
Scotland keeps popping up in the strangest of places, as in the minor
furore that arose when a bursary fund that had been operating since 1868
came under fire in April 1996 because its long dead benefactor, the
thread-maker, John Clark, had stipulated that no Catholics should be
allowed to apply for it. More ecumenical in his exclusiveness, Clark also
banned Moslems, Buddhists and atheists from his bursary. There were
calls for the 'bursary for bigotry', advertised at Strathclyde and Glasgow
universities, to be banned. And the Orange Order can always be relied
upon to make what they see as a principled stand on behalf of those they
have chosen to defend. One such case was in January 1996 when a
Catholic bishop had to cancel a visit to the Harthill Primary School to
speak to the dozen or so Catholic children who were about to take
confirmation and their first communion. Objections were raised,
including one promise that if Bishop Devine did turn up there would be
a flute band to meet him. As the *Sunday Mail* reported it, '12 little kids
had to trek through snow to meet their bishop' instead.[8]

Before the Findlay and MacMillan controversies of 1999, the
Monklands East by-election of June 1994 raised the greatest outburst of
sectarian breast-beating outside football. This by-election, called
following the death of the leader of the Labour Party, John Smith, on 12
May 1994, brought to light grievances that had been simmering beneath
the surface of local politics for years about bias in the way the Labour-

controlled Monklands District Council had run its affairs – above all that Catholic Labour councillors had favoured family and fellow Catholics. In a report issued shortly after the poll, Robert Black, professor of Scots Law at Edinburgh University, came to no fixed conclusion, but presented a litany of the complaints that had been made and in so doing allowed those who wanted to prejudge the issues to regard them as truth. His report was in turn criticised in a fuller investigation by William Nimmo Smith QC, who cleared the Monklands councillors of nepotism and religious bias, charges more than just a little redolent of religion on the eve of the Reformation, and apparently not altogether out of place in 1990s Airdrie and Coatbridge.

The Monklands East seat covered the two adjacent towns of Protestant-dominated Airdrie (whose football team has been accused of operating a no-Catholics policy) and Catholic-dominated Coatbridge (whose football team, Albion Rovers, despite a proud history and boasting Jock Stein among its playing talent, has almost passed out of the memory of Scottish football fans).[9] A faction within the Coatbridge Labour council was accused of discriminating against Airdrie, showing favouritism in regard to employment, job allocation and the issuing of licenses, all of which would have been branded as a masonic conspiracy except that the main actors were Catholics. The by-election campaign gave an opportunity for these resentments in the running of local government to come to the fore, and sectarianism was shown to be a reality in parts of Scottish society and in areas far removed from football. Resentment against the perceived bias of Catholic Labour councillors from Coatbridge, itself said to be a payback after previous discrimination by Protestant councillors from Airdrie, led to Protestant working-class voters preferring the Scottish National Party to Labour, whose candidate, Helen Liddell, came within 1,640 votes of losing what had been one of the safest Labour seats in Britain. Whatever the outcome of the official findings, at the core of discontent was the belief by many citizens of Airdrie that the Catholic-dominated Monklands District councillors discriminated against the people of Airdrie. It was more than another incident to add to the long-running saga of tales of suspected corruption in local government that can be found in all places and at all times since such democracy has been in existence, for in addition to the perennial accusations of jobs for the boys was that of religious preferment.

The Coatbridge councillors were castigated as the Monklands mafia, and in the by-election campaign a few of the more zealous workers on behalf of the two main parties played the sectarian card – albeit against the advice of the leaders, who knew better than to fish in such murky waters. Voters were made aware of the religious beliefs of Labour's Helen

Liddell, as it was pointed out that she was called Reilly before she was married and had gone to St Patrick's High, a Catholic school. On the other hand, some over-zealous Labour workers tried to spread the story that if the Scottish Nationalists won they would put an end to separate Catholic schools. One Conservative voter was threatened that if he voted for the SNP his 'vote against the Union' would be disclosed the next time he went to Ibrox to support Rangers. All of this was helped along by Tory imports from England anxious to distract attention from the sleaze activities that had become a permanent feature of their own party.

For those who liked to believe that sectarianism in Scotland was merely a matter of history, it was time to revise their opinions. Among these was the chief political editor of *The Scotsman*, Peter Jones. At the end of the campaign he wrote an article in which he criticised both George Galloway of the Labour Party and Alex Salmond of the Scottish National Party for the way in which they had reacted to the sectarian issue.[10] This they had done in *Flourish*, the monthly journal of the Roman Catholic Archdiocese of Glasgow, where Galloway blamed the SNP for bringing sectarianism into the campaign, while Salmond claimed that it was the conduct of the Labour councillors, and not their religion, that was the issue. The one was saying that sectarianism was an imported issue and was overturned by the result, the other that it did not exist at all.

Jones denounced both of these claims and appealed for a recognition that sectarianism did exist and had to be confronted. He claimed that the Monklands by-election was one of the first in which religion rather than social class, home ownership or age has decided people's voting preference: while 80 per cent of Catholics voted Labour, 65 per cent of Protestants voted SNP. For them, if not for the Black report and the Smith inquiry into the affair, religion was clearly an issue. For Jones, who once thought that 'real sectarianism in Scotland today had been locked away into the cul-de-sac of ceremonial marching bands and distasteful football songs', it was time for him and others like him to admit that they were wrong. Much of the old discrimination was gone, but much of it lingered on, and not only in Monklands.

THE CATHOLIC CHURCH AND THE SECULAR STATE

The Catholic Church no longer has the power it once had, either over its members or over society at large; even in Ireland it has lost much of its previous power to impose its religious morality on public policy. This has been in the face of resistance within the Church itself, which has never pretended other than that it has the right to a role in political as much as in moral matters, even in societies where the bulk of the population is non-Catholic and prefers that politics be secular and religion remain a private affair. The insistence of the Catholic Church, even in this secular age, on telling its members how to act on certain issues, has often been to the annoyance of Catholics themselves, and this even on issues with which they are in agreement with their Church. Despite this, Scots who hold such secular views have been denounced in some circles not only as being anti-Catholic, but as being anti-Irish and racist. Gerry Finn claims that people who hold such views are merely putting forward a recycled version of an earlier racism, while Joseph Bradley, another researcher unwilling to recognise the socially divisive policies of the Catholic Church, seems to have swallowed Finn's assertions.[11] Finn and Bradley are in the company of another academic, Willy Maley, who is also happy to add the tag of 'racist' to people whose objection to Catholicism has nothing to do with Catholics or the Irish, but much to do with the Church's interference in political and personal matters.

Abortion is a delicate subject, and Catholics have no monopoly on the outrage that it should be legalised, but it has generally been accepted that this is ultimately a matter for the woman and her doctor to decide. It is natural that the Catholic Church should make its opinion known on this matter, and should advise its members accordingly, it is another matter when it tries to impose this belief on non-Catholics or when it blackmails a political party into conforming with its religious beliefs on the issue. This was the case in July 1991, when an article in the journal of the then Archbishop (later Cardinal) Winning, threatened the Labour Party with a loss of Catholic votes if it went soft on the issue. In a banner headline, *Flourish* declared that, 'Abortion is a political test', and Archbishop Winning issued voters a 'challenge', the clear implication of which was that Catholics should reconsider voting for the Labour Party unless it came into line with the Church's policy on abortion.[12] We can expect a similar intrusion into private morality and the issue of suffering and terminal illness when the euthanasia debate comes to Britain.

The most sensitive issue for the Catholic Church today, as it has been since the time of mass literacy, is that all Catholics must be educated in Catholic schools: it was this that forced Mussolini to come to an agreement with the Church in 1929, and the only time the Vatican spoke out against the Nazis was in 1937 after they had ignored the provisions of the Concordat between the Church and Hitler that guaranteed the Catholic Church the right to independence in how young Catholics were being educated – and the only time a member of the Church used his office to thwart Nazi policy (as distinct from individual clerics and other Catholics who risked their lives in opposing the regime) was when Bishop Count Galen of Münster spoke out against the euthanasia programme. Since

1918 when the Labour Party won over the support of Catholics in Scotland with its support for the Conservative-dominated coalition government's introduction of fully funded Catholic education in Scotland, Scottish taxpayers have been helping to provide for the maintenance of a particular religion. This is an issue that has been sanctioned by time, and no party is seriously committed to changing it in its fundamentals. In recent years, however, as school numbers drop off and it has been necessary for some schools to merge, the opportunity to bring children of different religions together in the same classrooms has been strenuously resisted by the Catholic hierarchy (and minorities among the Protestants). This perennial source of conflict was brought to a head in a series of public debates in the middle of 1991 – and would erupt in even more fevered debate just over a decade later. (See Chapter 12)

It was at this time that the irrationality of the divided system was brought to the fore, as parents of either denomination refused to have their children mix with those of the other sort. Or even, as happened at a school in Glasgow's Easterhouse, Catholic and Protestant kids were taught under the same roof, but by different teachers acting under a separate administration. This situation arose when St Colette's RC school was destroyed by fire in 1986 and the pupils had to be accommodated in the non-denominational Commonhead school. The system actually seemed to work quite well, but at a time of cutbacks in education spending, the duplication of resources was something of an anomaly.[13]

The education of its young by its own priests is one of the most fiercely guarded demands of the Catholic Church. This is not for educational, but religious reasons. Cardinal Winning made this quite clear on many occasions, claiming that without Catholic schools he would lose Catholics to the faith. At the time of the problem discussed above, Winning declared openly:

> The Church would not be as strong as it is without Catholic schools . . . I know other denominations are envious of our schools and the great rapport we have with our kids. We would be foolish to throw away an asset like that.[14]

Catholic schools in Scotland are under no threat from any of the political parties: the only threat they are under is from a society that is increasingly free from bigotry and sees that one of the few ways in which bigoted attitudes grow is when children are brought up in ignorance of each other's way of life. Anyone who supports apartheid in education has little grounds for complaining of bigotry in society at large. This is neither an anti-Catholic nor a racist statement.

The recognition of freedom of conscience and opinion and the removal of religion to the private sphere are among the essential tenets of the modern democratic state. To hold to such beliefs is not to be anti-religious, and those who accuse critics of the Catholic Church's interference in secular affairs as bigots are really reflecting on themselves. Finn and Bradley's narrow views were taken up from a different angle by Willy Maley in a newspaper article entitled: 'Of saints, scholars and sectarians' that appeared in *The Herald* of 29 June 1991. Maley argues that 'reading between the lines' in regard to separate schools, 'integration' and 'secularisation' were an attempt to get rid of Catholic schools by a process of acculturation and assimilation. However, he then slews off on a non sequitur to declare that private schools are as 'divisive and exclusive as Catholic education'. This is certainly true, but the education of the rich and the privileged is not directly subsidised by the taxpayer. Maley's most controversial claim, however, is that 'anti-Irish racism and anti-Catholicism are inseparable in a Scottish context', a statement as unacceptable as his related one that the Catholic Church and socialist republicanism are not mutually exclusive: the socialism of the Catholic Church is that of Rerum Novarum, proclaimed in 1891 and practised by Mussolini a few decades later, while the socialism of James Connolly was damned by the Church along with that of all other political socialists, Catholic or otherwise, who dared to suggest that the fate of the people should be in their own hands.

There are no doubt Scottish Protestants who fit Maley's accusation, and no doubt he could find many of his examples at Ibrox or even in the columns of the broadsheet press, especially when the Wee Free writer John Macleod appears in the middle pages with a mind that is still locked somewhere in Scotland's medieval past. Much of what Macleod has to say was true once upon a time, and some of it is true today, but for him the Catholic Church remains, Vatican II notwithstanding, the same as that which happily sent heretics to be burned at the stake. Like Sam and Paddy in *Football, Faith and Flutes*, Maley and Macleod speak from oddly similar viewpoints.

CATHOLICS, PROTESTANTS AND PATRIOTS

Maley, who seems unwilling to distinguish between integration and assimilation, or at least chooses to overlook them in the Scottish situation, takes a swipe at Graham Walker for daring to suggest that 'Scotland is a Protestant country'. He makes the assumption that this statement leaves no room for those who are not Protestant. Here we have one of the ironies of multiculturalism, when the host country is turned on by those it had hoped to integrate and finds itself forced to justify itself before the more recent immigrants: Christians defending Christmas and Easter against Muslims; Protestants in Scotland having to apologise for having been there for a few hundred years and feeling that somehow the country of their forebears has something to do with them. Even the supporters of Glasgow Rangers, no blushing violets in defending their own position, have been assailed to such an extent that they now exhibit on occasion a paranoia more usually associated with their rivals on the other side of the city.

Scotland is many things. It is Protestant, but far from exclusively so. There was a time when this was a defining or a dominant characteristic: a Scotland where in his pre-teen years the young male went to Sunday School and the Life Boys, then when he was older to the Boys' Brigade followed by church service. At school he learned of the good work of missionaries like David Livingstone, the inventions of a host of people who can be found on tea-towels anywhere in the Scottish tourist market, the novels of Scott and the poems of Burns. At home he would be taught the virtues of hard work and the lessons of the Bible, all translated into simple language in the couthie columns of the *Sunday Post*. (Women, of course, did what they were told.)

Little of this has much attraction for Catholics whose heart is in Ireland, and even those whose heart was in Scotland would have been offended by Oor Wullie's comment in the middle of the Second World War[15] when he listed first among the great Scots, 'Bruce and Wallace and the Rangers . . .' (it is always overlooked that Bruce and Wallace were Catholics). Even the message of Burns, one of whose closest friends, William Maxwell, was a Catholic, has more in common with two great enemies of the Catholic Church: socialism and Freemasonry. But the Catholic of the 1990s is as different from the Catholic of the pre-Vatican II days as the hardline Protestant is of the pre-Souness days at Ibrox. As Bradley rightly says, there are many layers of Irish identity; what he seems less willing to recognise is that there are also many layers of Scottish identity.

The portrait of the Protestant in works of literature has often been that of the bigot or the narrow killjoy: the Orangeman in Hector McMillan's *The Sash*; the despair of the central character in Gordon Williams' sympathetic novel *From Scenes Like These*, and the narrow honesty of the innocent in the short stories of Alan Spence, brought together in his book, *Its Colours They Are Fine*. In his most brlliant work, however, *The Magic Flute*, he presents an intricately nuanced treatment of Protestantism with his four principal characters. The world of the Protestant work ethic is presented in dark hues in the works of A.J. Cronin, more sympathetically in works like George Blake's *The*

Shipbuilders, or the film loosely based on it that came out in 1949, *Floodtide*. These are the people who made Scotland into a country whose contribution to the developed world was immense. It was the Protestant Scots, educated in the religion of the Book, whose restless energies took them to the far-flung corners of the globe: engineers, clerks and tradesmen in the service of the industrial revolution, missionaries, civil servants and educators in the spread of the Empire, whose most lasting and perhaps greatest memorial is in the game they took with them (along with some Englishmen and others) to play in their leisure time – the contribution of Scots, both Catholic and Protestant, in the spread of association football is echoed in the names of teams and competitions and the foundation members of associations established throughout the world in the years up to and beyond the First World War.

By the 1960s the success of Scotland's Catholic football club was paralleled by the success of Scottish Catholics throughout the business and professional world, and this, along with the greater loyalty retained by Catholics to their religion, challenged the certainties of Scots who still believed in a Protestant ascendancy. For those who felt marginalised, comfort could be found in Rangers Football Club, or the control of local councils such as that of Airdrie. Since Souness, Protestant pride has been regained, although in the new-look Rangers there is less emphasis on the old Protestantism, and even less on the Scottishness that Rangers once boasted in opposition to the Irishness of their Catholic rivals.

It is one of the ironies of Scottish identity that its two biggest football teams are its least Scottish: Rangers with their British rather than Scottish identity, their red, white and blue of the Union Jack, the Queen and the National Anthem; Celtic with their green and white of Ireland, the Pope and the Republic. In contrast to countries like Belgium, Italy and Greece (but not Spain) where the immense differences between regions and communities are overlooked when the nation is represented in the colours of the national football team, support for the Scotland team has never been complete. Many Celtic fans have always been more likely to support club before country, now they have been joined by many Rangers fans. In the new Europe with its emphasis on regions rather than nation states, this has been emphasised, with the club taking pride of place over national identity. When Gascoigne scored that fantastic goal that sank Scotland's chances in the match against the Auld Enemy at Wembley in Euro 96 there were sporadic fights throughout Scotland as Rangers fans celebrating the goal angered other Scots fans – and even other Rangers supporters. Many Celtic fans, with no Republic of Ireland to support, supported no one.

There was a time, in the 1960s in particular, when what later became known as the Tartan Army was made up mainly of Rangers supporters, some of whom, unfortunately, could not stomach the sight of a Celtic favourite in a Scotland jersey. The disgust felt by these players at being abused by their own supporters is understandable, as is that of the Celtic supporters who witnessed it. Now the Scotland team of recent years is routinely dismissed as a Jacobite XI by the Rangers fanzines. The prominent Celtic supporter and later a writer for the *Celtic View*, Matt McGlone, spoke for many Celtic fans when he admitted to losing his last remnant of support for the Scotland team when he heard the Scottish crowd baying for Sandy Jardine to come on in place of David Hay during a Scotland international match, and Bobby Brown, the Scotland manager, caved in to the crowd.[16] Twenty years on and a Tartan Army less dominated by Rangers fans and Scotland was still not a top priority in the minds of many Celtic people.[17] Michael Kelly tells of the reaction of Celtic supporters, at an away match in Kirkcaldy, to the announcement that the Scotland rugby team had lost by a single point in the last minute of a Calcutta Cup match: to his disgust they immediately started jeering and taunting the Raith Rovers supporters.[18] On the other hand, in 1994 Scotland played Holland as part of the Dutch team's preparation for the World Cup in the USA, and this coincided with a visit of the Celtic Boys Club to the Netherlands for a youth tournament. The youngsters went along to cheer on the Scotland team, but were subjected to such a torrent of abuse from some Scottish supporters that they had to be removed by the Dutch officials and placed among the home supporters for their own safety.[19] None of this has been helped by the owners of the two big clubs, who, while they claim to be acting in the best interests of Scottish football, and not just the shareholders in their club and its followers, often give a good impression of wanting to have nothing to do with the game in Scotland.

In such circumstances it is easy to see how Rangers and Celtic can be scorned by other Scots, and while patriotism may be dismissed as the last refuge of the scoundrel, the rejection of one's 'native land' can just as often reveal a soul dead to more than just a field or forest. While Rangers and Celtic play within the Scottish system with only a secondary loyalty to Scotland, even more so as they rely on foreign imports at the expense of bringing on young local talent, they cannot expect to win over the support of agnostic Scots when they play abroad. It would be heartening if this were to be the case, and now that they have shed their religious baggage Celtic and Rangers should be able to enter Europe as ambassadors for the country as a whole. Neither the Unionism of Rangers nor the Irish associations of Celtic are necessarily antithetical to a Scottish identity – and above all in this age of multiculturalism. A Rangers fan who is British first and Scottish second is not in breach of loyalty to his own country, and there is no reason why Celtic supporters can't appreciate Irish culture, sing Irish songs and visit Ireland as a preferred place for holidays. This is the situation for many Catholics in Scotland and the 'Bhoys against Bigotry' campaign celebrates this. Scotland and Ireland have common Celtic roots and if it wasn't for religion would have very little to divide them – certainly not racism.

FAIR PLAY FOR JOCK TAMSON'S BAIRNS

The problem of new immigrants and their children holding onto their old ways and adapting to the new is one that has faced untold numbers of people in dozens of countries around the world. In Britain, football circles have come under criticism for the absence of players from an Asian background. The FA ran a conference at Oldham in October 1996 on the theme 'Asians in Football', concerned about the absence of Asians in the major English leagues despite there being Asian leagues and Asian teams in the country. The assumption was that it was prejudice against the Asians that had kept them out, under the excuse that gave the title to two Asian researchers' project: 'Asians Can't Play Football'. Much of this has echoes of the accusations of prejudice by Catholics of a few decades ago; but not all the blame rests with the host community.

Moves have been made to welcome Asians into the Scottish game, above all by Celtic, in line with their 'Bhoys against Bigotry' campaign, and *Scotland on Sunday*, engaged in active campaigns to integrate Asians through football. Even before they launched the campaign, Celtic worked closely with the recently appointed City of Glasgow's Ethnic Minorities Officer, Kash Taank, during the 1995–96 season. They helped him set up coaching sessions involving the club's players and invited groups to visit Celtic Park for discussions and as guests at some games. Celtic was the only high-profile club to become actively involved with the Scottish Asian Sports Association, and fully supported the plans to set up the Asian Soccer Academy in Glasgow, the first of its kind in the UK.

Scotland on Sunday began its campaign of 'Fair play for Asians' in its issue of 24 November 1996, and thereafter Jonathon Northcroft wrote regular articles trying to improve the opportunity for Asians to 'take part in football from the top level down'. Northcroft claimed that Celtic was the only high-profile club with initiatives targeting Asians, although he also pointed out that the only Asian playing in the Scottish League at that time was Rangers' Jaswinder ('Jazz') Juttla. He also noted that when the 'Let's Kick Racism out of Sport' campaign was opened in 1993, the Scottish League and the SFA thought that this had nothing to do with them.

Luckily not all of the clubs in the Premier League agreed, although not all of them entered the spirit of the campaign. Rangers struck the strongest possible blow against racism when Souness signed Mark Walters, but since then foul monkey chants have again filled the stadium, directed for example at Celtic's Regi Blinker, especially whenever he lined up to take a corner near the Copland Stand in his first Old Firm game of the 1997–98 season, and more recently at Bobo Balde and Momo Sylla. Little – if anything – of this was noted in official Rangers publications, and yet this is surely something that no one in sport can tolerate. Whether it is to be done by campaigns and words, or specific action, is up to those concerned. As Gerry McNee has pointed out, if someone like Richard Gough had gone up to Blinker and demonstrated to the fans that he was having nothing to do with racism, it would have been an action worth a million words.

Celtic and *Scotland on Sunday* combined both words and action. The newspaper backed a national sixes tournament to celebrate Asian football, planned to take place in Edinburgh in the spring of 1997 as part of a campaign called 'Fair Play for Asians'.[20] The idea was thought up by Sultan Mahmood, a designer retailer who has arrived in Edinburgh from Huddersfield and whose team, the Kurry Kickers, was just one of the many playing in the Asian leagues there. Mahmood's main wish is for the Asian teams to be integrated into the Scottish leagues and not to be forced into separate leagues as was the case in England. *Scotland on Sunday* claimed that Asians were forced out onto the margins of Scottish football by 'abuse, discrimination and ignorance',[21] and no doubt there is much truth in this: there are some communities, however, that prefer to keep to themselves. The absence of Asian footballers from the top grade is not necessarily an indication of prejudice against them. Some Asians, and Pakistanis in particular, do not see football as a high-status activity and encourage their male children into other pursuits: many of them find more important things to do than play football. It will be with the children, or the children of their children, that change is most likely to come.[22]

One of the few Asians to make the top grade in Scottish football was Rashid Sarwar, who made 21 first-team appearances for Kilmarnock between 1984 and 1987. By his own admission, football was not a driving obsession with him, and he pointed out that a couple of his mates who were better players than he was gave up football to concentrate on the family business. This has been reflected on the world stage, where Africa, despite a population that is a fraction of Asia's, has produced a multitude of top-class players; Asia by comparison has produced only a few. A Scots-Asian fan who wrote to *Not the View* saying how proud he was to have adopted Celtic as his team, confessed that although born in Scotland he was 18 before he knew about the Old Firm.[23] Admittedly his parents had preferred cricket, but any native-born sports-loving Scot who has not heard of the Old Firm by the time he is a young adult is surely living in another world.

Times change, and with the yuppification of football, the time might come when all these young Asians who can be seen kicking balls about the parks and wastegrounds of Scotland are encouraged to join the potentially lucrative and decidedly more socially acceptable status of professional football player. And in a world where Rangers employ Catholic players to help them win games, no team is going to turn down an Asian Maradona because of his ethnic origin. There are also signs of other cultural barriers coming down: Muslim women are no longer so prepared to abide by the strictures of their male 'superiors' who dictate that they should not be seen in immodest dress, such as a swimming costume, or gaze on immodestly dressed males, such as the bare knees on show at a football match. The one source of comfort to come from Australia's tragic elimination by Iran from France 1998 was when an estimated 5,000 Iranian women ignored the order to stay away from the celebrations for the heroes returning from Australia and burst past the guards set up to keep them out of the stadium.

There are Christians (and non-believers) today who find the Muslim attitude to women degrading, just as there are Muslims who believe that the adoption of liberal values by their womenfolk is a blasphemy. It is another version of the age-old problem of where religious belief ends and cultural contamination begins. Many who are uncomfortable with Muslim practices today need not be racists, although many are, just as Protestants who were once suspicious of Catholicism were not necessarily bigots, although many were. There are distinctions between culture, religion and race that can be easily confused, but this can never condone the open bigotry and racism that have too often scarred the face of football. On the other hand, if racism is to be measured by the exclusion of Asians from football, this must also have something to say about the countless numbers of blacks who are playing in football teams all over Britain today.

GLASGOW: DEAD BRILLIANT CITY OF CULTURE

Glasgow before the 1980s was a city with more than its share of problems. The transformation since the early 1980s has been little short of miraculous, as the city, despite some black spots that have won it recognition as being in need of special subsidy, not only smiles better but has presented its newly polished face to an admiring world. The savagely funny travel writer, Bill Bryson, thought no city more deserved its new reputation and, although he didn't understand a word anyone said to him while he was there, still commented: 'Glasgow was named European City of Culture, and no one laughed.'[24] Glasgow was the Garden City of Europe in 1988 and it won the right, against tough opposition, to the stewardship of the Year of Architecture and Design in 1999. The 'no mean city' image of Glasgow is now a thing of the past as it enters the third phase in its history as a world power, tobacco and heavy industry now being followed by its role as a centre for tourism and the arts.

In common with the rest of Scotland, whose writers in the last decade or so have won Booker prizes and produced award-winning films and television series, rediscovered Charles Rennie Mackintosh and revolutionised its attitude to eating out, Glasgow with its freshly scrubbed tenements and spectacular examples of urban renewal prepares to host some of the top cultural events in Britain. There is nothing that can be done about Glasgow's weather or its geographical position, but it has always been within a short distance from some of the world's best scenery, while within its confines it has more parks than most cities of the same size, including public museums and art galleries that for more than a century have been open to the public free of charge. Now it has the Burrell collection in Pollok Park to add to the Art Gallery and Museum in Kelvingrove Park and the People's Palace in the Glasgow Green. And still the entrance is by voluntary donation. The new Glasgow is also reflected in the all-seated, all-covered stadiums at Celtic Park and Ibrox, with the difference that entry is restricted to those who can afford the high admission charges.

Glasgow still has its eyesores, as anyone walking from the city to Celtic Park can see, and there will be those who will have to make do with fish and chips and a carry-out rather than the gourmet delights of The Ubiquitous Chip and the other quality restaurants in the West End and elsewhere, but unlike those who have been priced out of the new stadiums at Ibrox and Parkhead, those who can't afford chablis and choice seafood have not lost something that was once a cherished part of their life. It would be a welcome development if the dispossessed from Ibrox and Celtic Park were to reverse the trend of a century ago and return to following the other teams in and around Glasgow – and elsewhere in Scotland. Such wishful thinking, of course, ignores the reality of life not only in Glasgow and with regard to the Old Firm, but in Europe and the world at large.

In the wider world of European football, the Scottish Cup and the Scottish League are minor trophies that serve as little more than springboards to greater things. Realistically, only Celtic and Rangers can hope to hold their own with the giants of the world game. Scotland, and Glasgow in particular, has its world-class opera, theatre, museums and galleries, but no urban culture is complete without world-class football entertainment. The stadiums in place at Parkhead and Ibrox are fit to set before the elite of the world game: now all we need is for Rangers and Celtic to provide the teams that the money and nervous energy spent on them warrant.

Such were the rather romantic notions that inspired the hopes of those who believed that, as the century neared its close, sectarianism was no longer the problem it once was, that in terms of community relations Scotland had more to be proud of than ashamed. This applied to Celtic and Rangers as much as society at large, for the two clubs appeared to have done all that was in their power to clean up their image. Alas it was not to be. In the last year of the old millennium, in May 1999, the Rangers vice-chairman, Donald Findlay, plunged the club back into the days of yore when he was secretly filmed singing sectarian songs at a private Rangers social function and this was splashed across the media. Barely three months later, James MacMillan, until then a fairly anonymous Celtic supporter and composer of genius, appeared in his new guise of religious conscience for modern Scotland. This was in the speech he gave shortly after the opening of the new Scottish parliament in Edinburgh, in which he denounced his homeland for its attitude to Catholics and catholicism with accusations that made Scotland look as though it would have trouble entering the twentieth century, let alone the twenty-first. This was the beginning of a groundswell of opinion against sectarianism that was to gather strength in the years to follow. Caught in the middle were Celtic and Rangers, faced for the first time in their history by independent pressure groups, church dignitaries, the Glasgow City Council and members of the new Scottish parliament, a coalition of the righteous determined to cleanse the land of the 'scourge of bigotry'.

11. Into the New Millennium

When Jansen's Celtic averted the dreaded Ten-in-a-Row, the Stein chase seemed finally buried as the likelihood of either team setting out on a ten-season winning streak was the most distant of possibilities, especially as neither team hoped to be playing in Scotland in the decades to come. With that albatross removed, it looked as though some form of sanity might prevail between the world's oldest football rivals. But it was not to be. The architect of Celtic's triumph, Wim Jansen, left the club at the end of his triumphant season, and in what had become typical Celtic fashion it was a messy departure following a torrid time between the fans' favourite and McCann and his favourite, Jock Brown. Replaced by the anonymous Dr Josef (Who?) Venglos, worse disasters befell the club with the appointment of the dream-team-turned-nightmare pairing of former hero Kenny Dalglish and Jamaican-born England international John Barnes. When some heavenly light finally seemed to shine on the club, it came when they turned their eyes nearer to home to find a new coach: Ulster-born Catholic Martin O'Neill, who started off with what seemed to be becoming something of a tradition with first-time managers of the Old Firm clubs when he won a treble in his first season.

As Wim Jansen departed Scotland's shores for his native Netherlands, another Dutchman arrived to take up the reins at the Ibrox club, having controlled its destinies from the wings in the dying months of Walter Smith's last season. The Dutch Napoleon, Dick Advocaat, won the fans over with a treble in his first season, almost repeated the next, before he met his match with Celtic's Catholic Ulsterman. Until the near-glorious night of 21 May 2003 in Seville, however, none of the Old Firm managers was able to lay to rest the bogey of Old Firm disasters and disappointments in Europe. In Scotland, the domestic scene became more farcical than ever as Celtic and Rangers dominated the Scottish Premier League with an unprecedented stranglehold, their arrogance in this regard finally provoking their victims into resigning en bloc and leaving the possibility of Rangers and Celtic playing in the ultimate Scottish Super League, one in which they were the only two clubs.

And while the two teams battled on the playing fields of Scotland, England and Europe, off the field they found themselves constantly assailed by those who believed that the shame – apparently a 'secret' shame to some – of Scotland's continuing sectarianism lay at the front doors of their respective football stadiums. For those with some sense of history, even one that did not stretch as far back as the days of Struth and Maley, but just a couple of decades to the days before the arrival of Graeme Souness at Ibrox, it was all a bit puzzling to hear claims that the Scotland of the new millennium was as steeped in sectarianism as it always had been, and that Rangers and Celtic were as guilty of causing this as they had always been. There could be no denying the continued existence of sectarianism and that it could still be found in all its full-throated ugliness at Ibrox or Celtic Park, but no longer was this encouraged or tolerated as had once been the case, a couple of flute performances by a top player and a sectarian sing-along conducted by a top director notwithstanding. Lapses like these brought attacks on Rangers more savage than that of Ian Archer's rather isolated condemnation of the club in 1976 when he had called them 'a permanent embarrassment and an occasional disgrace'; they were also better orchestrated as Rangers were assailed by a horde of critics, from editorialists and letters to the editor to talk-back stirrers and pronouncements from the high and mighty among Scotland's political and other leaders.

Leading the morally indignant were some of Scotland's most prominent Catholics, including Cardinal Winning's successor, Mario Conti, as well as veteran anti-Rangers critic, emeritus Professor Pat Reilly, and a newcomer in the field in the form of Scotland's Celtic-supporting music composer, James MacMillan. More neutral commentators were happy to damn both clubs, Rangers gave signs of still being caught in the warp of their say-nothing past, while Celtic clung precariously to the moral high ground they had once occupied so firmly in the days before Souness. Specially created pressure groups were formed to deal with the problem, politicians entered the fray as they had never done before, inevitably causing some alarm as to their motives and methods, while an umbrella group called Sense over Sectarianism promised in its reach and its aims to live up to its simple title. Scotland might have entered the new millennium with more to be proud than ashamed of in regard to communal relations, but in a world where community attitudes are more enlightened than they have ever been, the slightest sound, sight or scent of sectarianism was something to be sought out and suppressed. At Parkhead and Govan the two clubs, while understandably at the centre of any discussion of the subject, might well have wondered what more they could do, especially when Rangers entered the lists in belated response to Celtic's 'Bhoys against Bigotry' with their own campaign under the slogan 'Pride over Prejudice'.

Beyond the reach of the two clubs, Ulster will continue to gnaw ulcerously at Scottish social life while the problems of a divided Ireland remain, and Scotland's divided education system remains as an object of continuing scrutiny by anyone concerned about whatever levels of sectarianism still exist in Scotland. Ibrox and Celtic Park will continue to be a haven for those who wish to express their sectarian bile without losing their jobs or incurring the contempt of their fellows at work or play, but an increasingly uncomfortable haven, the last resort of the bigot in a world where he (or she) has nowhere else to run or hide.

FIRST THE FOOTBALL

When Fergus McCann raised the League flag at Celtic Park at the beginning of the 1998–99 season, he was greeted by a storm of abuse from Celtic fans who were upset at the appointments and dismissals he had made over the previous months. In November 1998, he was forced to sack Jock Brown, who was constantly at odds with Wim Jansen during Celtic's dramatic bid to halt Rangers' march to a tenth flag. Around the central figures in what should have been Celtic's triumphant year there had been much collateral damage, and among the crowd abusing McCann on a day when he should have been hailed as the architect of Celtic's post-1994 revival were some fans who claimed on a large banner to be Celtic supporters, but not bigots. They were replying to McCann's criticism of the 'Catholic bigots' at Celtic Park, people whom he thought were too tied to an Irish and religious past that had no relevance in the modern world. When he left the club at the end of that season, however, his final departure delayed until the following April, The Bunnet left with the best wishes of the vast majority of the Celtic faithful. He had come, saw what had to be done, did it and then left, as he promised he would, to enjoy a new life with a new wife and family far from the trials and tribulations of a public more interested in 'hopes and dreams' than dollars and cents, as well as Scottish football authorities who thought they knew better how to run the Scottish game.

Over at Ibrox David Murray looked likely to continue to up the ante on all that Celtic did, promising to put in a tenner for every fiver of theirs. And under the disciplined leadership of the new Dutch coach, Dick Advocaat, who seemed intent on ridding the club of what its own supporters saw as the laxness and lack of professionalism that had marked the last two seasons of Walter Smith's reign, it looked as though Rangers might at last attain their dream of being regular players in Europe rather than bit players with hopes dashed before Christmas. In his first season he won the treble at home, was eliminated by Parma in the UEFA Cup, but returned the next year to defeat the Italians on a 2–1 aggregate to gain entry to the Champions League proper. What followed was anguish on German soil on an epic scale: needing only a draw to proceed to the second round, Rangers lost to Bayern Munich, the previous year's beaten finalists, then in the UEFA Cup they took a 2–0 lead to the second leg against Borussia Dortmund only to be eliminated in a penalty shoot-out after extra time, in a game in which they several times were within an inch of wrapping it all up.

At home in his second year a win for Celtic in the League Cup prevented a second Rangers treble. Well might the Rangers faithful have cause to celebrate, and how better to honour their new hero than by wearing the colours of his country at the Scottish Cup final of May 2000. And so they came decked out in orange tops in a display of colour that paid tribute to the reigning House of Orange and that of an Order that belonged to the more ancient traditions of the club. The colours may have been fine, even old and beautiful, and at Hampden on that sunny May afternoon worn in a spirit of fun, but when the club decided to take commercial advantage of a fan initiative they turned a one-off joke into a sectarian sell-out.

While Advocaat enjoyed his triumphal second season at Ibrox, Rangers fans had the additional joy of seeing Celtic sink to a level even lower than during the worst days of the old board. Against the wishes of McCann, the new board at Celtic, led by the millionaire Irish businessman Dermot Desmond, appointed Allan MacDonald to take over as chief executive in 1999. MacDonald was to prove, if proof was ever needed, that success in the business world, even at the highest levels, is no great recommendation for running a football team, any more than a brilliant career as a footballer is any guarantee of making even a half-decent manager. All these truisms were to come to pass in Celtic's most traumatic year, under the guidance of former Celtic hero Kenny Dalglish and brilliant English international John Barnes, but such disasters cast their shadows before them when the club brought ridicule on itself by some ill-advised actions off the field.

In the last Old Firm game of the 1998–99 season, on 2 May, Rangers, for the first time in an Old Firm game since Celtic drew 2–2 at Ibrox in 1967, were in a position to win the championship at their rival's ground. They duly did, by 3–0, but in a tempestuous game in which referee Hugh Dallas drew the ire of the Celtic support by awarding Rangers a penalty from which they scored and then sending off Celtic defender Stéphane Mahe for a double dose of stupidity when the fiery Frenchman was unable to contain his anger at what he perhaps thought was masonic malevolence. In the lead-up to Rangers second goal Dallas again appeared to favour Rangers, enraging Celtic supporters who let fly with a hail of coins, at least one of which hit Dallas on the head and brought him to his knees. Caught on camera it was an image shown around the world as he tried to staunch the blood oozing out of the wound. Amid the mayhem, at least four Celtic supporters invaded the field, but were cut short by the stewards, one of whom was himself felled by a coin or coins. Another Celtic supporter fell from an upper stand and had to be carted away on a stretcher, all the while yelling his abuse at the iniquities of the referee. It might not have been Dallas's best game, but it was not his worst. However, MacDonald, under what he claimed to be an attempt to make a good referee better, sent a video of the game to a psychologist in England for his analysis. It all fed the notorious Celtic paranoia, while one Celtic fan took more direct retribution by sending a couple of bricks through Dallas's window after the game. Many were left wondering just who needed a psychiatrist.

But MacDonald's biggest mistake was the appointment of Dalglish as technical director, who in turn appointed Barnes in one of these dual managerial appointments that more often serve to cause conflict than consensus. Barnes was an untried rookie with no knowledge of the Scottish game, on a typically obscene salary, all of which was paid out to him when he departed as Celtic's shortest ever managerial appointment, beating the record set by Lou Macari. His end came after a catastrophic 1–3 defeat at home in the Scottish Cup in February 2000 at the hands of the recently formed club from the Highlands, Inverness Caledonian Thistle. Catastrophic in that it came in a season where Celtic had already given up the League chase and in the midst of turmoil in the dressing-room that was reflected on the field of play. Dalglish, who had graced Scotland's football fields as few before him or since, took over after Barnes's departure, but he seemed more intent on making a fool of the media than lifting Celtic's image on the field. In one highly publicised encounter, he barred Hugh Keevins from a press interview conducted in a pub, the gentlemen of the press not failing to report that the bouncer (and vice-president of the social club) who barred one of Scotland's most venerable reporters and in his private life an unapologetic Celtic supporter, was a man alleged to have a criminal record involving dealings with the IRA.[1] Dalglish, despite his obvious failings at Celtic Park, also walked off with a substantial payout, and for a while it looked as though Allan MacDonald might do the same, but he agreed to forego part of the money the club offered him.

This left Celtic in the familiar situation of having to find a new manager over the summer, but this time their troubles were about to come to an end, when the club decided to give up wild-goose chases on the continent and returned to more familiar soil. Martin O'Neill was at Leicester City when Celtic approached him, a young and successful manager tipped one day to take over at Manchester United. In coming to Celtic he put such ambitions on hold and instead embraced another ambition, for although O'Neill was not as fanatical about soccer in his native Kilrea as most of his peers, preferring Gaelic football, and although he did not necessarily share the enthusiasm of his Catholic friends for the hoops from Glasgow, he grew up among the troubles of Northern Ireland in a Catholic environment that helped shape his outlook on life. A player of distinction with Nottingham Forest in their glory years in the 1970s, thoughtful enough to hold his own in verbal battles with Brian Clough, he captained his country and after stints with Norwich City, Manchester City and Notts County he went on to coach several non-league clubs and Norwich City before ending up at Leicester. At Leicester, the club was as furious as it was confounded when he left at the end of May 2000, for O'Neill spurned their offer of an increased salary to beat Celtic's, and when this was refused Leicester chief John Elsom disparaged O'Neill for 'a personal dream related to his Roman Catholic heritage'.[2] Such are the values of the new age, that a talented manager is criticised for preferring to follow his heart rather than his wallet.

Like Advocaat in his first year, O'Neill went on to win the treble, and although he won the league in his second season at Parkhead he narrowly lost the two other top trophies to Rangers. His success spelled the end for Advocaat, who fell into a strangely impotent period at Ibrox, hamstrung it might have appeared by his penchant for Dutch players and an inexplicable lassitude in startling contrast to his early impact on the club. O'Neill made a sensational Old Firm debut when on 27 August 2000 Celtic thrashed Rangers 6–2 in a strange game where, it has to be said, with a bit of luck and better refereeing Rangers might well have salvaged a draw – certainly they did not deserve to be down 1–3 at half-time. A 5–1 loss to Rangers at Ibrox the following November ended Celtic's run of 16 games without defeat, but this only postponed O'Neill's race for the flag, which was over by early April 2001. In the following season it was another one-horse race for the flag, which was virtually over by Christmas 2001, when Celtic led the league by ten points. By now Advocaat's time at Ibrox was up, and in the New Year he was euphemistically moved 'upstairs' and allowed to continue on the payroll of the club as a Director of Football. In the meantime he occupied his spare time with the job of coaching the Dutch national team, a position that he took over on a full-time basis in November 2002.

Advocaat was replaced in mid-December 2001 by a low-key

appointment, Alex McLeish, then managing Hibs but best remembered
as a player for Aberdeen. Whether it was because of his association with
a club for which many Rangers supporters have a peculiar aversion, or a
realisation that Rangers were no longer operating from an open cheque
book, his welcome at Ibrox was somewhat muted. Two trophies in his
first six months and a succession of triumphs in Old Firm games, capped
by a treble in his first full season at the club, was greeted as much with
relief as joy in a 2002–03 season that will forever go down as one of the
most exciting in Scottish football history.

Celtic ended the 2002–03 season without a trophy, and yet for most
Celtic fans it was one of the most exhilarating seasons they had ever
known. In the League Cup Celtic lost the final 1–2 to Rangers after John
Hartson sent a penalty wide in the last minute, previously having had
what many saw as a perfectly good goal disallowed for off-side. In the
Scottish Cup they came up against Inverness Caledonian Thistle in the
quarter-final in Inverness, but instead of wreaking vengeance for the
humiliation of three years previously, were eliminated in a 1–0 loss. Then
when it appeared that Celtic had no chance of winning the League, being
eight points behind Rangers on 19 April, albeit with a game in hand, the
League leader dropped two points to Dundee in a 2–2 draw and in the
last Old Firm game of the season lost 1–2 at Ibrox. On the last day of the
season, both teams were on the same points, with Rangers ahead on goal
difference by a single goal. As a result there was an outside possibility that
the two clubs could have ended with exactly the same record and so been
involved in a play-off for the title. In a pulsating finish it was the team
that won by the biggest margin in the last game that would win the
League, although Rangers kicked off one goal ahead and with more goals
scored. Fortunes seesawed over 90 minutes as all of Scotland sat at home
or in pubs, eyes popping and ears straining as they tuned in to
combinations of two television channels (BBC1 and BBC2) and radio
broadcasts as Rangers battled it out at home to Dunfermline, while
Celtic travelled to Kilmarnock to knock in as many goals as they could.
Rangers won the goal-scoring battle, beating Dunfermline 6–1 while
Celtic could manage only 4–0 against Kilmarnock, being awarded two
penalties but making only one count.[3] Rangers completed the treble a
week later when an Amoruso goal took an exhausted team to a 1–0
victory over Dundee in the Scottish Cup final.

But in many ways the highlight of the season was on the Wednesday
before the climactic two-ground shoot-out to see who won the League.
This was Celtic's UEFA Cup final played in Seville, Spain, on 21 May
against Portuguese champions, Porto, which was transformed into a
historic event by the invasion of the Andalusian capital by an army of

Celtic fans estimated to be at least 50,000, possibly 80,000, while
Spanish papers, who could not believe what they were seeing before their
very eyes, claimed that there were 100,000. Of the green-, white- and
tartan-clad invaders, only about 25,000 arrived with tickets, although an
estimated 35,000 outnumbered the Porto supporters in the 53,000
capacity ground: the others simply wanted to be near the action. Hotels
were booked to overflowing for anything up to a hundred miles from
Seville, the park benches offered alfresco accommodation for the less
fortunate, while those serving drinks in the Spanish heat did their best to
keep up with what seemed an unquenchable thirst on the part of their
unexpected but welcome guests. Never before in the history of football,
as one Celtic supporter observed, had so many people come so far to see
a game on television.[4] In 1967, Celtic had astonished Europe when their
fans travelled in a cavalcade of cars, coaches and aeroplanes to see the
European Cup final against Inter Milan in Lisbon, the final total being
estimated at anything between 12,000 and 15,000. Over 30 years later it
was the Celtic fans who again astonished footballing Europe with a
travelling support that arguably could not be equalled by any other
football team – even Manchester United did not bring so many fans to
Barcelona to see their team's 2–1 triumph over Bayern Munich in 1999.
Whether Rangers fans could equal the feat of their Glasgow rivals
remains a matter of speculation – one that it would be pleasing to see
put to the test in the near future.

What made the Celtic adventure in Spain so uplifting, despite the 3–2
loss in the last minutes of extra time, was the list of victories on the way
to Seville. Having been eliminated from the Champions League in the
third qualifying round by Basel in Switzerland on the away goals rule
(3–3), Celtic won the consolation prize of a place in the UEFA Cup,
known to some as the 'losers cup', where they met a string of exalted
opponents. First up were easy victories against Lithuania's FK Suduva,
but this was followed by victories in both legs against Graeme Souness's
Blackburn, an away goals win against Celta Vigo of Portugal, then an
equally tense victory over VfB Stuttgart in Germany on a 5–4 aggregate.
This set up a tantalising fixture against Liverpool, Celtic's nemesis in two
previous European encounters. This Battle of Britain was decided clearly
in favour of Celtic who drew 1–1 in Glasgow then triumphed with a 2–0
victory in Liverpool. This took Celtic to a semi-final with Portuguese
club Boavista, but despite the prospect of this formidable opposition a
wave of optimism surged through Celtic fans throughout the world as
they started making their plans to get to Seville, in the process nearly
jamming the daily affairs of any travel office that had any dealings with
travel to Spain. In 1970, Celtic had made the fatal mistake of thinking

when they beat Leeds United over two legs in the semi-final that they had won the European Cup, but this time the club and the fans had no illusions that a victory over English opposition, however satisfying that may be, was as good as a victory in Europe. In the game against Boavista, Celtic drew the first leg in Glasgow, 1–1, then went through to the final with a 1–0 victory in Portugal. Thousands of plane flights and hotel bookings remained uncancelled as Spanish tourist and other authorities prepared for the second wave of enquiries from Celtic supporters around the world.

Celtic's 3–2 loss in the closing minutes of extra time proved to be only a temporary dampener on the spirit of their fans, who realised that Europe is a bigger field than Scotland, and the string of victories that took them to a close second place gave the lie to the claim that winning is the only thing. When Porto scored their winning goal, however, there was as much rejoicing in parts of Scotland as there was in Portugal, while a collective sigh of relief is said to have emanated from Larkhall, where a pub window reminding Celtic fans that they had won 'hee-haw' that season remained unsmashed – the Celtic supporters presumably having used up all their energies on the march to the final itself. (I report this story on the evidence of my cousins in Larkhall, as ever dispassionate witnesses to the surreal events that surround their home town.)

Prior to the Seville adventure, both clubs had come close to breaking the hoodoo that had long hung over them – staying in Europe beyond Christmas. The season after their heartbreak in Germany, Rangers in 2000–01 came third in their Champions League section behind Sturm Graz of Austria and Galatasaray of Turkey, then fell 1–3 on aggregate to Kaiserslautern in the UEFA Cup. In the following season they lost 1–2 on aggregate to Fenerbahce of Turkey in the third qualifying round of the Champions League and then, after a win on penalties over Paris St Germain in the UEFA Cup, lost 3–4 to Feyenoord of the Netherlands in the fourth round. At least this allowed their European adventure to last into February. In the 1998–99 season Celtic lost 1–3 to Croatia Zagreb in the Champions League qualifiers, and were then beaten by Zurich of Switzerland on a 3–5 aggregate in the UEFA Cup. In the following two seasons, Celtic fell early victims in the UEFA Cup to Lyon in the second round (0–2 on aggregate) and then to Bordeaux of France, again in the second round, 2–3 on aggregate. Under Martin O'Neill Celtic seemed set to stay in Europe after Christmas for the first time since the 1979–80 season when they beat Ajax of the Netherlands (3–2 on aggregate) to qualify for the league section of the Champions League, but came a close third behind Juventus and Porto. Dropping into the third round of the UEFA Cup they were eliminated on penalties by Valencia in Spain after a 1–1 draw on aggregate. That same December night Rangers qualified to stay in Europe until the following February 2002, when they lost to Feyenoord. It was an early exit for Rangers the next season, and to opposition that raised few fears among the big clubs of Europe: the modest Viktoria Zizkov of the Czech Republic lost 3–1 in Scotland but won 2–0 at home to eliminate Rangers from the UEFA Cup on the away goals rule. For Celtic the adventures in Europe that season had a different story to tell.

On the domestic scene, the Old Firm stranglehold closed tighter than ever, and the old debate about where they could best show off their talents was again entered into. Atlantic leagues were justifiably dismissed by *Not The View* as Atlantis leagues – lost 20,000 leagues under the sea. The English Premier League possibility was raised again, appealing to the one ideal that all the top clubs have in common (greed), while for the ordinary fan there remains the tantalising thought of Celtic and Rangers engaged in competition with teams that challenged them on a regular basis. Few would doubt their ability to keep in the top half of the English Premier League and the more romantic might justifiably expect that the Glasgow giants would more than hold their own against Arsenal, Manchester United and Liverpool, but for the moment UK and UEFA regulations present insuperable barriers. Entry to the Premier League through the Nationwide League remains a remote possibility, a British Cup still warrants the occasional dusting-off, but a more likely alternative to the Old Firm playing in a league that reflects their status in the game would be some sort of regional European league replacing the UEFA Cup and running with, or instead of, the present European Championship.

However that may be, the big two in Scotland made little effort to hide where their ambitions lay, and their efforts to keep all the money and power to themselves eventually provoked the ten other members of the Scottish Premier League into pre-empting the constant threats of an Old Firm departure by themselves in April 2002 giving notice of their intention to resign from the Scottish Premier League. This left Celtic and Rangers with the prospect of playing in a league of their own, a new Super League of two clubs. Bluff or exasperation, the sorry state of Scottish football continues: the would-be self-excised ten formally gave notice in August 2002 to resign at the end of two years, but this was withdrawn in June 2003 after a reconciliation agreement. In the debate that accompanied all this, the thought of Scottish football without Rangers or Celtic continued to gain a more favourable airing than previously as the 'Old Firm GTF' brigade promised to help Celtic and Rangers to move elsewhere and leave the other teams to get on with their own competition unburdened by the bloated two.

The most irksome aspect of the Old Firm's inability to get into England was the chasm between television money in the Premier League and the comparatively trivial returns in Scotland. If the lure of television money was denied to the big two north of the border, it was available but hard to achieve in Europe. In July 2002, David Murray, without relinquishing his shareholding control, passed the direction of the club over to John McClelland. Murray had often set his goal as seeing Rangers playing regularly in Europe, with the domestic game a mere sideshow. His departure, however, was said to be hastened by the precarious financial situation of the club. Reports of Rangers' impending financial doom have usually sounded like the stories of Mark Twain's death, greatly exaggerated, and in the summer of 2003 the club's debts were variously said to be anything from £21 million (by the club itself) to £80 million (by others who might have had a more realistic appraisal).[5] It is a well-known axiom that messing around with your own money is one thing, messing around with someone else's is another matter, and so it was whispered that the banks were getting frightened about Murray's emotional involvement in football, telling him that he had to act more like a businessman and concentrate on the profitable parts of his empire. Murray's promise to double any investment made by Celtic had been quietly shelved some time previously, and for those investors who had bought Rangers shares hoping to make a profit, the news was not good, while Murray's old financial enemy and former Rangers director, Hugh Adam, unloaded his shares with undisguised malice at the way Murray, according to him, had lived up to his estimation of the Rangers' chief's (lack of) financial wisdom. Apart from listing various ways in which Celtic were superior to Rangers, above all in their international appeal, Adam claimed in an article in *The Scotsman* of 2 February 2002, captioned 'Adam shakes Ibrox pillars with warning of bankruptcy', that the reason for unloading what remained of his shares was to get some money for them before they dwindled away to nothing. In 2001, he sold 12,000 of his 59,000 shares, and the balance of 47,000 for £1.15 a year later. Three years previously they had been worth £3.45.[6]

At Celtic Park it was the faceless green men who controlled the club's fortunes, with Dermot Desmond, the major shareholder, suggesting on television shortly before Celtic's date with destiny in Seville that the club should be playing in a bigger league. It was a rare appearance by Celtic's major shareholder, rarer even than his visits to Celtic Park, and one that reminded some of the differences in approach at the club since McCann, whose achievements are likely to stand alone for a long time. One reason why no other Celtic figure has loomed so large was that in his five years at the club McCann achieved a turnaround that no one else would ever again be required to make. Just as Souness, in Murray's words, had 'turned the big ship round' at Ibrox, so McCann had rebuilt the club out of the ruins left by the old board. He also had a deep personal interest in the Bhoys against Bigotry campaign, which was not taken up with the same enthusiasm by his successors, whose concerns were more with victories on the field and performance on the stock market. When McCann left Celtic, the influence of his fellow antagonist and sometimes fellow warrior, David Murray, also seemed to decline. If on the field of play, however, the fortunes in both camps were mixed, in the wider world from which the Old Firm can never extract themselves, the achievement in removing the dead hand of history remained similarly mixed, especially when Rangers made a spectacular re-entry into the Days of Yore with a musical performance by their vice-chairman that filled the airways and columns of the press as no other story since the signing of Mo Johnston.

DAYS OF YORE REVISITED

Throughout the 1990s Rangers had celebrated their many victories with songs and chants at venues around Scotland which were often described as being of a sectarian nature in which an unnamed member of the board was said to take part. That this anonymous person might have been Donald Findlay QC was left to the imaginations of friend and foe alike. Such suspicions appeared to be given full justification when the man himself was caught in full voice at a private Rangers function, spurning the claim that Rangers were no longer a sectarian club and leading the happy throng in choruses of a few Rangers favourites in which any words offensive to more delicate ears were not replaced by their more politically correct version.

It was a private function, held at the Rangers Social Club on the evening of 29 May 1999 after Rangers had beaten Celtic 1–0 in the Scottish Cup final and in doing so repeated their treble season of three years earlier. It was a meeting of friends in a celebratory atmosphere and not where you would expect a camcorder to be at work secretly recording events on video in order for someone to sell them to a newspaper. But so it was that a particular Rangers supporter saw the chance of a small fortune to be made even at the cost of his social well-being among those soon to be former friends. The Scottish media, feeding as it does off Old Firm stories, accepted the Judas offering, the *Daily Record* breaking the news the following Monday with splashes on its front pages with the video image of Scotland's top QC leading the chorus, the words of the songs conveniently added for those unfamiliar with them. And all replayed on television and taken up by the rest of the press.

Findlay's fate was sealed, and when Murray was warned of what was about to appear in the press he had little option but to accept Findlay's resignation, which was on his desk even before the story broke. It was one thing to be suspected of being a bigot, another to be caught acting like one, and so it was that those bearing no feelings of goodwill towards Rangers swelled with justifiable indignation at this proof that Scotland's largest sporting institution was the den of sectarian vice they had always known it to be. To them, Gascoigne's flute performances and Goram's black armband tributes were all part of a whole that denied Murray's efforts to cleanse Rangers of its sectarian past.

For Findlay it was the worst time in his life and he was even reported to have contemplated suicide. His professional life was also clouded over as his peers at the Dean of Faculties fined him £3,500 and he was rejected for an honorary degree by the University of St Andrews, at a time when this would otherwise have been a formality as he had served two terms as rector. Students at St Andrews came to his aid, but support also came from an altogether more illustrious quarter of that ancient institution in the form of the distinguished professor of philosophy, John Haldane. Haldane, son of a convert to Catholicism, suggested that although Findlay had been 'irresponsible, foolish and vulgar', the university should not revoke the decision to award the degree until it had looked further into the matter and ascertained whether Findlay intended to 'embark on a course of social reparation'. Such thoughts appeared in *The Herald* under the heading 'A matter of honour', and for this suspicion of Christian charity, Haldane was assailed by at least one correspondent as a Protestant-lover and traitor to the faith.[7] As for the man who sold the damning images to the media, he was said to have been forced to leave the country when his name was revealed to spare the feelings and safety of others who had mistakenly been suspected of being the Judas.

Findlay's actions came as a major setback to the club's anti-sectarian endeavours, one of which might have been a small step for any other club, but was a giant leap for Rangers: this was when their players were allowed to cross themselves on the pitch within view of the Rangers supporters (although cautioned that this was not recommended as a good idea). Basile Boli had claimed that Murray advised him not to cross himself, Mario Jardel sportingly agreed not to do so if the club signed him and Marco Negri unburdened himself on Italian television about how his love of celebrating a goal with the sign of the cross was denied him, resulting in his sullen reaction to goal scoring, even when he scored a magnificent five against Dundee United on 23 August 1997. The ban, like the former refusal to sign Catholics, was never official and was denied by the club, but however that may be it was finally jettisoned in

August 1998, when Gabriel Amato crossed himself after scoring against PAOK Salonika at Ibrox – and was even applauded by a small group of fans; reassured that his life would not be under threat for such indiscretions, Tony Vidmar felt safe to indulge himself in the practice as was his wont. And so it appeared that one of the sectarian ghosts of Ibrox past had been laid to rest.

Within a few months of Amato's public declaration of his faith another ghost of Rangers' sectarian past seemed to be fully exorcised. This was in December 1998 when Rangers signed Neil McCann, a Greenock-born, Celtic-supporting Catholic, from Hearts: the first Scottish-born Catholic to sign for Rangers since Mo Johnston. Rangers had been home to many Catholics since the 'Mo surrender', but they were all foreign: several Italians, from the curmudgeonly Marco Negri to the massive figure of error-prone but amiable Lorenzo Amoruso who became Rangers' first Catholic captain, antipodeans like Tony Vidmar and the exotic French-African Basile Boli, as well as the German Jörg Albertz, The Hammer, whose love for the club, complete with all its anti-Catholic baggage, was reciprocated by the faithful. The club might have expected that critics such as Gerry McNee, who had long called for a Scottish Catholic signing, would now ease up, but no one was holding their breath on that one. McCann's fortunes at Ibrox have fluctuated, but any sectarian abuse he has had to suffer came from fellow Catholics.

Prior to McCann, Rangers had even appointed a Catholic to a top-level post at the club. Bob Brannan, a Dundee supporter from a prominent Catholic family in that city, was appointed on 16 March 1998 to look after commercial matters and allow Murray to get on with the more interesting aspects of running a football club. His stay was short, but when he left on 8 January 1999 it was for failing to make as much as the club hoped he would out of its TV and marketing potential. His religion had nothing to do with the decision. Commerce was now a higher priority than religious purity.

Indeed, Rangers' willingness to allow former strangers through the gates at Ibrox seemed to be developing into what looked like a policy of banning Bluenoses from positions in the club where emotion might get in the way of hard-hearted business decisions. High priest of this new philosophy was Martin Bain, who came to the club as a marketing and media manager and who openly boasted that he came from a rugby-playing school and as such presumably had at best only a passing interest in Rangers as a boy. He saw a clear distinction between the playing staff and those involved in the more mundane affairs of the club: the accountants, the public relations people and the business managers. He believed that since some people 'can get so passionate' it was best that the staunch supporters be kept out of the business side of the divide.[8] Perhaps Bain had enough examples from the staff at Ibrox in his own time, but had he been aware of the recent history of the club he could have pointed to the disastrous relationship between dyed-in-the-blue Alan Mongomery and Graeme Souness back in the early 1990s.

Remnants of the past continued to hang around the club, and when Claudio Reyna, Rangers' new Catholic signing from the United States, appeared at training with a green sweater shortly after his arrival in late 1999 it was suggested he choose a different colour. In this case it was friendly advice to help the newcomer settle in. He came from a land where an individual could be killed for the colour of his skin, but even he would have had difficulties comprehending that in Scotland an individual could be killed for the colour of his clothing. Despite the efforts at Ibrox and Celtic Park to clamp down on the objectionable behaviour of their fans, resulting in a funereal lack of enthusiasm at some games where another Old Firm team was not involved, they came under increased pressure from sources outside football to eliminate all banners, flags, chants and songs that were deemed to be of a sectarian nature.

For most people in most countries the national emblem, the flag of the nation, is something about which you can be proud. Not so simple in Scotland where national and religious rivalries continue to muddy the issue. Rangers fans claimed to be outraged when it was suggested that their waving of the Union flag was in some way provocative and should be banned. Their Unionist and royalist sensitivities were similarly outraged when it was declared out of order to wave flags portraying the Red Hand of Ulster, the Irish province from which Rangers drew much of their support and which they see as an integral part of the Union. Some Rangers fans even wave the English St George's Cross, although the prominent waving of such a flag, as depicted in one of the most dramatic photographs of Rangers' Cup-Winners' Cup victory in Barcelona in 1972, probably owes more to political correctness later in the century than prescience on the part of a particular Rangers fan in 1972.[9] In similar ways Celtic fans could claim, albeit with more historical accuracy than a serious attempt at mutual understanding, that their tricolour, inspired by the French Revolution, represented feelings of goodwill to the Orangemen whose colours along with the green of Ireland and the white of the papacy, were a symbol of peace between the Catholics and Protestants, just as the blue, white and red that made up the tricolour of the French Revolution represented union between the white of the monarchy and the blue and red of the city of Paris, a symbol that the former subjects of the king were now citizens of France. The Irish tricolour dates back to 1830 and became more widely accepted during the year of revolutions in 1848; it appeared prominently alongside the more traditional green flag with the gold harp in the 1916 uprising, but it was not until the proclamation of the Constitution of the Irish Republic in 1937 that it was officially recognised as the national flag of the new Republic, a country from which Celtic drew much of their support.

Patriotic ardour may account in part for the vigorous waving of such flags at Old Firm games, but just as often it is to provoke the opposition. Opposition fans waving the Saltire flag, the cross of St Andrew, do so in defiance of Rangers' Unionist associations, just as Rangers fans reply with choruses of 'God Save the Queen' and 'Rule Britannia', although no doubt the fan who added a message in sympathy with the death of the Queen Mother, 'gone but not forgotten', was expressing his personal grief rather than trying to upset anyone. At times more sinister messages are added to these otherwise innocent symbols, above all those with a paramilitary slogan praising the IRA or UDA/UVF, or more sickening like the 'RIP Neil Lennon', directed at Celtic's Northern Ireland Catholic when he was forced to give up the captaincy of his country. At times like these the boundaries of good taste as much as political correctness have been crossed.

Some flag waving defies definition, although it may have its own logic, above all the Rangers fan with an Israeli flag being challenged by a Celtic fan with that of Palestine. This could be seen to fit in to the traditions of the two clubs, with Rangers on the side of the bully-boys, the US-backed Sharon government, and Celtic brandishing what they see as the flag of the dispossessed and oppressed Palestinians. On the other hand there was a delightful ambiguity in the spectacular blaze of provocative colour that brightened up the 2000 Scottish Cup final when Rangers fans appeared in their thousands decked out in orange: few people believed that this was solely in honour of their then favourite Dutchman's home country, more saw it as a deliberate flaunting of the colours of the Orange Order and for some it was a salute to the club's anti-Catholic past. The club's claim that this was in fact a 'tangerine' strip only made them look foolish – orange at least had some association with the club, however unwelcome, tangerine had nothing to do with any team in Scotland except Dundee United.

Some displays of colour in support of the team or even sticking it up the opposition are not without their humour. One such occasion was when Rangers fans appeared at Celtic Park in March 2000 with red, white and blue safety helmets for the first Old Firm game after a match at Celtic Park was postponed in the previous month because part of the roof had fallen in. In this category, too, could be placed the Celtic fans who came to Ibrox for the last Old Firm game before the Seville adventure with their sun hats and beach balls, happily overlooking the fact that Seville is more than a hundred miles from the sea: to Scots who had long forgotten the charms of Ardrossan, Troon or Saltcoats for the annual summer holidays, Spain was the new Mecca and that meant sunshine and sand as well as lots of cheap grog. When the Seville adventure ended with no trophy, Rangers replied at the first opportunity to the Celtic fans' ditty to the tune of 'The Entertainer' by turning up at the climactic end-of-season encounter a few days later wearing police hats. This was their reponse to the taunt that while the Celtic supporters were in Seville, Rangers fans would be at home watching *The Bill* – 'for we're goan tae Seville and your no'.

The singing that accompanied the banners was more difficult to control, but under pressure from outside bodies the two clubs were told to act against provocative songs and chants. Celtic Chief Executive Ian McLeod wrote to every Celtic shareholder in September 2002 asking them to uphold the dignity of a Scottish club 'proud of our Irish roots' by refusing to take part in any political songs and do their best to stop others doing so. His letter drew the praise of some, but angered others who thought his accusations unjustified, especially when Rangers fans engaged in their own particular brand of aggressive hymn singing. Rangers continued to fiddle with alternative words to replace the more objectionable allusions to drowning in Fenian blood and damning the Pope as a sexual object, but to have arrested every Rangers fan who took part in such choruses would have just about emptied the stadium. When Dick Advocaat arrived at Ibrox and removed Gascoigne and Goram, it seemed to signal not only a new approach to the lack of discipline that had had untold consequences on the club's playing record, but also that the club was intent on eliminating the most conspicuous performer (apart from the vice-chairman) of sectarian mimes and the one man whose associations with the hard men in Ulster was openly proclaimed. Some of these hard men would make the odd well-publicised visit to Ibrox, but never as official guests. When UDA member John Gregg was murdered shortly after leaving the Stranraer–Larne ferry in early February 2003 by what were said to be supporters of his factional enemy, Johnny 'Mad Dog' Adair,[10] few papers missed the chance to say that he had attended a game at Ibrox that afternoon. It has to be assumed that any Republican or Unionist extremist who has an interest in football would support one or other of the Glasgow giants, but it is a long time since such people would be welcome as official guests of the club.[11] Under McCann at Celtic Park not even the Irish Premier was welcomed into the directors' box. Nevertheless, pride was steadily making its inroads against prejudice at Ibrox.

The elimination of what some saw as Rangers' traditions did not go down well in the offices of *Follow, Follow*, which saw the club capitulating to the forces of political correctness, and while it was particularly bilious about the apparent policy of denying employment at Ibrox to men of the purest royal blue blood, the fanzine continued to make blistering attacks on the men mismanaging Rangers. Fulsome condemnation fell even on some of the club's employees whose credentials as 'one of us' could scarcely be queried.[12] This included John Greig, once photographed performing a flute mime with a beer bottle before an audience of amused Rangers supporters in Canada at a convention of the North American Supporters Association, but best known as the Greatest Ever Ranger and his burly body majestically captured in bronze outside the stadium in the tribute to the victims of the Ibrox disaster of 1971.[13] In view of the savage criticism aimed at those running the club it was hardly surprising that the fanzine and its editor would not be welcome at Ibrox, but when it was finally banned and its editor refused entry to the press box, this was not made public until two years after the event, and the reason given for this was what was called the fanzine's racist and sectarian content. Dingwall was quick to respond. His refutation of the accusation that the fanzine was racist was fully justified, as it has opposed racism from its first number to its latest, although his claim that it is not a bigoted or sectarian publication was based on less solid ground: the fanzine abounds with abusive references to Celtic supporters, although I have never seen them referred to as 'taigs' or 'tarriers'. In fact, it would appear that the club was bringing this matter to public attention – it was picked up by the press – to win anti-sectarian brownie points, for there was nothing new in *Follow, Follow*'s banishment from Ibrox: the fanzine had been banned from the press box from 17 August 2000 for refusing to have its independent voice crushed, after which 'the bluenose fanzine' appeared with the subtitle: 'unofficial, unauthorised, uncensored and unashamed'. It was only at the AGM of 30 September 2002 that the reason for the ban was given as moral rather than commercial, and Dingwall had no qualms about setting Martin Bain straight. He said that the whole issue was about 'money and control', and that Bain had 'offered me a seat in the press box if I signed the *FF* domain name and fanzine over to him and gave the club editorial and advertising control over the site and the fanzine'.[14]

The business and the bigotry are forever tangled.

THE BEST SUPPORTERS IN THE WORLD

The behaviour of the Celtic fans at Seville in May 2003 won the universal praise of all who were there and resulted in them being put forward for the FIFA Fair Play award, the other contenders being the fans of AC Milan and Juventus – bringing them into the same category as the Tartan Army of 1992 and 1998 and Dundee United of 1987.[15] The Rangers fans might be just as faithful as those of Celtic, but they still have some trouble winning over football fans outside the club. Even within the club they have been severely criticised at times, such as David Murray expressing his horror when he heard the foul chants of 'fenian scum' that accompanied his club's great victory over Parma in the Champions League qualifier of 25 August 1999, while both he and Advocaat have each expressed the wish that Rangers supporters were as faithful as Celtic: the latter's comment came in April 1999 when Rangers were strolling towards an easy League flag and the stadium was not reverberating with the cheering of a delirious following. Such comments did not go down well with fans who thought the owner and the coach were out of touch with the culture of the club, and were irrelevant to those supporters who belonged to the 'No one likes us, we don't care' brigade.

Chief purveyor of this attitude is Dingwall's *Follow, Follow*, which entered its 14th year in 2003 with as much zest and vituperation as had marked it since the days when it first defended the rights of the hardcore fan to follow the club in what they saw as the traditional manner. Indeed *Follow, Follow* could lay claim to being the most successful fanzine in Britain: not only have its sales reached as high as 14,000, but it has appeared regularly since 1988 without any apparent diminution in its support for the club and condemnation of all who do not see it in the same light. One voice of moderate bigotry, the Dowanhill Hack, seems to have moved to other watering holes, but the Gub and the Major are still happy to associate themselves with the extremists in Ulster, proud not only of Rangers' recent renewal of contacts with Linfield FC, but of the way the fanzine was regarded as the best read in Belfast's H Block, where news of Rangers victories helped to keep spirits up – echoes of Father McRory's imprisonment on suspicion of being involved in the Duke Street shoot-out of 1921, when gunmen fired on a police van taking IRA prisoners to the gaol, in the process killing one police officer and injuring another: the young priest and other Celtic supporters held in prison were said to have had their spirits lifted by news of Celtic victories.[16] *Follow, Follow* has outlasted those of many other clubs as well as other Rangers fanzines, although out Larkhall way the anonymous editor of *Number One* continues to support the club in his own idiosyncratic way, now on a weekly basis.

The official Rangers history that came out in 1998, *The Spirit of Ibrox*, is a lavish production with top-quality paper, print and binding, while the research that went into it is most admirable. The more is the pity then that more pride was not taken with the text, in its style, expression and basic grammar. In the Rangers fanzines in particular this is a fault where the Rangers writers could learn from their Celtic counterparts, and should give them pause before dismissing Catholics – the Mankie-Mob, the Soap-dodgers, the Beadrattlers, the Great Unwashed, the Scabby ones, the Beggars of the Beggardome/Piggery/Stydome/Scumdome – as cultural illiterates.

That Rangers fans are not all politically reactionary continues to be exposed. Among those presenting the Rangers support in a more civilised light is Ronnie Esplin, whose *Down the Copland Road* was published without any support from the club, which banned him from using its copyrighted names, hence the ingenious title. This book is based on a wide range of opinions of the Rangers fans brought together in a most readable format to show that while Rangers fans do embody many of the attributes that Dingwall and company like to perpetuate, there are probably more Rangers fans whose political opinions stray left of centre and whose vision of Scottish football acknowledges the presence of clubs other than Rangers, Celtic and Aberdeen. His follow-up book, *Barcelona Here We Come! The Story of Rangers' European Cup-Winners' Cup Win in 1972*, written with Alex Anderson and superbly illustrated with photographs by Eric McCowat, did have the support of the club, but – give or take a doctored photograph – has not suffered for that as it portrays, again from an admirable range of interviews, what is still – perhaps with the exception of 1993 – the greatest year in Rangers' recent history. Another history written without the shackles of the past is Rab MacWilliam's *Rangers: An Illustrated History* (London, Aurum Press, 2002), a welcome addition to the Rangers output. But we still await the book that will fill in the biggest gap in Scottish history, and not just sports history: a detailed history of the Rangers Football Club that places it with pride, without concealing its prejudice, in the rich tradition of Scotland's industrial past.

The works on Celtic continue to roll off the printing presses for what would appear to be an insatiable audience. *Not the View* went through a period of uncertainty but is still there to poke fun at the Forces of Darkness emanating from Castle Greyskull and ponder over the manifest mysteries of following the men in the Hoops. Matt McGlone has re-entered the fanzine scene with *The Alternative View*, a classy production which takes up where he left off on *The Celtic View*, his increasingly independent views rubbing ever more uncomfortably against the grain of a club less willing to permit deviance from the party line. The players might have been the single group most opposed to McGlone's independent spirit, at one time refusing to cooperate with him and demanding that he be sacked, but others thought he was too much of 'a Celtic man' and in the end his gradual ostracisation forced him to return to the role of a terracing Tim: like Dingwall at Ibrox he was still more in tune with fans on the outer limits than the suits in the plush seats.[17]

Veteran Celtic historian Tom Campbell continues to investigate the vagaries of his favourite team, most recently with a thorough investigation of the commonly held view that many Celtic fans have been afflicted with a terminal dose of paranoia. *Celtic's Paranoia . . . All in the Mind?* (Ayr, Fort Publishing, 2001) comes to a conclusion that might not please all Celtic fans. He argues that whereas in the past Celtic have had to put up with the bias of the ruling bodies in Scottish football and a Protestant-dominated media that barely tried to conceal its support for Rangers, too many Celtic people – directors, managers, players and supporters – have used the mantras of the past to rationalise setbacks in the present. At times they may have been justified, but it is essentially a cop-out and in the end a dangerous practice. Famous barneys between Celtic and the authorities, through to the running confrontation between McCann and Jim Farry, and above all with a clutch of referees, are thoroughly investigated. As for the Masons in Black, the demons who haunt the tortured minds of those trying to explain Celtic losses on the park, the occasions when there have been dodgy decisions have not added up to a conspiracy and, as he suggests, it is time Celtic fans woke up to this. It is not advice that seems to have been taken to heart at the club: first Ian McLeod, shortly before his departure, accused the Scottish Premier League of bias in rescheduling a game against Rangers for 27 April 2003, just three days after Celtic's second leg of their UEFA Cup semi-final game against Boavista; Martin O'Neill added his version of the conspiracy theory by suggesting that the SPL board was ruled by a pro-Rangers bias; and then Chris Sutton reacted petulantly to Celtic's narrow loss in the title chase by claiming that Dunfermline had lain down to Rangers in the final game of the season. All three men made fools of themselves and reinforced the suspicions of those who believe there is still a persecution complex at Celtic Park into which newcomers are soon initiated.

There were also some fans, perhaps believing they were following the lead of those in high places, who decided to take more direct action. One of these was the individual accused by Dunfermline goalkeeper Derek Stillie of sending him a death threat for conceding six goals in the League decider against Rangers (no death threats were recorded about the six let in by Dundee's goalkeeper in Celtic's 6–2 win at Celtic Park a couple of weeks before), some others were said to have tried to confront Dunfermline chairman, John Yorkston, at his home address, but he had left for Spain on an end-of-season trip and so avoided what was unlikely to have been a friendly discussion on the merits of the game.[18] It should be pointed out, too, that there was a strange delay in reporting these incidents in the press, while Stillie never actually produced the letter, which he said he threw in the waste-paper bin.[19] In early July 2003, a mob said to be Celtic supporters, although they were not wearing identifiable clothing, attacked four Rangers players – Barry Ferguson, Robert Malcolm, Kevin Muscat and Maurice Ross – leaving a wine bar in Uddingston. The players avoided trouble, but one of their protectors was severely beaten up. The alleged perpetrators, the Uddingston Young Team, were said to be notorious Celtic supporters who often wore the team's tops, but it is just as likely they were young thugs looking for an outlet for their adolescent aggression – and the press were happy to pick up a story that helped fill in the dead period at the beginning of summer when there was no actual football to report.[20]

While the players and the management of the two clubs have not always comported themselves with dignity and good grace on every occasion, the supporters have continued at times in their own uninhibited way. The most spectacular example of this was the game at Celtic Park when Rangers clinched the 1998–99 championship. The fans travelling to away games continue to be the biggest problem, at games in Scotland at any rate. Free from the surveillance to which they are subjected at home games, they can give full vent to their feelings in loudmouth glory at away matches and at times disturb the peace on the way to and from the game. Some fans have given up going to away games for this reason. The jury is still out, however, on whether it was fan behaviour or the pilot's overreaction that was behind the emergency landing in Wales of a plane bringing Celtic fans back from their nerve-wracking win on away goals against Celta Vigo in Spain on 12 December 2002. The days when plane travel was a novelty, and Celtic fans took up collections for the 'driver' on the way to Lisbon, or asked the stewards if it was all right to hang their scarves out the window, are long gone. The terrorist attacks of 11 September 2001 added a new dimension to plane travel thereafter, and so whether it was a Celtic fan aggressively refusing to put out his cigarette or a fight between a couple of fans, or the aggro they had to face getting on the plane, it was hardly behaviour to be tolerated 30,000 feet in the air.

Other fans have disgraced themselves in the manner of certain hooligans in high places, and the morons will always be among us, those for whom the only answer is permanent exclusion from the game. Among these are those who wreck silences commemorating tragedies such as the Omagh bombing, the Ibrox disaster or the death of a former player. Or even simple tributes, such as the death of a 100-year-old woman with no interest in football but who was once the queen (and played a heroic role when London was being bombed, in contrast to some of today's would-be leaders who disappear at the first sign of the trouble they have brought on their nation). The Rangers fanzines became quite weepie at the death of the 'Queen Mum', but this was a harmless piece of nonsense that did not deserve the ridicule it met when referee Willie Young had to cut the royal tribute short after 32 seconds when a section of the home support at Celtic Park continued to boo and whistle throughout the silence.[21] Equally tasteless were the actions of the Celtic fan mocking Rangers' American signing, Claudio Reyna, after the 11 September 2001 terrorist attacks by running around making himself out to be an airplane. The clubs can do little to prevent fans who besmirch their reputation in this way, but they can take – and have taken – exemplary action when those who dishonour the club are identified or caught.

Transgressions beyond the stadiums are further beyond their reach, but still within their moral milieu: the Rangers bravehearts who planted a Union flag in Martin O'Neill's garden shortly after the club's semi-final victory in the League Cup against Celtic in February 2002, the Celtic fan who threw a brick through referee Dallas's window after the Coin-Throwing game at Celtic Park in May 1999 (and who was identified and lost his season ticket), the abuse of and death threats against Neil Lennon in Northern Ireland and in Scotland, not so much because he was a Catholic but rather because he played for Celtic and supported a united Ireland, and forced him to give up playing for his country. Then there were the petrol bomb and other threats made against the Rangers Dublin Loyal supporters club shortly after it was founded in 2001, or the cars vandalised because they were the wrong colour or belonged to a particular player, Tore Andre Flo and Neil Lennon being prominent victims for owning a BMW, or players who cannot be left in peace when seen in public on a night out – and not even sporting the club's colours as Barry Ferguson was the night he was involved in a brawl after the 6–2 thrashing in Martin O'Neill's first Old Firm game. The most detestable and unsupportable fan behaviour, however, is still that of racial abuse, most recently exhibited by the Rangers fans making monkey chants against Bobo Balde and Momo Sylla, for which they were roundly condemned in *Follow, Follow*.

More sinister are the death threats, anonymous or otherwise, such as that said to have been received by Derek Stillie after Rangers' 6–1 clincher over Dunfermline, more seriously those that forced Lennon to give up his Northern Ireland captaincy, while the threats against the personal safety of Gascoigne after his first flute performance were taken very seriously by him. And Amoruso tells us in his autobiography, *L.A. Confidential*, that a letter was sent to him and his fellow Italians, Rino Gattuso, Marco Negri and Sergio Porrini, with veiled threats against them for putting money before faith and playing for a club that sang songs against the Pope and the Catholic people. Such threats, by phone or letter, can be made by the most empty-headed crank, but there is always the chance that the threats are not empty.

There are deaths that have been directly related to Old Firm tensions. Certain statistics claim there were eight sectarian murders in 1999 and 2000. This was the period when Donald Findlay was 'outed' by the *Daily Record*, which did not neglect to tell its readers that that same night a young Celtic supporter, Thomas McFadden, was stabbed to death after taunting, or being taunted by, two Rangers supporters; and another, who had been wearing a Celtic top, lay seriously injured after being hit by a bolt from a crossbow. Less publicised was the death earlier in that month of a Rangers supporter who was beaten to death in West Lothian after the Old Firm game of 2 May 1999, while another Rangers fan was later killed in the Glasgow suburb of Pollok, allegedly in retaliation for the killing of McFadden. Three years after the chilling murder of Mark Scott by Jason Campbell, one of Campbell's friends slashed the throat of another innocent victim to the cry of 'fenian bastard', and in November 1999, a man described as a 'crazed Rangers fan' was given a life sentence for the fatal stabbing of a neighbour for 'wearing a Celtic shirt'.[22] A man was stabbed to death a few days after Rangers beat Celtic 5–1 in November 2000, the reasons for the attack going back to the accused, Mark Fox, calling the deceased's father an 'Orange bastard' shortly after the game. The Celtic fan, Mark Fox, was given ten years for culpable homicide, claiming that Frank Forrester and his brother had attacked him with a knife which he had picked up and used to defend himself. On the evening of that match, a Celtic supporter, Michael Cusick, was in hospital fighting for his life after he was viciously attacked in his own home in Fife. No motive could immediately be ascribed to the assault, but it came shortly after the end of the game which Cusick had watched while 'drinking in several pubs around the town'.[23] In October 2002, a Celtic supporter, Jeffrey Robertson, was given five years for a glass attack on a Rangers fan, alleging in his defence that he had been subjected to sectarian taunts and insults over a long period.

The list could go on, and while some would question the direct relationship between football and sectarianism in these cases, others would emphasise that there were 'hundreds' of other cases that passed unreported. Many continued to come before the courts, the victim at times alleged to have started the trouble, the extent of the injury not always intentional, the colours of the victim or the accused as much an excuse as a reason for the crime. In all of this it is assumed that the fans of the Old Firm, presumably motivated by sectarianism in a way other supporters are not, are worse than those of other teams, in Scotland or elsewhere. The conclusion to the McElhone report into football hooliganism that was published in 1977 and based on the 1975–76 season is likely to apply to the game in the new century. It claimed that the actual violence by hooligans was more in perception than reality, while in proportion to the numbers involved the Old Firm fans were no worse than those of other clubs.[24]

However that may be, it was in reaction against crimes by people identified with Celtic or Rangers that Nil by Mouth was formed in 1999 to combat the 'scourge' of sectarianism and put pressure on politicians at local and national level to do something about it. The group's persistence resulted in the problem being raised in the Scottish parliament, while the Glasgow City Council instituted several initiatives to investigate the problem. Much as the problem of sectarianism has been a constant in Scottish history, this was the first time that concerted efforts had been made across several fronts to combat it. It was also the first time that Rangers and Celtic were forced to come together within the same body to do something about it, somewhat reluctantly at first, but bending before the inevitable: public opinion in the new millennium was not to be brushed aside as in the past.

12. Pride, Prejudice
and the New Crusaders

Cara Henderson is a young woman whose life was brutally ruptured by the callous killing of her close friend, 16-year-old Mark Scott, by a Loyalist thug while returning through Bridgeton Cross on his way back from a Celtic game against Partick Thistle in 1995. Four years later she still could not erase the memory of this senseless killing, images of which were flashed back to her when she saw Donald Findlay singing sectarian songs on television. This was the catalyst that channelled her grief into a determination to take action against the forces behind the killing, forces that she believed began with mindless slogans and ended up with murder. So it was that she founded Nil by Mouth, a voluntary organisation that set out to uncover and take action against religious hatred wherever and in whatever form it was to be found. She soon attracted support and the attention of the media and in July 2000 her organisation received charitable status. Nil by Mouth's objectives were clearly set out in an all-encompassing attack on 'sectarianism and bigotry within Scottish society', challenging people to 'take responsibility for the language they use and the way they behave', in general to strive for a multicultural Scotland in which differences of race and religion would be respected.[1] Cara devoted much of her spare time to speaking engagements, in schools and in prisons and wherever her message could get through. With the support of the *Evening Times* she was invited as a guest to an Old Firm game at Ibrox in November 2000, her one and only such experience. It was not one she enjoyed, having her worst fears confirmed in an atmosphere which she found hate-filled and worse, one in which she herself (a Protestant) was insulted as a 'Fenian bitch'. Eventually she galvanised those with more political clout to involve themselves in her crusade to outlaw bigotry, racism and sectarianism. She left Nil by Mouth in 2002, departing from an organisation to which she had given so much of her life unstintingly and for the most part without financial support, to take a necessary and deserved break, but also a calculated decision to remove her personal involvement in a movement that had become too closely associated with her name.

Nil by Mouth's message did not fall on deaf ears and in February 2001 the Glasgow City Council took upon itself the responsibility of investigating the moral disease that was, however unjustly, so closely associated with the city. In October 2001, in partnership with the Glasgow City Council, the various parties touched by sectarian issues were brought together in a new initiative called Sense over Sectarianism. Along with the Glasgow City Council and Nil by Mouth, this partnership included the Roman Catholic Archdiocese and the Glasgow Presbytery of the Church of Scotland, as well as Rangers and Celtic. Under the dynamic leadership of Alison Logan, Sense over Sectarianism received a millennium grant of £402,000 over three years to fund 'an awards scheme for locally based anti-sectarian projects'. The result has been a remarkable array of imaginative ideas, from plays to cross-cultural football matches and a 'peace garden', to an absorbing children's novel, *The Drums of Hampden,* in which Mark Frankland tells the story of a black Scottish captain who, during a break from football because of injury, travels to Africa and comes back with a promising young talent whose innocent questions about some of the tribal passions of the natives leads to further questions about Scotland's problems and how to solve them.[2] Practical projects like these among children at an impressionable age – education in the best sense of the word – are where the best hopes for the future lie.[3] In March 2003, pupils from across Glasgow, aged nine to sixteen, were invited to join a project in which they had to think about religious bigotry and consider ways to combat it, by way of a debate on the topic 'Stop the Hate', culminating in a parliamentary style debate in the Glasgow City Chambers in April, the conclusions of which would be sent to every member of the Glasgow City Council and every MSP to ponder over – and take action. Prominent in promoting the initiative were former Old Firm heroes Mark Hateley and Paul McStay.[4] Both Old Firm clubs are now fully involved in the project, with groups of young people visiting Celtic Park and Ibrox, meeting the players at training and even attending matches as special guests.

ENTER THE POLITICIANS

It is an old cliché that 'sport and politics do not mix': in fact they have always mixed, most notably in international competition. It is the intrusion of politicians into sport that is often more of a problem. In Scotland the traps for any politician who takes on sectarianism are obvious, as two leading Scottish politicians were to discover. John Reid, Secretary of State for Northern Ireland in the Labour government, seemed to be floundering out of his depth when in a radio broadcast on

BBC Ulster he urged the Old Firm to make more commercial capital out of their international connections. And when Jack McConnell, First Minister of the Scottish Executive, breezed into debate on the subject and referred to sectarianism as Scotland's 'secret' shame, it raised some doubts about his grasp on a subject some thought more 'synonymous' with Scotland than a 'secret'. And yet both Reid and McConnell are not only Scots, but football men – perhaps it was their very intimacy with two of Scotland's greatest passions that interfered with their judgement. However that may be, the initial embarrassments were overcome, the issue was turned into a 'battle against bigotry' and on 11 December 2002 the Scottish parliament's Justice 2 Committee decided to support an amendment to the Criminal Justice (Scotland) Bill introducing offences aggravated by religious prejudice.

It was the Liberal-Democrat Member of the Scottish Parliament (MSP), Donald Gorrie, who first raised the issue in parliament. A man more interested in the arts than football, in early March 2001 he tabled a motion in the Scottish parliament calling for a commission on sectarianism with the aim of making discrimination on the grounds of religion a criminal offence. In doing so he criticised the relationship between the Scottish Labour Party and the Catholic Church as 'cosy and incestuous', but also turned on his fellow Protestants when he said that 'in terms of sectarianism, Protestantism seems the more pervasive force'. Scotland needed a law, he claimed, in which songs, insults and flags that caused religious offence would be treated as intolerable, as was the case with racism.[5]

Gorrie's proposals met with a mixed response, but his intervention came at a time when Nil by Mouth was gaining wide publicity, and the Glasgow City Council had just formally recognised that sectarianism continued to be an issue and commissioned NFO Social Research to complete a comprehensive research report on the subject. It also came at a time when Celtic's Catholic internationalist from Northern Ireland, Neil Lennon, threatened to retire from international football after being booed when Northern Ireland were beaten by Norway that February – insults that would continue and worsen until eventually, after threats to his life and that of his daughter, he did retire from international duty in August 2002. Football and religion were also at the centre of a major embarrassment when a visit by the Irish Premier, Bertie Ahern, was cancelled because it coincided with an Old Firm match, played on 11 February 2001. Ahern had been invited to unveil a monument to the Irish famine at the Carfin grotto in Lanarkshire on that day, but Frank Roy, a Celtic-supporting Labour MP, said by some Rangers followers to have had links with the Ancient Order of Hibernians, and who had been

Private Personal Secretary to John Reid and would soon be former PPS to Helen Liddell, sent a letter on his own initiative to the Taoiseach advising him that the visit should be put off as its clash with the Old Firm game might spark sectarian violence. There was still some simmering bitterness – as much to do with local politics as Roy's ham-fisted intervention – when the Taoiseach was able to come back in June to perform his task, accomplished without any danger to himself or damage to the surrounding neighbourhood. And overhanging it all was the bid by Scotland and Ireland to jointly host the 2008 European Championship, the SFA and the politicians hoping, perhaps, to keep it a secret from UEFA that games played in Glasgow were not always marked by peace and decorum. When that bid ultimately fell through, it had nothing to do with sectarianism.

Word was also leaking out at this time of a Channel 4 documentary that promised to show Cardinal Winning as having too much power over Scotland's Labour Party and in which the presenter, Kirsty Wark, complained of how Scotland's divided education system had separated her from her best friend at age five. The issue of Scotland's divided education system and full state funding for Catholic schools brought the usual defensive reaction from the Church, and speaking for the Cardinal, Ronnie Convery, at the same time as he dismissed claims that the Orange Order and the Ancient Order of Hibernians were equally sectarian, said that segregated schools were the 'best antidote to sectarianism'. The Orange Order, in the increasingly curious position of speaking with a voice of reason at odds with the behaviour of some of its adherents, expressed its determination to get rid of the 'idiots' who gave the Order a bad name. At Parkhead and Ibrox, where the two clubs were increasingly being forced to speak out on the subject, Celtic director Kevin Sweeney expressed his wish that the government do something, although he preferred to locate the problem of Scotland's sectarianism in the continued existence of the 1701 Act of Settlement which banned Catholics from ascending to the throne. In his eyes this was institutionalised sectarianism – a delightful gift for any Rangers fan who wanted to claim the Queen as their Number One Bigot. No such thoughts passed the mind of Rangers secretary Campbell Ogilvie, of course, who in addition to suggesting that fans acting in a non-bigoted way be rewarded with free tickets to away games, put the main problem down to religiously segregated schools.[6]

In June 2001, Gorrie's bill making sectarian behaviour an aggravation of a criminal offence was proposed in the Scottish parliament, and in November a cross-party working group was convened by the Scottish Executive to investigate 'possible legislation to tackle religious hatred in

Scotland'. It was while this group was meeting that a voice from across the Irish Sea was heard suggesting that the passions of the Old Firm might be more fully exploited as a means of making lots more money. The voice was that of John Reid, Blair's man in Northern Ireland, and it was heard courtesy of an interview conducted on BBC Ulster at the beginning of January 2002.

Born into a Catholic family in Bellshill in 1947, son of a postman and factory worker, Reid grew up in a working-class Scottish environment before embarking on an ideological odyssey that took him through the shoals of extreme left-wing politics at Stirling University in the 1970s, collecting on the way a doctorate in history with a thesis on the Marxist interpretation of the West African slave trade in the nineteenth century, before finally coming to a safe haven in the more placid waters of Blair's ideology-free New Labour. Said to be as well versed in Hegel and Gramsci as in the deeds of his favourite footballers, Reid was a devoted Celtic supporter as well as a Unionist.[7] It was perhaps in an attempt to satisfy these normally contradictory positions that he ended up pleasing no one. Dismissing the other teams in Scotland as irrelevant, he said that Rangers and Celtic had to ignore them and get on to the 'bigger stage'. Not only that, but they should make full market advantage of their international appeal, Rangers with their Ulster Protestantism and Celtic with their Irish Republicanism. It is true, as Seville in May 2003 showed, that Celtic have an international attraction beyond the reach of most clubs, one that is based on an Irish diaspora that across the generations has never lost the romantic appeal of a people who always seemed to come up smiling regardless of what they had to put up with. On the other hand, Scottish Protestants, with their energy and ability to exploit the resources of Empire, have more often become identified with place and power. The appeal of Rangers abroad is largely restricted to Scots who were Rangers supporters when they left Scotland (or Ulster), and unlike Celtic, who retain some sympathy with those who do not support the club, Rangers are often disliked. Reid's linking of Rangers to Ulster Protestantism was particularly unfortunate in that while he was offering his advice to the two clubs the image of Ulster Protestantism that was being flashed around the world was that of the terrified faces of the wee girls on their way to Holy Cross primary school in north Belfast having to walk the gauntlet of big men with hate-filled faces trying to prevent their attendance.

Jack McConnell was elected First Minister of the Scottish Executive on 22 November 2001, and among the host of tasks that awaited the new young leader of Scotland's parliament was the gathering tide of opinion against sectarianism, especially as it was attached to Rangers and Celtic.

It was in October 2002 that he was said to have declared a 'war on bigotry' as the city braced for the second Old Firm game of the season. He called representatives of Rangers and Celtic to a special meeting to discuss the issue and took the 'wraps' off some of his ideas, which involved a crack-down on the waving of banners and singing of songs deemed sectarian, as well as the restriction of the sale of such emblems around football grounds. On the eve of the next Old Firm game, on 7 December, he issued a 12-point plan in which he described bigotry as 'Scotland's secret shame' and in announcing the publication of the report of the Scottish Executive's cross-party working group on religious hatred, promised to 'toughen the law so that courts can more severely punish crimes motivated by sectarianism'. On 19 February 2003, the Scottish Executive passed a law giving the courts the power to impose stiffer penalties for such offences.[8]

When it came to taking action against the Old Firm, especially the antics of their supporters, McConnell had the full support of Scotland's newspapers, which tried to outdo each other in denouncing the blight, the cancer, the curse, the evil, the scourge . . . or whatever other images they could think of to express their righteous anger. When police at a Hearts–Celtic game at Tynecastle on 20 October 2002 tried to act on the clamour for the banning of flags and the eviction of supporters singing sectarian songs and chanting sectarian obscenities, the outcome was fairly predictable. Police attempts to act against the banners and chants met with as much confusion as anger, with the police in the perplexing position of having to judge what was sectarian about a Union flag in the hands of a Hearts supporter, or a Palestinian flag being waved by a Celtic supporter. At the first Old Firm game after the crack-down, on 7 December 2002, the threats were treated as a challenge by the Rangers supporters in particular, who called on their comrades to make it a 'flag day' to surpass all others. To add to the colour, some Rangers fans even appeared with Scottish saltires, which surely was more an attempt to claim some Scottish identity for the club than an exotic sectarian statement.

ENTER THE PRIESTS

In all the discussions about sectarianism, Celtic and Rangers were never far from the main focus of attention: they were an easy target. It was inevitable – and reasonable – that they would be at the centre of any discussion of sectarianism; it was just as inevitable that the issue of Catholic schools would come into it. And above all it was inevitable that the Catholic Church would spring to the defence of what it believes to be one of its main means of maintaining the faith. Some might say that it was also inevitable that when McConnell was faced by the wrath of the Church for even mentioning the subject, the politician would back off. It all began when McConnell, himself a Protestant married to a Catholic and aware of the obloquy that can befall such miscegenetic relationships, innocently suggested that there were benefits both social and financial in Catholic and non-Catholic schools sharing some of their facilities. The united front demanding action against the Old Firm fans, Orange Walks and republican parades started to crumble as the Catholic Church condemned what it saw as another attempt to drive into the education system the wedge of abolition.

At the beginning of 2002, when the proposed Gorrie bill was still a topic of hot debate, a survey by the National Council for Social Research claimed that four out of five Scots, including six out of ten Catholics, believed that Catholic schools should be phased out.[9] Rising to the defence of faith schools came Peter Kearney, director of the Scottish Catholic Church's media office, who claimed that bigotry was taught in the home and not in the classroom.[10] This was one of what would be frequent appearances by the young Catholic lawyer in the months ahead. Kearney had made an unsuccessful challenge to become deputy leader of the Scottish Nationalist Party and came second as an SNP candidate for the constituency of Coatbridge and Chryston in the May 1999 elections, part of his programme being to help the aged and the unborn. And in between, no doubt, Catholic schoolchildren. Into the torrent of words Kearney was to bring all the exaggeration and misinterpretation that was to typify the arguments of those who felt that any surrender to the secularists would result in the destruction of the Catholic Church itself. Kearney claimed that faith schools had no part whatsoever to play in causing bigotry, because sectarian bigotry preceded faith schools and so the schools could not have caused it: the argument, however, had nothing to do with first causes, but perpetuating or sustaining an existing problem – everyone knows that bigotry did not suddenly appear in 1918. Kearney went on to ridicule what he said the 'abolitionists' claimed: that 'children who are not schooled together can never interact or relate harmoniously with each other in adult life'. For proof of what seems to be a claim that was of his own invention, Kearney pointed to the Balkans, to Bosnia in particular, where integrated schools were unable to prevent the slaughter there. 'Surely,' sneered Kearney, 'the panacea of the abolitionists' "shared campuses" should have prevented such intolerance and hate, as they promised they will do in Scotland.' Persevering with his determination to label all critics, however mild, as 'abolitionists', he said it was time 'for the abolitionists to concede that scrapping Catholic schools in a knee-jerk and simplistic attempt to end sectarianism would be a facile and superficial step, based on the alarmingly naïve proposition that shared buildings will of themselves end generations of entrenched hostility'. Such was the intellectual level of argument that faced the First Minister. But welded to the political power of the Church it was not a weakness that could be lightly dismissed.

In his former post as Education Minister, McConnell had praised Catholic schools as a model for the rest of Scotland, but when his proposed measures to combat bigotry and sectarianism threatened to go beyond the Old Firm and Orange Walks, the Catholic Church heard the alarm bells ring and started to close ranks on the issue of shared campuses, a system in which dining rooms, playgrounds and assembly halls would be held in common, but the children would be taught in separate classrooms. In September 2002, a weakening in the front seemed to appear when the Bishop of Motherwell, Joseph Devine, president of the Church education committee and a man who often seemed to be at intellectual and commonsense odds with his brethren, suggested: 'Denominational education is an enabler of sectarianism. Roman Catholic schooling is divisive.' With an honesty notably absent in the debate to come, he went on to say that this was a price worth paying as it combined the academic with the moral and spiritual life.[11]

It all came to the boil at the time of the Old Firm game of 7 December 2002, when Kirsty Wark again entered the headlines with a speech at an awards ceremony for aspiring teachers where she called for debate on Scotland's education system and the way it separated children on the grounds of religion. This coincided with McConnell openly giving his support for shared campuses, and this time the Church's response was immediate and uncompromising. And it came from the top. Archbishop Mario Conti, who had succeeded to the post of Archbishop of Glasgow at the beginning of 2002, following the death of Cardinal Winning the previous June, was the son of an Italian who had taken a typical road to acceptance by immigrant Italians at the turn of the century, selling sweeties and then running a fish and chip shop, in his case in Elgin in the north of Scotland. In personality, Conti was far removed from the populist priest who had preceded him, allegedly more of an intellectual than the doughty fighter for his people that had won Winning the love of many and the respect of all. On the issue of Catholic schools, however, Conti and Winning were as one. Winning had used his position to block any attempts to bring Catholics and Protestants together during school hours, and Conti added his condemnation of any such plans, adding his resentment that Catholic education should be raised in the context of the national debate over sectarianism. For him, the problem arose out of poverty. Faced by the wrath of the hierarchy and their threats to turn this into action at the polls, McConnell felt the need to moderate his opinions. He could hardly have been surprised at the reaction, as the Archbishop was speaking as he had to speak, on a matter of faith, as Winning and his predecessors had done.

At the beginning of January 2003, the NFO System Three report commissioned by the Glasgow City Council was published, the most extensive independent survey of the sectarian issue until then.[12] Said to be controversial in some quarters, because it did not present the sectarian Scotland some people wanted to see portrayed, it showed that close to half of those consulted favoured bringing an end to state-funded Catholic schools, and this included one-third of Catholics surveyed. In other areas it showed that sectarianism in and around Glasgow was a problem, but in some ways more in the mind than in reality – many of those who believed bigotry and sectarianism played a big part in Scottish life had in fact not experienced this personally.

In early March 2003, McConnell's plans received a setback when the Catholic Church claimed that the Scottish Executive had no 'moral authority' to tackle sectarianism. This was in a paper prepared by Scotland's eight bishops, which elevated the problem above the 'superficiality' of the education system, the Old Firm and marching bands to place it where it really belonged – with the Act of Settlement of 1701. Since this was a meeting of men no longer restrained by medieval mindsets, it can only be assumed that this was a diversionary tactic to take the heat off the schools issue, especially when the new anti-sectarian laws were seen as a threat to Catholic 'freedoms' and it was feared that a Catholic making the sign of the cross could find himself or herself up on a charge.[13] With the elections to the Scottish parliament due to take place the following May, the church organised a task force to deal with the problems it faced, and to issue instructions to its members about what the important issues at the election would be: this included the distribution to its parishioners of a quarter of a million leaflets highlighting the benefits of faith-based education in Scotland's 412 Catholic primary, secondary and special needs schools.

The ongoing debate over the schools issue brought out some of the old warriors with their well-rehearsed debates: Conti in a mismatch against the atheist Oxford Professor of the Public Understanding of Science, Richard Dawkins; Peter Kearney repeating his Bosnian analogies and excited exaggerations in response to Fred Forrester, the former Depute General Secretary of the Educational Institute of Scotland; and members of the public usually talking more sense than their ideological champions.[14] Peter Kearney came out in March 2003 with some views

that had even his fellow Catholics wondering where he got his ideas
from. This was when he claimed, speaking as a private citizen, that it was
time the Church reappraised its 'outdated and offensive' relationship
with Celtic Football Club. He was particularly angry at the way some
priests offered prayers for a Celtic victory against Rangers and at the end
of the mass advertised raffle tickets in which the main attraction was a
prize item that had been signed by a Celtic player.[15] When no Catholics
were included in the doling out of Orders of the Thistle by Buckingham
Palace in 2003, he complained angrily that he was going to demand an
explanation for this. As a devoted Scottish nationalist, it is perhaps
surprising that he was concerned about baubles dished out by the
monarchy in London, but Kearney saw it as part of the bigger picture, as
a conspiracy against Catholics and as such a monarchical equivalent of
the Masons in Black. However that may be, he had no trouble linking
this snub to the Act of Settlement which showed that the British state
was 'institutionally anti-Catholic'.[16] This was the same state, through its
Scottish branch, that had granted full government funding to Catholic
schools, but Kearney did not allow such trivia to interfere with his
judgement.

Kearney was merely the most prolific in a list of defenders of faith
education whose exaggerations and misinterpretations had been
foreshadowed by James MacMillan in his August 1999 speech at the
Edinburgh Festival. Typical of these were the claims that separate schools
'breed' or 'teach' sectarianism, that 'bigotry is on the curriculum', that
they were the 'sole cause' of sectarianism. All of this was said to be a
'knee-jerk reaction' by those who believed that if separate schools were
abolished this would be a 'panacea' for all of Scotland's ills. But if a low
point was reached in the debate it surely came from the Archbishop,
when Conti compared the issue of shared campuses to the Church of
Scotland's notorious 1923 report published as 'The Menace of the Irish
Race to our Scottish Nationality'. This report alleged that Scotland was
on the verge of committing race suicide by allowing the Irish to flood
into the country and that the only remedy was to send them back to
where they had come from. With this in mind, Conti dismissed the
claim that 'religion is the cause of division among us' and then claimed
that to seek a solution in 'the abolition or amalgamation of Catholic
schools is tantamount to asking for the "repatriation of the Irish", and
just as offensive'.[17] Not only was Conti's comparison an insult to a
Church that had already issued an apology for past faults and was doing
all it could to act in brotherhood with its Catholic fellow Christians, but
to compare Scotland of the early twenty-first century to that of the
1920s, when Catholics were a beleaguered minority, or even the 1930s

when sectarian strife was rampant, above all in Edinburgh, tells us more about the Archbishop's commitment to his faith than his intellectual credentials.

Into the debate against the continuation of faith schools came several prominent Catholic personalities. In the course of the debate in 1998, Peter Broughan, leading film producer and Celtic fanatic who refused to go to away games because of the moronic behaviour of the fans, claimed that although he had had an excellent education at St Mungo's Academy, the time had come to end 'religious apartheid in education'. He believed that this was the only hope for a better and more integrated future.[18] Fellow Catholic and famous actor Tom Conti said that the state 'should not put a penny into these schools' which, he said, created 'separatism, hatred and for nothing; they should be abolished, completely abolished'.[19] From the world of football came Celtic hero and captain of the Lisbon Lions, Billy McNeill, while Rangers' departing Catholic captain, Lorenzo Amoruso, perhaps coached by the same people who taught Gascoigne how to mime a flute performance, claimed that his saddest encounter in his six years in Scotland was the problem of sectarianism, which he blamed on 'the system of separate schools for Protestants and Catholics'.[20] Those in positions of religious authority suggested he should stick to football, while Nil by Mouth asked more players to speak out against bigotry.

Most significantly of all, came James Boyle, Arts Council chairman and the happy product of a Catholic education in Glasgow in the 1950s. At Holy Cross primary and Holyrood secondary, 'the overwhelming emphasis in religious studies was on learning catechism and adhering to the daily rituals of prayers and the weekly observance of Sunday'. Priests made regular visits and plaster saints and crucifixes were everywhere to be seen, but he felt that the social cohesiveness that came with this religious unity had positive academic results. That was back in the 1950s, however, when Catholics were still under siege, still trying to gain status as first-class citizens, as Scots even. At the beginning of the twenty-first century this was no longer the case, as Catholics integrated into the classes, rich or poor, while 'apart from a few Celtic-crazed bigots, their Scottishness is indisputable'. Christian charity no doubt prevented him adding and 'a few Rangers-supporting bigots'. The school system that had served him well 'has had its day', he said, separate schooling was part of the past and should be left that way. Catholics no longer needed the protection of a religiously based education: the time had come 'to let go of separate schools; time to secularise education. Time for the Catholic Church to put its energies into defending high-quality, liberal and prejudice-free education for its flock and for the rest of Scottish society'.[21]

Whatever the justice of the case against faith education in Scotland, nothing justifies its sudden abolition. Change has to come gradually and by winning over the consent of those most concerned, the parents and not the priests. At the purely educational level, the success of Catholic schools is well testified, historically it is too entrenched to be suddenly uprooted and in justice it would have to be given restitution for the property it gave up to the government after 1918. None of this, however, is to deny that the dual education system has been a major source of division and as such a contributor to, or even 'enabler' of, sectarianism in this time. Through to the 1980s the Scottish education system and Rangers Football Club were the most obvious forms of institutional sectarianism. The education system is still with us, but Rangers since 1989 have gone to great lengths to change their ways: with the Pride over Prejudice campaign launched in May 2003 they made a resounding declaration that they would have nothing to do with their sectarian past.

PRIDE OVER PREJUDICE

The launch of the Bhoys against Bigotry campaign in 1996 had added to the constantly simmering rivalry between Celtic and Rangers in regard to their community responsibilities. Celtic supporters would obliquely criticise Rangers for not following their lead, or for 'piggy-backing' on their initiatives, Rangers would reply by saying that their good deeds were done in private and without the blaring of trumpets; on another level Celtic would claim that Rangers' hooligan problem was worse than Celtic's in that their worst offenders were political deviants, while those of Rangers were religious: you never heard Celtic supporters expressing the wish to be wallowing in Protestant blood – and so, presumably, when they sang about the deeds of the IRA, the blood of the victims, including women and children of all faiths and none, was less tainted. Such logic could be carried further by claiming that insults against the Queen, a political figure, are less obnoxious than insults against the Pope. There is logic in the madness, but logic by itself has never been a laudable moral trait.

With the launch of the Pride over Prejudice campaign in May 2003, Rangers came through with an open and unambiguous statement that many of their fans had been waiting for. It was a complete break with their sectarian past, challenging their supporters to behave in a manner that befitted the club they supported and promising to take action against those who brought shame on it by acting in a bigoted or sectarian way. It also helped set the seal on the goals of Sense over Sectarianism: Celtic and Rangers speaking with one voice on these issues is still the most effective antidote to the 'poison of sectarianism'. It is as true in 2003 as it had been in 1903 that the influence of football clubs and their players is greater than the passing of any law or the exhortation of any number of priests and ministers. If the Old Firm are to work together in this way, and if Scottish schools could similarly work together instead of in parallel, there is little doubt that Scotland's problems in regard to sectarianism could be reduced to a minimum.

Central to the campaign was a Blue Guide to be issued to every Rangers season ticket-holder, pledging them to act according to the club's motto, 'Ready'.[22] In this spirit the fans were to be 'Ready . . . to welcome players, officials and fans of all teams to Ibrox, regardless of race, religious background or country of origin.' This clear break with its recent past went on to urge True Blue Rangers people to be 'Ready . . .': to show respect and courtesy to the general public, on the way to and from wherever the club was playing; to oppose bigotry, racism and inappropriate behaviour arising from all forms of prejudice, and reject emblems of an offensive, racist or paramilitary nature; to sing traditional songs which 'glorify the history of the club' and reject 'obscene or bigoted words that cause offence'. Those not prepared to act in accordance with the Blue Guide would face bans of varying degrees of severity: loss of season ticket without compensation up to a life ban for the most serious offences. This applied to supporters clubs that transgressed, as much as individuals.

The club also produced a video, *Playing for Everyone*, highlighting its new image, although in view of the centrality of the problem, Celtic and anti-Catholic bigotry are given rather short treatment. The Pride over Prejudice launch also highlighted some of the ways that the club had already been tackling the problem, and other features of the club's activities that might have escaped the notice of the public. Foremost among these is the Study Support Centre at Ibrox, launched in partnership with the Glasgow City Council in November 2001, which takes on the task of educating teachers and pupils in various skills involving literacy and numeracy as well as the latest IT innovations. This is all within an environment that emphasises the spirit of fair play at the heart of any sporting enterprise. Under the guidance of two full-time teachers and the involvement of some star players, 110 teachers and 1,500 children had taken part in the exercise by May 2003. The formal education was complemented by football tournaments, stadium visits and complimentary tickets for some games. Under the heading Football in the Community, the club set out its efforts to help with the more serious issues in society such as behavioural problems, alcohol and drug abuse and homelessness. It also promised to extend to new levels its involvement in community football with a 'New Opportunities Fund' to run from July 2003 to 2006. Coaching, encouragement of girls' football and bringing the game to the disabled were all part of a scheme aimed at influencing 'future generations towards healthy lifestyles and team working'. Rangers had always been involved in charity work, but from October 2002 the Rangers Charity Foundation selected three specific charities for special attention: Maggie's Cancer Care, Shelter's Families Project and Childline Scotland. Some areas of health and welfare can only seriously be tackled by the government, but football clubs with their star players have something unique to offer: visits to the sick, the disabled or the disadvantaged, where the joy of seeing and talking with a star player is beyond monetary calculation.

It is all very laudable – and out in the open!

NIL BY MOUTH

The club still had its critics, for some of whom this was just another piece of flannel to disguise the more commercial goals of the club. Others doubted that the club would take the promised action. Foremost among these is Nil by Mouth, where Peter McLean played a key role alongside Cara Henderson, and continued to do so after her departure. As Celtic's public relations officer in the McCann years, he was very close to his boss and disliked by the more 'Celtic-minded', who claimed that he 'did not have a Celtic bone in his body'.[23] He was a driving force in the Bhoys against Bigotry campaign and as such speaks with a voice of authority when it comes to understanding the inner workings of and problems faced by the two big clubs. To the outsider, however, the demands of Nil by Mouth at times tend to zealotry, setting goals that it would (perhaps even 'should') be impossible to achieve.

Nil by Mouth will always deserve the praise of all those who are concerned about sectarianism in Scotland. Starting with nothing more than the determination and the drive of a redoubtable young woman, Nil by Mouth brought the issue of sectarianism to the attention of bodies which in the past had tended to skirt the issue. It not only brought them all together under a single umbrella but, most importantly of all, it brought Celtic and Rangers together to act in common, a major stumbling block to all previous such endeavours to force the two clubs to face up to their responsibilities. There are, however, some problems in the approach taken by Nil by Mouth.

The first of these is in Nil by Mouth's definition of 'sectarian', which they seem to interpret in the broadest possible sense. From the eight deaths in a single year over 1999–2000 they have gone on to record every

attack which they claim had some sectarian intent or influence. This is a
term which while clear enough in some circumstances is less clear in
others – the banners and the chants and the songs at Celtic Park and
Ibrox, as discussed elsewhere, are not always clearly sectarian. Not every
brawl or altercation involving Celtic or Rangers fans is sectarian, although
fighting for a 'cause' can add some holy justification for what would
otherwise be drunken youths looking for a fight. On the evening of 21
May 2003, when Celtic fans in their tens of thousands were winning
praise for their behaviour in Spain, in Glasgow there were sporadic fights
and skirmishing involving split skulls and bloodshed that was barely
reported in the press the next day. One drunken youth in the pub where
I saw the game smashed his full pint glass against the wall when Porto
scored their winning goal, showering his fellow Celtic supporters with
broken glass and beer. He was prepared to follow up his idiocy by
attacking those he had offended, but others intervened and he was ejected
from the pub – three others then left with what looked to me like
vengeance on their mind – possibly one of the motives for the fights that
followed around George Square and accounted for the two split skulls and
one fan standing slightly dazed but unperturbed in a Celtic top drenched
in blood. It was a strange experience to wander around Glasgow's central
square, looking rather bare since the removal of its trees, with well over a
hundred fans at one end singing and dancing as though they had won the
UEFA Cup, while others at the Cenotaph end, to quote one bystander:
'suddenly started to kick the fuck out of each other'. Throughout the
entire evening the only likely Rangers fan I saw was someone who refused
to come into the pub to watch the game with his girlfriend, despite her
pleas that 'Celtic are a Scottish team'. At no time did I hear any anti-
Rangers abuse, nor did I hear any political songs or chants. But if any
Rangers fan had appeared and somehow got involved in the battles, no
doubt the headlines would have been screaming 'sectarianism'. And
despite the triumph and despair that brought the 2003 League
championship to its dramatic close the following Sunday, the fans
flooding out of the venues where they had watched the dramatic end to
the season celebrated or despaired without reports of any serious incidents
to spoil the drama that had just taken place.

There were no doubt many incidents of a less serious nature in the sense
that there was no bloodshed. One of these reported in the Scottish *Catholic
Observer*, albeit more than two weeks later on 13 June 2002, described a
scene of unadulterated sectarian behaviour. This happened at St Luke's
Catholic church in Motherwell, one hour after the League chase was
decided, when Catholics at mass were besieged by yelling and chanting
youths in Rangers tops who abused them and spat on them as they

returned to their cars, many of which had been vandalised. On the other hand, the death threats to the Dunfermline goalkeeper Stillie and the gang said to be out to attack the Dunfermline chairman in his home, as suggested earlier, were more likely the expression of twisted individuals or hate-filled young men who could not accept a defeat.

There are some actions which are clearly sectarian, others which are not. It is certainly 'sectarian' for a football club to ban players on the sole grounds of their religion – and in the days before Souness the Rangers Football Club was rightly condemned for encouraging bigotry with its attitude in this regard. The murder of young Mark Scott was decidedly sectarian, although there is nothing that Celtic or Rangers can do about deranged individuals who carry out such attacks. To attack someone simply because of the colours they wear is sectarian, but a fight in which epithets like 'Orange' or 'Fenian' are used may be more an excuse for a fight than a reason. It is not sectarian to support the Unionist position on Northern Ireland, or the Republican claims for unification: these are matters for debate, not bombs. To disagree over religion is not sectarian, although acts based on this belief may be. Or not. Not to believe, as the Catholic Church teaches, that birth control or divorce or marriage outside the faith is a sin, abortion a crime and homosexuality evil, is not sectarian; nor is it sectarian (or bigoted) to oppose the Church's attempts to have its private morality passed into the law or encouraged through the education system. Nor is it sectarian (or prejudiced) to regard with dismay the role of the Catholic Church in secular affairs over the past two centuries. There are some people who will hold any of these views in a bigoted way, and in their actions display sectarian behaviour in such regard, but they are not all bigots as some among their Catholic opponents would claim.

In its tally of sectarian deaths in 1999–2000, Nil by Mouth noted that there had not been a single racist murder in that time. The association of racism with sectarianism is again more subject to confusion than clarification. Despite areas where the one can shade into the other and the undoubtedly racist attitudes of some Protestant bigots to (Irish) Catholics, there is a fundamental difference between racism and sectarianism. Racism, the belief about someone based on their biology, in particular skin colour, is in all places and at all times unacceptable. People die with the skin colour they are born with, and there is nothing they can do about it. Those who judge people on this basis are judging them on a complete irrelevance and reveal their own ignorance. Religious or political opinions can tell us something about someone in a way that skin colour never can, but what people believe is their own affair: it is how they act on their beliefs that is the problem.

Sectarianism stems from many causes, chief among which are ignorance and fear, the one often based on the other and leading to hatred. Attempts to eliminate such personal inadequacies by draconian action from above can result in a cure worse than the disease, and there are times when Nil by Mouth's strictures on what it sees as sectarian acts, threatening to eliminate every fault in the human condition, give off echoes of Robespierre's attempts to establish his Republic of Virtue, or Big Brother in Orwell's *1984* – or more appropriately, perhaps, Calvin's Geneva. No one can legislate happiness or purity into existence, while bans are not so much a solution as a recognition of despair. Most Scots would be happy to see the end of Orange Walks, or parades by the Ancient Order of Hibernians or the James Connolly Society, but it would be better if they could be left by themselves to toot on their flutes and bang on their drums, to wither away on their own irrelevance – although as bands and marchers massed in their thousands to cross the sea from Stranraer to the Ulster Mecca in Belfast in the summer of 2003, with drunkenness and foul language in flagrant contradiction with the ideals of the Orange Order, this is perhaps a rather forlorn hope. Again it could well be that the uncommonly large gatherings were a defiant challenge to the attempts to silence the Order over the previous couple of years.[24] There are practical problems in regard to policing marches that might get out of order, but the already existing laws are there to take action against offensive or threatening behaviour. Much the same applies to the printed word and graven images. Banning the sale of political, paramilitary or material judged sectarian is the last resort of a society that has given up on its faith in democracy – more redolent of the Inquisition and Index of the past, or the Ayatollahs and their like today.

The Holy Willies of today's PC pack have reached into the workplace and determined that banter involving terms like Tim and Hun can result in dismissal, but so far they have not made their way into the privacy of the home. The closest they have come to this is with the pubs, which for some are a home away from home. Stories are constantly cropping up where this pub or that has had to take down a sign or change a name or part of its colour scheme. But what goes on in the inside – unless fragrantly in breach of the law – should surely be as free from the morally pure as what goes on in the privacy of the home – again unless this in flagrant breach of the law, as is often enough the case. Many pubs are unpleasant places, but by and large no one is forced to visit them. The IRA and Celtic pubs, like the Orange and Rangers pubs, are usually well known and can soon be left on entering if the material inside offends. If walls draped in the politics of Ireland do not suit your sense of décor; if you are offended by songs praising the IRA or Bobby Sands, or making fun of the Pope or honouring 'King Billy on the Wall', or if you feel menaced by battle-scarred men with tattoos of 1690 or 1916 emblazoned on their forearms, the simple answer is to walk out and find a pub more in tune with your own tastes. And it could well be said that a Rangers social club function is a private affair where members should be free to voice their opinions, however unsavoury.

Undercutting all of Nil by Mouth's efforts, however, is its unwillingness to see Scotland's divided education system as being part of the problem. In defence of this position they claim that other countries have a similar education system but do not have Scotland's problems in regard to sectarianism. This is not true. Other societies have their problems, many much worse than Scotland's far from secret shame, but that is not the issue here. Only in Scotland has a democratic society privileged a specific religious minority by granting it full funding from the state, and this over a period of many decades. In the anglophone democracies of the later nineteenth century which introduced 'free, secular and compulsory' education, the 'secular' clause was usually included because the various Protestant groups could not agree on which version of Protestantism should be taught – in Catholic societies there was no question of education being other than Catholic, for them pluralism was an anathema. In France, as in Spain and Italy, the most divisive question in the century after the French Revolution was that of the competing rights of the Catholic Church and the secular State. In France the dispute over 'godless' schools was particularly bitter and came to an unsatisfactory conclusion in 1905 only with the complete separation of Church and State. Like the United States, France has a near total separation of the two, especially in education. In Scandinavian countries the Catholic minority has always been small, in Belgium and Canada the language problem complicated that of religion, in de Valera's Ireland the power of the Church was so strong that it did not need safeguards in regard to its control over education (and everything else). Bavaria in Germany had special privileges for Catholics, like the Netherlands, but this has since been abolished: outside of Northern Ireland the situation in Scotland is unique.

There were good reasons for Scotland giving full funding to Catholic schools in 1918. As a large minority with voting power the Catholics were able to exert strong political pressure on the Labour Party, but it was justice as much as anything else that persuaded Scotland's educational authorities to take Catholics out of an inferior education system, a system marked by overlarge classes and poorly trained teachers to which they were condemned by the strictures of a Church that warned them of the most condign consequences if they did not do what the Vatican or the priest told them in regard to education (and marriage). Even then, the Roman bishops and the Archbishop of Glasgow were suspicious of accepting the gift of a Protestant state, but they were forced by the teachers to take up the offer of 'Catholic schools for Catholic children taught by Catholic teachers under Catholic control so far as religion is concerned'.[25] The price to be paid for decades to come was the division of Scotland's boys and girls at age five into 'them' and 'us'. In recent years, many governments, partly out of their mania for privatising, partly because the rich have lost any guilty conscience in regard to the poor, have increasingly subsidised private schools, including Catholic schools. Only in Scotland, however, has this been full funding, and only in Scotland has it been going on for more than 80 years.

In Scotland today, the institutional barriers that once deprived Catholics of their rights as individuals, in jobs, in educational opportunities, in the media . . . and in the Rangers Football Club, have all fallen. When Rangers practised their sectarian policies through to the 1980s, this allowed Celtic and the Catholic community at large to bask in the moral sunshine of a club and a group that did not discriminate against people who were not of the right religion – unless perhaps they wanted to become a director at Celtic Football Club. In Scotland today, unless you are a Catholic who aspires to the top job in the monarchy, there is no institution that actively or openly discriminates against a religious group, and the only institutional bias in favour of a particular religious group is in the education system; in defence of this system have appeared a new brand of crusaders, all Catholics, many of them Celtic supporters, whose attacks on those with whom they disagree at times takes on all the appearance of a new sectarianism.

THE NEW CRUSADERS

In physics there is a law which says that to each and every action there is an equal and opposite reaction. This can apply at times to the natural world and some could find instances of this in the wonderful world of the Old Firm. One notable example of this came shortly after the Findlay furore, when James MacMillan left the podium and exchanged his conductor's baton for a big stick with which he proceeded to get stuck into Scotland as a sink of sectarian iniquity. This was at the lecture he gave as part of the celebrations surrounding the opening of Scotland's new parliament in Edinburgh in July 1999, and delivered on 9 August 1999 as part of the series on Cultural Reflections at the Edinburgh Festival.

In his diatribe, for the speech could hardly have been called a reasoned discussion, MacMillan painted a picture of Scotland which might have taken some of the older folks back to their young days, but bore only passing resemblance to Scotland in the dying days of the twentieth century. His themes and some of his images had the clear signature of Professor Patrick Reilly, leading crusader against the iniquities of Protestantism and the Rangers Football Club, and while Cardinal Winning was criticised by MacMillan along with some of his 'cronies' it all had the blessing of the Cardinal. MacMillan painted a picture of a succession of vandals from the Reformation on who had committed a cultural holocaust so complete that it would have won the praise of Pol Pot and Mao Zedong. The vandals were still at work in 1999, where the clear and present danger came in the form of the Educational Institute of Scotland, the biggest teaching union. According to MacMillan, this body was 'slavering' at the mouth 'at the prospect of the new parliament being involved in this vandalism [attacks on faith education]' which had become 'a frightening spectacle for many of us'. It was religion itself that was at risk, from enemies motivated by such a deep-seated hatred of the Church that it amounted to 'racism'.[26]

In the debate that followed, above all in Glasgow's *Herald*, there were some who showed sympathy for MacMillan's motives, others praised him for 'sticking his head above the parapet', and while some could have given additional evidence to back up some of what MacMillan said, most prominent Catholics agreed that while sticking his head above the parapet he had also gone over the top. The various opinions of the time were brought together in a book edited by Scotland's leading scholar on the subject, Tom Devine, Director of the Research Institute of Irish and Scottish Studies at the University of Aberdeen, and launched before an overflow audience at a Glasgow bookshop in the spring of 2000. Entitled *Scotland's Shame? Bigotry and Sectarianism in Modern Scotland*, there were no references to a 'secret' shame.[27] On the contrary, a particular group of contributors, granted remarkable latitude to expound on their pet obsessions, thought that the question-mark in the title was a complete irrelevance. These included a typical rambling piece by Gerry Finn that was twice as long as every other article, an astonishing piece by Joseph Bradley that reads more like a sermon, a lament from Patrick Reilly about the perils of kicking with the left foot in Scotland, and introductory and concluding comments by MacMillan that showed little evidence of him having learned much since he launched his attack the previous August.

There are also some articles of eminent good sense in the book, from authors of a Protestant as well as an atheist or Catholic bent, but it is the authors mentioned above, Celtic supporters all, who stand out for their extreme opinions. They belong, perhaps, to the intellectual wing of what

McCann might call 'Catholic bigots', and this is how they are judged in an excoriating review of the book by Owen Dudley Edwards, entitled 'Is the Cardinal anti-Catholic?'.[28] Dudley Edwards is a historian and writer of deep Catholic faith, and it is this very faith that roused his anger against co-religionists whose ideas he labelled as 'Cromagnon'. Dudley Edwards has no sympathy for Rangers supporters ('thugs'), whose behaviour in a train carriage he was forced to share with them made him feel for the only time in his life what it might have been like to have been a Jew in Nazi Germany. His attack, combining piercing wit with scintillating scholarship, reflects his dismay at the way the Church he loves seems to have fallen into the clutches of 'our loathsome media', in which he includes *Flourish*, 'a journal chiefly devoted to the interests and personality cult of its Archbishop, His Eminence Thomas Cardinal Winning'. His harshest judgement, however, falls on the authors of 'Devine's clutch of five Cromagnon Catholic essays', denouncing 'MacMillan, [Andrew] O'Hagan [no football fan], Reilly, [Tom] Gallagher (alas!) and Finn [who] may be intellectually beneath contempt, but they certainly provide devastating evidence of the sickness of modern Scottish Catholic culture'.

In the 'Scotland's Shame?' debate it was mainly the issue of Catholic schools that seems to have affected minds which in other areas are quite brilliant. There is a fine old Scottish hymn that tells us to be 'Ever faithful, ever sure', but while loyalty or faith is a fine quality, dogmatic certainty seldom is – better to be faithful but never sure. (Well, hardly ever . . .) The defenders of the present system of education in Scotland seem to have allowed their faith to overtake their reason. In the case of Archbishop Conti and his bishops this is understandable: they not only have a right, but they have a duty to defend their faith, and if they believe that Catholic schools are needed for this purpose then they must fight for their preservation tooth and nail. But they should admit this openly and not make claims about 'freedom' and 'choice' and 'multiculturalism', which logically would lead to the establishment of Hindu, Muslim, Jewish, Sikh . . . and even Wee Free or other Protestant schools all fully funded by the state. In 2003, as in 1903, the prime duty of the Archbishop is to keep his charges in the One, True Faith: all that has changed is how to achieve this. In the dark days of the past it involved the killing and public torture of people who waved the wrong banners, sang from the wrong hymn sheets and bowed before the graven images of a false god; before Vatican II it involved keeping Catholics as much as possible apart from those who may have tempted them into apostasy. Today it is the retention of fully funded Catholic schools. Without Catholic schools, and Cardinal Winning said this on more than one

occasion, he would have lost people to the faith. Keeping its people in
the true faith is the first duty of the servants of the Catholic Church, and
it was for this purpose that the Celtic Football Club was founded in
1887.

SHOULD YOU KNOW YOUR HISTORY?

It is most unlikely that the Rangers Football Club has ever suffered
because it has lived for most of its history in the mistaken belief that it
was founded in 1873. For some of its followers who care about such
things, however, they have had to admit that this is wrong and that the
club was in fact well under way with regular games and properly
organised meetings in 1872. Celtic followers have had to live with a
much more serious historical error, albeit of more recent invention: this
is that the club was founded to bring together the Protestant and
Catholic communities of Glasgow. If the Celtic fans know their history,
and many of them do, or should, for some of the best football histories
have been written about it, they should be well aware that the club was
founded to keep young Catholics out of Protestant soup kitchens and
away from the perils of Protestant leisure pursuits.[29] This historical
distortion was reinforced by the Mission Statement that launched the
Bhoys against Bigotry campaign and since then has been swallowed by
some journalists. Among these are the leader writers for Glasgow's
Herald, who claimed in an editorial of 24 March 2003 that Celtic 'was
founded in the east end of Glasgow by an Irish Marist brother who
wanted both to raise money for the poor and to build bridges between
immigrants and the local population. Brother Walfrid wanted everyone
to support his club – be they Catholic, Protestant, Scottish, Irish or of
another faith and nationality entirely.' The easy acceptance of this myth
is because it is more in tune with today's moral climate than that of 1887,
when any suggestion of Catholics welcoming Protestants into their inner
sanctums was as unthinkable as Protestants extending such courtesies to
Catholics. Even Rangers have allowed themselves to be drawn into the
thraldom of political correctness, such as their tampering with historical
truth in a rather Stalinesque way by changing a flag depicting the Red
Hand of Ulster to that of the Saint George cross in one of the books
about them – in some ways a worse sin than their former refusal to
acknowledge their 'no Catholics at Ibrox' policy. This may sound like
historical pedantry, but at a time when 'small' lies are peddled by our
prime ministers and presidents in order to pursue particular political
purposes, it should be borne in mind that a nation or those in a position
of authority who distort or suppress historical 'truth' are heading at least

some small way in the direction of truly corrupt societies, like those of the former Soviet Union or South Africa under apartheid, or the nightmare world of Orwell's Big Brother.

Rangers were landed with their wrong foundation date because of the faulty memory and sloppy attention to detail of their first historian, John Allan. Celtic's direct relations with the Catholic Church ended soon after Brother Walfrid left Glasgow and the devout Catholics who got the club going and wanted to make it a truly Catholic club were ditched by those who preferred to make it a more commercial entity. Relations between the club and Church remained close, but while Celtic over the years increasingly became a source of integration of Catholics and Protestants, the Church is as committed today, as it has to be, to maintaining the primacy of the Holy Roman and Apostolic Church. Today, however, the danger lies less in Catholics becoming Protestants, but lapsing into secular-humanism or non-belief. This is the reason why the Church is fighting blindly against any reform of an education system that has served it well over the years, but whether it is wise to do so in the belief that all reform is aimed at religion itself is to fall prey to the paranoia it shares with its favourite football club.

THE END OF THE ROAD?

I saw my first Old Firm game in the summer of 1979, a Drybrough Cup match at Hampden which will always be remembered for the ball-juggling skills of Davie Cooper. I also remember it for the demented Celtic fan at the end of the game screaming his abuse and spitting on the Rangers supporters through the separating fence, and the Rangers man accompanied by his son who looked in disgust at 'these people'. But I also remember the concern of some other Celtic fans who pushed away their deranged brother, and especially the wee man who made a point of congratulating the Rangers fans for their victory and wishing them all the best. My initiation into Old Firm relations started just before the kick-off when two young lads I had been talking with left, one to join the Celtic supporters, the other his Rangers pals. The reason that it had taken so long for me to see an Old Firm game was not that I had spent most of the previous 20 years in Australia, but because as a child in Glasgow in the late 1940s and early 1950s my father would not let me go to these games because he thought they were too dangerous. He worked in the shipyards and as a special constable during and after the Second World War he had attended many Old Firm games in that capacity; it was from these experiences that he told me stories of the police on horses with their batons drawn wading into troublesome supporters, the days of the bottle parties, images that have since been reinforced by consulting the written record. Born in Greenock to parents who had recently arrived from Belfast, he was a Morton supporter and it was at Cappielow that I saw most of my games as a youngster, bedazzled by a host of heroes like Billy Campbell, Jimmy Cowan and Tommy Orr, unsurpassed by the Baxters and Johnstones still to come. But living in Whiteinch (later Nitshill) I saw many games at Ibrox, as well as Firhill (and Hampden); to me the East End was another country and people lived a different life there; they were after all Catholics and supported Celtic, a team I never saw unless they were playing Morton.

Since that first Old Firm game in 1979 I have now been to many, as well as games involving Celtic or Rangers, especially if they were playing Morton (as they did once upon a time). At these games I always tried to position myself between the two warring sets of supporters. This has involved a few hair-raising moments, verbal aggression verging on the physical and always obscene language and abuse enough to make one mourn for the mindlessness of one's fellow man. But it was not until the evening of 21 May 2003 that I actually saw football supporters covered in blood as a result of fights with other fans, in this case Celtic fans fighting with each other. A few days before that I met a wee Glasgow man at a bus stop late at night where I was waiting to see a friend off. Probably in his forties and aggressively drunk, he soon let us know his allegiances with a well-intoned 'We arra Pee-pul' followed by a chorus of 'The Sash'. A bigot, no doubt, and beyond the pale, but what about the Rangers fan I met the day after the Seville game? He was helping me into the cab that was taking me to the airport and in reply to my mumbled greeting about the cold, wet and windy weather, replied with the broadest of smiles: 'No, sir, it is a beautiful day, Celtic did not win the UEFA Cup.' On the way to the airport he responded to my story about the Celtic supporters the night before more in sorrow than in anger about 'these people', but if this man was a bigot, perhaps there is such a thing as a 'benign bigot'. Not so the young couple whose memory is still printed on my mind more than 20 years after the event. It was in the subway on the way home from a game at Ibrox and the carriage was invaded by a foul-mouthed group of Rangers youths bellowing out their sectarian hatred. Opposite me were a well-dressed young couple and their wee boy, a Rangers scarf unostentatiously draped around his neck. When the singing and chanting came to that most foul of effusions, 'If you hate the fuckin' Fenians clap your hands', the wee boy joined in, tentatively at first but with more confidence when his parents gave him a hug, bent over and smiled their approval.

Could a young couple so blithely allow their children to enter into the world of bigotry today? James MacMillan and others would say that they could, and in MacMillan's case point to at least one incident involving his children that was obscenely sectarian. Statistics can show (well, anything actually) that while Catholics have reported more incidences of sectarian abuse, Protestants have more often been the victims of physical violence. As a historian cut adrift from his childhood who enjoys his frequent return visits to Glasgow and the football, and tries to make some sense of it, there is also a yearning to believe that life is better now than it has ever been, that the youngsters of today have better chances than they ever had before. That sectarianism is less of a problem than it once was. That Rangers and Celtic are genuinely committed to healing the wounds that they lived off in the past. Unfortunately the most ardent hope cannot replace the meanest reality, but on paper at least, and in my view in practice as well, the Old Firm are today closer to being a benefit to Scottish society than a blight. The battle is far from over and to the victims of sectarian assault there is no salve in the statistics. For such reasons the practical efforts of Sense over Sectarianism, and the moral prodding of Nil by Mouth, must continue to be encouraged by the Glasgow City Council and the politicians and the public at large. The Church of Scotland and the Catholic Church have long forgotten the differences that once made them mortal enemies, and perhaps the Catholic Church might realise one day that it can keep its people in the faith without having to resort to hi-jacking young minds at age five, that the home and the church are the proper places to pass on the faith of the fathers, whatever that faith may be. In a similar spirit of the hope that springs eternal, perhaps we will soon see Rangers and Celtic triumph in Europe with the main aim of their supporters being to outdo in goodwill what Celtic did for Scotland at Seville in 2003.

It would be nice to be able to say Amen to all that – but there is a voice in my head, speaking with a distinctly Scottish accent, that keeps saying instead: 'Aye, that'll be right . . .'

Notes

1. The Greatest Club Game in the World?

1. Story told in the history of Rangers audio-tape that came out in the summer of 1993, narrated by Roddy Forsyth: 'Glasgow Rangers Revisited'

2. Stephen Walsh, *Voices of the Old Firm* (Edinburgh, Mainstream, 1995), p. 222

3. Ibid., p. 223

4. See in particular Vic Duke and Liz Crolley, *Football, Nationality and the State* (London, Longman, 1996)

5. For Jews in football see Bill Murray, *Football: A History of the World Game* (Aldershot, Scolar Press,1994), *passim*

6. See, for example, *Tiocfaidh Ar La*, Issue 8

7. This is recounted in several of the club histories. For an account in English see the excellent coverage of Spanish football in Duke and Crolley

2. A Catholic Comes to Ibrox

1. On Ure Primrose and Rangers, see Gerry P.T. Finn, 'In the Grip? A Psychological and Historical Exploration of the Social Significance of Freemasonry in Scotland', in Graham Walker and Tom Gallagher (eds), *Sermons and Battle Hymns: Protestant Popular Culture in Modern Scotland* (Edinburgh, EUP, 1990), pp. 179–80. Finn has also pointed out that J.F. Wilson, the chairman of Rangers who supported Celtic in the 1952 Flag Flutter controversy, was a leading member of the Scottish Vigilance Society directed against the 'Irish enemy within'. Further work on the associations of high-ranking Rangers with such links would be most interesting

2. The change was more a matter of style than a concession to essential truths. See in particular the opinion of two prominent academics who are also Celtic supporters: Pat Reilly in an illuminating article, 'The mirror of literature: the development of Catholicism in Scotland since 1845', *Scottish Affairs*, 8 (Summer 1994), pp. 86–95; and for a simple reminder that the Catholic Church is still unable or unwilling to compromise on Christian unity, Michael Kelly in his regular column in *The Scotsman*, 21 April 1997

3. For comments on Rush and Sheridan, see Rob Brown and David Cameron, *Scotland on Sunday*, 16 July 1989

4. Chick Young, *Rebirth of the Blues: The Story of a Rangers Revolution* (Edinburgh, Mainstream, 1987), p. 26

5. Told to Pete Davies in his marvellous coverage of England's

1990 World Cup campaign, *All Played Out: The Full Story of Italia 90* (London, Mandarin, 1990), p. 45

6. Stephen Walsh, *Voices of the Old Firm*, p. 220

7. Joanna Macdonald in *The Herald*, 16 December 1996

8. *Shoot*, December 1996

9. *Daily Record*, 24 July 1989

10. 'Glasgow Rangers Revisited' audio-tape

11. *Follow, Follow*, No.8

12. *The Herald*, 12 July 1989

13. *Rangers News*, 2 August 1989

14. *Follow, Follow*, No.57

15. Bob Ferrier and Robert McElroy, *Rangers: The Complete Record* (Derby, Breedon Books, 1996), p. 7

16. 'The Dowanhill Hack', *Follow, Follow*, No.57

3. The End of the Biscuit Tin

1. *Glasgow Herald*, 23 December 1986

2. Hugh Keevins, *Twists and Turns: The Tommy Burns Story* (Edinburgh, Sportprint Publishing, 1989), p. 69

3. Michael Kelly, *Paradise Lost: The Struggle for Celtic's Soul* (Edinburgh, Canongate Press, 1994), p. 150 on car phones, p. 168 on catering

4. Tom Campbell and Pat Woods, *Dreams, and Songs to Sing: A New History of Celtic* (Edinburgh, Mainstream, 1996), p. 250

5. Brian Wilson, *Celtic: A Century with Honour* (London, Willow Books, 1988), p. 97

6. Kelly, *Paradise Lost*, p. 14

7. Wilson, *Celtic*, p. 108

8. For a brilliant evocation of the changes in Glasgow in the 1980s, see 'The Repackaging of Glasgow', in Ian Jack, *Before the Oil Ran Out: Britain 1977–87*, (London, Flamingo, 1987)

9. Archie Macpherson, *Blue and Green: Rangers v Celtic: A Personal Look at the Glasgow Derby* (London, BBC Books, 1989), pp. 139–50 for a detailed and incisive analysis of the game and its outcome

10. *Mail on Sunday*, 5 March 1989

11. See especially *Follow, Follow*, No.9

12. Tom Campbell and Pat Woods, *A Celtic A–Z* (Glasgow, Greenfield Press, 1992), p. 143

13. Callum G. Brown, 'Popular Culture and the Continuing Struggle for Rational Recreation', in T.M. Devine and R.J. Finlay (eds), *Scotland in the Twentieth Century* (Edinburgh, EUP, 1996), pp. 211–15

14. James E. Handley, *The Celtic Story: A History of the Celtic Football Club* (London, Stanley Paul, 1960), p. 62

15. Wilson, *Celtic*, p. 182

16. Kelly, *Paradise Lost*, p. 56

17. Tom Campbell and Pat Woods, *The Glory and the Dream: The History of Celtic FC 1887– 1986* (Edinburgh, Mainstream, 1987)

18. In addition to *The Glory and the Dream*, Kevin McCarra and Pat Woods, *One Afternoon in Lisbon* (Edinburgh, Mainstream, 1988)

19. *Not the View*, No.17

20. Campbell and Woods, *Dreams, and Songs to Sing*, p. 299; the date of the first offer and the year in which McCann went to Canada (1963 or 1964) have been challenged: the information given

here comes from Campbell and Woods, but also from the account given by David Low, who was to become an intimate of McCann's, and who wrote, with Francis Shennan, a history of the McCann takeover. There were two other books on the issue (see Chapter Five), but the most important player in the takeover, McCann himself, has said very little publicly on his role

21. Kelly, *Paradise Lost*, pp. 16–17

4. The Souness Legacy

1. *Sportsweek*, 11 September 1986
2. *Daily Star*, 17 April 1991
3. *Daily Express*, 17 April 1991
4. For Murray's frank appraisal of Souness, consult 'Glasgow Rangers Revisited'
5. *Sunday Post*, 21 April 1991
6. *The Sun*, 25 October 1989
7. *Sunday Mail*, 30 August 1987
8. Sandy Jamieson, *Graeme Souness: The Ibrox Revolution and the Legacy of the Iron Lady's Man*, Mainstream, Edinburgh, 1997, pp. 185–88
9. See the *Sunday Times*, 21 April 1991
10. *Follow, Follow*, No.13
11. Ferrier and McElroy, *Rangers: The Complete History*, p. 131
12. For further discussion of this see Bill Murray, *Football: A History of the World Game, passim*, but especially pp. 108–10
13. *Daily Mail*, 24 July 1996
14. Bob Crampsey, *The Scottish Football League: The First 100 Years* (Glasgow, Scottish Football League, 1990), pp. 164–66
15. See for instance *The Herald*, 26 June 1992

16. Kelly, *Paradise Lost*, p. 64
17. He said this in 'Glasgow Rangers Revisited', and in the *Daily Record* of 24 December 1993 Murray admitted that he would 'like to think that my connections with Rangers will become a family dynasty'

5. Uncivil War at Parkhead

1. Michael Kelly, *Paradise Lost*
2. Ibid., p. 172
3. *Not the View*, No.1
4. McGlone's relationship with Celtic and his role in toppling the old board is told in his highly readable *Emotionally Celtic* (East Kilbride, GD Communications, 1995)
5. Kelly, *Paradise Lost*, p. 62
6. *Sunday Times*, 14 April 1991, where Jim Craig quotes him as saying that Rangers were '"too stupid and too slow" to make an approach for him'.
7. Kelly, *Paradise Lost*, p. 98
8. David Low and Francis Shennan, *Rebels in Paradise: The Inside Story of the Battle for the Celtic Football Club* (Edinburgh, Mainstream, 1994)
9. Allan Caldwell, *Sack the Board: Celtic the End of a Dynasty* (Edinburgh, Mainstream, 1994), pp. 21–2
10. Cyclops in *The Celt*, 32 (May 1991)
11. Bill Murray, *The Old Firm* (Edinburgh, John Donald Publishers, 2000), p. 253

6. A New Firm: Murray and McCann

1. *Evening Times*, 7 February 1997
2. Article by Ken Gallacher in

The Herald, 27 January 1997

3. See David Murray interview with Mike Aitken, in *The Scotsman,* 9 November 1994

4. On Sugar and other individuals who have made windfall profits out of their investment in (English) football, see David Conn, *The Football Business: Fair game in the '90s?* (Edinburgh, Mainstream, 1997)

5. *Daily Mail,* 23 January 1997

6. *Daily Record,* 23 January 1997

7. Ibid.

8. *The Scotsman,* 23 January 1997

9. Ibid.

10. See in particular the article by Christopher Sims in *The Herald,* 20 November 1997

11. *Evening Times,* 28 March 1997

12. *Evening Times,* 29 January 1997

13. *Daily Record,* 18 December 1996

14. Full details of the letter in the *Daily Record,* 6 February 1997

15. Tom Campbell, *Celtic's Paranoia . . . All in the Mind?* (Ayr, Fort Publishing, 2001) pp. 111–29

16. S.G. Checkland, *The Upas Tree: Glasgow 1875–1975* (Glasgow, University of Glasgow Press, 1976)

7. The Chase for Ten: End of an Era

1. Kenny Dalglish, with Henry Winter, *Dalglish: My Autobiography* (London, Hodder & Stoughton, 1996)

2. *Daily Record,* 9 January 1998

3. *Follow, Follow,* No.72; see also No.71

4. Quote paraphrased from Ed Horton, *Moving the Goalposts: Football's Exploitation* (Edinburgh, Mainstream, 1997), p. 83. This impassioned denunciation of the impact of television as viewed by an obsessive Oxford United fan overlooks some of the good that television has brought to football, especially in the way it has made games available to those with no chance of getting to the ground

8. Battling the Bigots

1. For further details on this see *The Old Firm* or any of the histories of the club by Pat Woods, but in particular his article, '1887 and all that', which appeared in the *Celtic View,* 2 February 1983. In Ireland those who accepted charity from Protestants in the Famine were condemned as 'soupers' for many decades thereafter, as Frank McCourt has recalled in his best-selling memoir of a Catholic childhood in Limerick, *Angela's Ashes: A Memoir* (London, HarperCollins, 1996), p. 65 and *passim*

2. *The Scotsman,* 10 May 1997

3. There can be no doubting the seriousness with which McCann took all aspects of the Bhoys against Bigotry campaign, as several bound cuttings of press and other extracts provided by Peter McLean make clear. The club has also, in collaboration with the Scottish Education authorities, compiled a set of primary and secondary class teaching aids on the theme of 'Youth against Bigotry'

4. *Tiocfaidh Ar La,* Issue 8

5. *Follow, Follow,* No.9

6. Campbell and Woods, *Dreams, and Songs to Sing,* p. 323

7. Handley, *The Celtic Story,* p. 173

8. Roddy Forsyth, *Blue and True: Unforgettable Rangers Days*

(Edinburgh, Mainstream, 1996), p. 25

9. *Daily Record*, 23 April 1990

10. *The Sun*, Nine-in-a-row souvenir pull-out, p. 48

11. Forsyth, *Blue and True*, p. 35

12. *Frankfurter Rundschau*, 13 January 1997

13. *The Sun*, 19 February 1996

14. *Evening Times*, 30 April 1996, which seems to be one of the few newspapers to comment on this

15. See, for example, the Celtic fanzine *Bhoyzone*, No.5, and following, where each game is listed and analysed

16. *Flourish*, February 1997

17. In the pub in Paris (The Auld Alliance) where I saw this game live, in the company of mixed Celtic, Rangers and French football fans, none of us saw any infringement by Cadete, yet when I first saw this in a replay, a long time afterwards, I thought that Cadete did handle the ball. Instead of another one for the lodge ('wan mair upfirthi luj' as Tom Leonard puts it in his poem 'Crack'), perhaps this was just another example of how the referee or his assistant will in the vast majority of cases see much more clearly than the fans

18. *Scotland on Sunday*, 29 September 1996

19. *The Sun*, Nine-in-a-row souvenir pull-out, p. 20

20. Ibid., p.33

21. *Daily Record*, 12 October 1995

22. Apart from the press of the time, *Tiocfaidh Ar La*, Issue 14, gave its own, obviously coloured, version of the events

23. *Daily Record*, 7 August 1993

24. *Daily Record*, 29 January 1997

25. *Daily Mail*, 19 February 1996

26. *Evening Times*, 27 October 1995

27. *The Herald*, 4 March 1996

28. *The Sun*, 22 April 1997

29. My grateful thanks to Else Bongenaar for finding these articles and sending them to me

9. No More, the Bygone Days of Yore . . .

1. This is the title of Graham Walker's study of the two nations, *Intimate Strangers: Political and Cultural Interaction between Scotland and Ulster in Modern Times* (Edinburgh, John Donald Publishers, 1995)

2. Kelly, *Paradise Lost*, pp. 15, 179

3. *The Independent*, 20 October 1992

4. See Bob Ferrier's obituary on his father, reproduced in John Swinburne, *Motherwell Football Club: A History of the Steelmen, 1886–1986*, published by the club, 1985, pp. 57–61. The son of an expatriate Scot who played for Sheffield Wednesday, 'Rabbie' Ferrier returned to his native Dumbarton three weeks too late to permit his son to play for Scotland. Bobby Ferrier spent his entire career with Motherwell, from 1918 to 1940, and the (George) Stevenson/Ferrier partnership is recognised as one of the greatest in the Scottish game

5. Bob Ferrier and Robert McElroy, *Rangers: The Complete Record*, p. 6

6. Joseph M. Bradley, *Ethnic and Religious Identity in Modern Scotland: Culture, Politics and Football* (Aldershot, Avebury,

1995), pp. 68–71

7. *The Rangers Historian*, 2: 10

8. Graham Walker and Tom Gallagher (eds), *Sermons and Battle Hymns: Protestant Culture in Modern Scotland* (Edinburgh, EUP, 1990), pp. 137–59

9. Ferrier and McElroy, *Rangers*, p. 7

10. See the special four-part series on 'Freemasons in Scotland today', in *The Scotsman*, especially 'Part 4', 4 July 1996

11. J.M. Roberts, *The Mythology of the Secret Societies* (London, Secker and Warburg, 1972), p. 1

12. Walker, 'There's not a team . . .', p. 144

13. Bill Murray, *Glasgow's Giants: 100 Years of the Old Firm* (Edinburgh, Mainstream, 1988), pp. 30–1

14. David Bennie, *Not Playing for Celtic: Another Paradise Lost* (Edinburgh, Mainstream, 1995)

15. *Gazza's Coming Home*, Channel 4 video

16. Story told in Roddy Forsyth's audio history

17. *Follow, Follow*, No.60

18. *Follow, Follow*, No.9

19. *Follow, Follow*, No.17

20. H.F. Moorhouse, 'Shooting Stars: Footballers and Working-Class Culture in Twentieth-Century Scotland' in Richard Holt (ed.), *Sport and the Working Class in Modern Britain* (Manchester, MUP, 1990), p. 190. Moorhouse has published several articles since 1984, all of which he refers to in his successive works: five of these are listed in the bibliography to his article: 'From 'zines like these, tradition and identity in Scottish football,' in Grant Jarvie and Graham Walker (eds), *Scottish Sport in the Making of a Nation: Ninety-Minute Patriots?* (Leicester, LUP, 1994)

21. Among his publications, Gerry P.T. Finn has contributed an excellent article on Freemasonry, 'In the Grip? A Psychological and Historical Exploration of the Social Significance of Freemasonry in Scotland', in Walker and Gallagher (eds), *Sermons and Battle Hymns*; and on Rangers, 'Faith, Hope and Bigotry: Case Studies of Anti-Catholic Prejudice in Scottish Soccer and Society', in Jarvie and Walker (eds), *Scottish Sport in the Making of the Nation*. He was to write three articles for the *International Journal of the History of Sport*, but the third of these did not appear. It is in the two published articles for that journal that Finn made his attacks on *The Old Firm* and *Glasgow's Giants*, together with other odd scraps of anything I might have said or was reported to have said, all of which he treats as being of equal value: 'Racism, Religion and Social Prejudice: Irish Catholic Clubs, Soccer and Scottish Society – I: The Historical Roots of Prejudice' (1991), 8: 1, pp. 70–93; 'Racism, Religion and Social Prejudice: Irish Catholic Clubs, Soccer and Scottish Society – II: Social Identities and Conspiracy Theories' (1991), 8: 3, pp. 370–97. It would take too long in a footnote to point out all the crass misinterpretations that make up these articles, so I will make do with one which typifies the rest. In the introduction to *Glasgow's*

Giants (p. 13) I wanted to illustrate the ludicrous nature of some aspects of the Old Firm rivalry and gave three examples of this. Finn then ridicules me by ascribing to me the opinion of one of the people I was quoting. *IJHS*, 8: I, p. 91

22. Bradley's book is unfortunately littered with serious faults in basic English and his documentation is often sloppy. While he is dismissive of earlier works on the subject, Bradley does not advance very far beyond them himself, and his history is patchy. His articles, usually made up of large chunks of material that have appeared in his book or his other articles, have appeared in various journals: Joseph M. Bradley, 'Religious Cleavage and Aspects of Catholic Identity in Modern Scotland' in *Records of the Scottish Church History Society*, vol.XXV (Edinburgh, 1995), pp. 442–68; 'Ethnicity: The Irish in Scotland – Football, Politics and Identity', *Innovation*, 7, 4, 1994, pp. 423–39; 'Football in Scotland: A History of Political and Ethnic Identity', the *International Journal of the History of Sport*, 12, 1, April 1995, pp. 81–98; 'Integration or Assimilation? Scottish Society, Football and Irish Immigrants', the *International Journal of the History of Sport*, 13, 2, August 1996, pp. 61–79

23. Bradley, like several other writers more sympathetic to Celtic or the Irish, has seized on a cartoon from the *Scottish Referee*, which I reproduced in *The Old Firm*, and used it as an example of anti-Catholicism in Scottish society. He goes to great pains to point out how he discovered this cartoon, in his book and in all of his articles taken from the book (see footnote above). It would appear that he took it from *The Old Firm* and not at source. The giveaway for Bradley, and the others who did the same, is that he attributes my (ironic) title, 'Apes and Aryans' to the *Referee*. The cartoon was bad enough in its depiction of the sub-human Irish/Celtic player against the handsome Rangers player, but, as I pointed out, only two such cartoons appeared, whether because readers objected or common decency took over, we don't know. And with some reflection, those writers who used this cartoon and blamed the *Referee* for the caption, must surely have wondered at its prescience, for while Nietzsche's works were being read by an elite few, Hitler's rise to fame was still a couple of decades off

24. *Sunday Post*, 13 May 1945

25. There is an excellent recapitulation of the *Oor Wullie* and *The Broons* comic strips in the 60th anniversary celebration that was brought out by the *Sunday Post: The Broons and Oor Wullie: 1936–96* (London, D.C. Thomson & Co Ltd, 1996)

26. See especially article in *The Scotsman* (Weekend Magazine, 29 November 1997)

27. *The Economist*, 1 November 1997

10. The Old Firm at Century's End

1. *Daily Mail,* 19 February 1997
2. Kenneth E. Collins, *Second City Jewry: The Jews of Glasgow in the Age of Expansion* (Glasgow, Scottish Jewish Archives Committee, 1990), p. 14
3. Ibid., p. 11
4. Callum G. Brown, *The Social History of Religion in Scotland Since 1730* (London, Methuen, 1987), pp. 243–7. Bruce and Gallagher have articles in Walker and Gallagher (eds), *Sermons and Battle Hymns,* and this should be consulted for a fuller bibliography of their works. See in particular: Steve Bruce, *No Pope of Rome: Militant Protestantism in Modern Scotland* (Edinburgh, Mainstream, 1985); Tom Gallagher, *Glasgow: The Uneasy Peace* (Manchester, MUP, 1987)
5. Archie Macpherson, *Action Replays* (London, Chapman, 1991), p. 251. A prospective buyer of *The Old Firm* claimed to detect the book's bias by comparing the number of Celtic fans on the cover to those of Rangers
6. *Scotland on Sunday,* 12 November 1995
7. *East End Independent,* 12 October 1995
8. *Sunday Mail,* 26 January 1996
9. It can also boast an impressive history written by one of its fans: R.W. Marwick, *The Boys from the 'Brig: The Life and Times of Albion Rovers* (Coatbridge Monklands Library Services Division, no date, but covers through to the 1985–86 season)
10. *The Scotsman,* 5 August 1994
11. Joseph M. Bradley, 'Integration or Assimilation? Scottish Society, Football and Irish Immigrants', *IJHS,* 13: 2 (August 1996)
12. *Sunday Times,* 7 July 1991
13. *Scotland on Sunday,* 5 May 1991
14. Ibid.
15. *Sunday Post,* 10 October 1943
16. Matt McGlone, *Emotionally Celtic* (East Kilbride, G.D. Communications Ltd, 1995), pp. 60–1
17. On this see also the work of Raymond Boyle: 'Faithful Through and Through: A Survey of Celtic FC's Most Committed Supporters', National Identity Research Unit, Glasgow Polytechnic, August 1991; '"We Are Celtic Supporters . . .": Questions of Football and Identity in Modern Scotland', in Richard Giulianotti and John Williams (eds), *Game Without Frontiers: Football, Identity and Modernity* (Aldershot, Arena, 1994), pp. 73–101
18. Kelly, *Paradise Lost,* pp. 148–9
19. As reported in *Tiocfaidh Ar La,* Issue 10
20. *Scotland on Sunday,* 1 December 1996
21. Ibid.
22. See the article by Sanjeev Kohli in the *Sunday Herald,* 7 April 2002
23. *Not the View,* No. 64
24. Bill Bryson, *Notes from a Small Island* (London, Doubleday, 1995), p. 272

11. Into the New Millennium

1. *Sunday Mail,* 7 May 2000
2. *Daily Record,* 2 June 2000
3. Scotland was not the only place where tensions were at breaking point over the results of two

simultaneously played games. In Germany, the third spot for promotion to the Bundesliga had to be decided between Eintracht Frankfurt and Mainz, both on the same points and Eintracht with a one-goal advantage on goal difference. Both played teams at the bottom of the league, and the scores seesawed right into injury time. With ten minutes to go, Eintracht fans had lost all hope, as they needed three goals depending on scores at the other game, but they then scored the goal that ensured promotion in the third minute of injury time. (With thanks to my German friend Ulrich Matheja for keeping me up with the adventures of his beloved Eintracht Frankfurt.)

4. The actual quote, in the magazine *FourFourTwo*, August 2003, was: 'This is the first major exodus to a foreign country to watch a football match on television'

5. See in particular the article by Scotland's foremost young journalist, Michael Grant, in the *Sunday Herald*, 1 June 2003

6. *The Scotsman*, 2 February 2002

7. For Haldane's Protestant background, his response to the Findlay episode and a balanced treatment of sectarianism in Scotland, see his chapter in Tom Devine (ed.) *Scotland's Shame? Bigotry and Sectarianism in Modern Scotland* (Edinburgh, Mainstream Publishing, 2000) pp. 89–104. Ironically his article is followed by one from Bernard Aspinwall, whose idiosyncratic ideas and distortion of those of others are nowhere more bizarre than when he discusses the Old Firm. Among my own file of crank mail I particularly treasure one from a 'Polish Fenian' on embossed paper of the highest quality filled with the most lurid mental lucubrations and foul language

8. See *Follow, Follow*, No. 135, p. 44

9. See the double-spread picture in Ronnie Esplin and Alex Anderson, *Barcelona here we come!* (Glendaruel Argyll Publishers, 2002) pp. 96–7

10. *The Scotsman*, 3 February 2003

11. On a tour of Celtic Park I could not help but notice the way our group was hustled past a private box under the name of James (Jimmy) Boyle: the reformed inmate of Scotland's harshest prisons, but not known for any outspoken opinions on the sectarian issue

12. See above pp. 132–3

13. This was a photograph dredged up from an event held nine years previously and which appeared in the *Sunday Mail* of 8 August 1999 – at the time of the MacMillan controversy. It was no doubt nothing more than a fleeting gesture, a jocular response to one of the guests at the gathering.

14. See in particular *Follow, Follow*, No. 135, p. 7, also nos 120 and 136

15. In the Spanish and Portuguese press they were criticised for booing Porto at the end of the game, but this was more for what the Scots saw as the time-wasting and gamesmanship of the Portuguese players – in turn the Portuguese criticised the brutal play of the Scots

16. See above pp. 174–5, and Bill Murray, *Glasgow's Giants: 100 Years of the Old Firm* (Edinburgh, Mainstream Publishing, 1988), pp. 30–1

17. *Alternative View*, Issue 1, 5 March 2002

18. *The Sun*, 5 July 2003; *Daily Mail*, 5 July 2003

19. It is unclear from *The Sun's* extensive report of this incident (5 July 2003) whether Stillie then retrieved the letter from the bin and took it to the police. *The Sun* did not show a photograph of the letter or reproduce its wording

20. *News of the World*, 6 July 2003

21. *Sunday Mail*, 7 April 2002

22. *The Old Firm*, 2000 edition, p. 300

23. *Daily Mail*, 28 November 2000

24. My thanks to Roy Hay for reminding me of this report and its conclusions

12. Pride, Prejudice and the New Crusaders

1. For information on Nil by Mouth I am indebted to its full-time coordinator, Helen Miller, who supplied me with detailed information on the organisation, and to Peter McLean for discussing issues with me in a long telephone conversation

2. Mark Frankland, *The Drums of Hampden* (Dumfries, Glenmill, 2002). It should be noted, however, that the 'history' discussed is somewhat suspect

3. I would like to thank Alison Logan, full-time coordinator of Sense over Sectarianism, for discussing her work and supplying me with various documents

4. The *Evening Times* was the project's media partner, see 3 March 2003

5. For a full discussion of these issues, see the Sunday Herald, 11 March 2001: 'Sectarianism . . . will it ever end?

6. Ibid.

7. See in particular the article by Kevin Toolis in *The Guardian Weekly*, 2 March 2002, 'The Operator'

8. See especially article headed 'End our secret shame' in the *Daily Record*, 6 December 2002

9. *Daily Mail*, 4 March 2002

10. *Scotland on Sunday*, 24 February 2002

11. *Sunday Herald*, 22 September 2002

12. I am particularly grateful for the help given to me by Doreen Montgomery, Principal Policy Development Officer of the Glasgow City Council, for sending me a copy of the report and discussing it and related matters with me while I was in Glasgow, as well as for supplying me with a file of press cuttings

13. See for example, *Daily Mail*, 12 March 2003

14. For examples of this see in particular *The Herald*, 14 December 2002, and the Sunday Herald, 15 December 2002

15. *Sunday Herald*, 23 March 2003

16. *Scotland on Sunday*, 9 March 2003

17. *The Herald*, 11 December 2002

18. *The Herald*, 29 August 1998

19. *The Scotsman*, 5 February 2003

20. *Daily Mail*, 20 June 2003

21. *Sunday Herald*, 15 December 2002

22. I would like to thank the Rangers Football Club for sending me a copy of the media package launching Pride over Prejudice

23. McGlone in the *Alternative View*, No. 1, although McLean is not mentioned by name

24. For samples of extreme moral outrage against the marchers, see in particular the Scottish *Daily Mirror* of 10 July 2003, where the page-one headline denounced the 'Silence of the shams', taking McConnell to task for vowing 'to stamp out sectarian hate' but refusing to 'discuss this summer's 800 marches'

25. See James Scotland, *The History of Scottish Education* (London, University of London Press, 1969), vol. 2, p. 45

26. Quoted in the preface to Tom Devine (ed.) *Scotland's Shame?*, p. 8

27. I have discussed this book and the issues involved in much greater detail in *The Old Firm*, 2000 edition, pp. 285–92

28. In *Scottish Affairs*, 33, Autumn 2000, pp. 1–22

29. Ibid., pp. 139–41

Bibliography

There has been a profusion of books on football since 1984, to add to the videos and fanzines that have also come on the market. I have indicated in the text the use I have made of fanzines, videos and the contemporary press. I have not always indicated where I have drawn on material from my other football books, where many points touched on in this book are explained in more detail:

Murray, Bill, *The Old Firm: Sectarianism, Sport and Society in Scotland* (Edinburgh, John Donald Publishers, 1984; updated and revised 2000)
—— *Glasgow's Giants: 100 Years of the Old Firm* (Edinburgh, Mainstream, 1988)
—— *Football: A History of the World Game* (Aldershot, Scolar Press, 1994)
—— *The World's Game: A History of Soccer* (Urbana and Chicago, University of Illinois Press, 1996)

The explosion of publishing in books on football can be seen in the comprehensive guide to books on football that came out in 1995, updated 2000, complete with useful comments on the works listed, from general and club histories to fanzines and music and film.

Sedden, Peter J. (compiler), *A Football Compendium: A Comprehensive Guide to the Literature of Association Football* (Boston Spa, The British Library, 2000)

The following is a selective list of books dealing with the Old Firm, Celtic, and Rangers that have appeared since 1984; the above works should also be consulted for further information.

ON THE OLD FIRM

Macpherson, Archie, *The Great Derbies: Rangers v. Celtic: A Personal Look at the Glasgow Derby* (London, BBC Books, 1989)
The Herald *Book of Old Firm Games: A Complete Record of all the Old Firm Matches Fought since the Second World War* (Edinburgh, Canongate, 1995)
Walsh, Stephen, *Voices of the Old Firm* (Edinburgh, Mainstream, 1995)

ON CELTIC

Burns, Peter, and Pat Woods, *Oh, Hampden in the Sun . . .* (Edinburgh, Mainstream, 1997)

Campbell, Tom, and Pat Woods, *The Glory and the Dream: The History of Celtic Football Club* (Edinburgh, Mainstream, 1987)

—— *Rhapsody in Green: Great Celtic Moments* (Edinburgh, Mainstream, 1990)

—— *A Celtic A–Z* (Glasgow, Greenfield Press, 1992)

—— *Dreams, and Songs to Sing: A New History of Celtic* (Edinburgh, Mainstream, 1996)

Campbell, Tom, *Celtic's Paranoia . . . All in the Mind?* (Ayr, Fort Publishing, 2001)

Forsyth, Roddy, *Fields of Green: Unforgettable Celtic Days* (Edinburgh, Mainstream, 1996)

Kelly, Michael, *Paradise Lost: The Struggle for Celtic's Soul* (Edinburgh, Canongate, 1994)

MacBride, Eugene, Martin O'Connor, Sheridan, George, *An Alphabet of the Celts: A Complete Who's Who of Celtic FC* (Leicester, ACL and Polar Publishing, 1994)

McColl, Graham, *Celtic: The Official Illustrated History, 1888–1996* (Edinburgh, Mainstream, 1996)

McColl, Graham and George Sheridan, *The Essential History of Celtic* (London, Headline Book Publishing, 2002)

McGlone, Matt, *Emotionally Celtic* (East Kilbride, GD Communications, 1995)

Potter, David, *Our Bhoys Have Won the Cup! 30 Times Scottish Cup Winners* (Edinburgh, John Donald Publishers, 1996)

Wilson, Brian, *Celtic: A Century with Honour* (London, Collins, 1988)

ON RANGERS

Anderson, Alex and Ronnie Esplin, *Barcelona Here We Come! The Story of Rangers' European Cup-Winners' Cup Win in 1972* (Glendaruel, Argyll Publishing, 2002)

Esplin, Ronnie, *Down the Copland Road* (Glendaruel, Argyll Publishing, 2000)

Ferrier, Bob, and Robert McElroy, *Rangers: The Complete Record* (Derby, Breedon Books, 1996)

Forsyth, Roddy, *Blue and True: Unforgettable Rangers Days* (Edinburgh, Mainstream, 1996)

Halliday, Stephen, *Rangers: The Official Illustrated History* (London, Arthur Barker, 1989)

Jamieson, Sandy, *Graeme Souness: The Ibrox Revolution and the Legacy of the Iron Lady's Man* (Edinburgh, Mainstream, 1997)

McElroy, Robert, *The Spirit of Ibrox*, (Lancaster, Newton Abbey, 1998)

MacWilliam, Rab, *Rangers: An Illustrated History* (London, Aurum Press, 2002)

Young, Chic, *Rebirth of the Blues: The Story of a Rangers Revolution* (Edinburgh, Mainstream, 1987)

FOOTBALL, RELIGION AND SCOTTISH SOCIETY

Bradley, Joseph M., *Ethnic and Religious Identity in Modern Scotland: Culture, Politics and Football* (Aldershot, Avebury, 1995)

Conn, David, *The Football Business: Fair Game in the '90s?* (Edinburgh, Mainstream, 1997)

Devine, Tom (ed.), *Scotland's Shame? Bigotry and Sectarianism in Modern Scotland*, (Edinburgh, Mainstream Publishing, 2000)

Devine, T.M., and Finlay, R.J.(eds), *Scotland in the Twentieth Century* (Edinburgh, EUP, 1996)

Frankland, Mark, *The Drums of Hampden* (Dumfries, Glenmill, 2002)

Gallagher, Tom, *Glasgow: The Uneasy Peace* (Manchester, MUP, 1987)

Horton, Ed, *Moving the Goalposts: Football's Exploitation* (Edinburgh, Mainstream, 1997)

Jarvie, Grant, and Graham Walker (eds), *Scottish Sport in the Making of the Nation: Ninety-Minute Patriots?* (Leicester, LUP, 1994)

Macpherson, Archie, *Action Replays* (London, Chapman, 1991)

Marshall, William B., *The Billy Boys: A Concise History of Orangeism in Scotland* (Edinburgh, Mercat Press, 1996)

Walker, Graham, and Tom Gallagher (eds), *Sermons and Battle Hymns: Protestant Popular Culture in Modern Scotland* (Edinburgh, EUP, 1990)

Walker, Graham, *Intimate Strangers: Political and Cultural Interaction between Scotland and Ulster in Modern Times* (Edinburgh, John Donald Publishers, 1995)

Index